HERODOTUS
AND
GREEK HISTORY

HERODOTUS
AND
GREEK HISTORY

John Hart

Published in 1993 by
John Hart

in association with
The Self Publishing Association Ltd.

First published in 1982 by
Croom Helm Ltd, 2-10 St John's Road, London SW11

British Library Cataloguing in Publication Data

A catalogue record for this book is available
from the British Library

ISBN 1 85421 226 5

Produced by Images.
Printed and Bound in Great Britain.

CONTENTS

List of Illustrations

This work took its origin in a course of lectures I gave to a group of pupils in 1968 on Herodotus and his subject-matter; I gave another course covering somewhat similar ground, but with a different emphasis, in 1976/7. When I embarked on the former, the student of Herodotus had very little accessible material in English to help him. On the Persian Wars themselves, and the earlier relations of Greece and Persia, there was an outstanding book in A.R. Burn's *Persia and the Greeks*, but Herodotus himself was poorly served. The title of J.L. Myres' *Herodotus, Father of History* promised much, but it was a work of disappointingly restricted utility. How & Wells' commentary, in particular its introduction and appendices, remained an indispensable tool in the hands of the student, despite its advanced age.

In 1971 there appeared C.W. Fornara's *Herodotus, an Interpretative Essay*. This short work offered some brilliant insights, and I am pleased to acknowledge my indebtedness to it more than once in the course of the present work; but it did more for the teacher than for the student of Herodotus, assuming as it did a thorough familiarity with the content of the *Histories*. Then there has been a steady flow of article – many of them in English – in the German periodical *Historia* over the past twenty years, which have made a varied and valuable contribution to Herodotean studies.

The present work is simply intended to help the student of Greek history. To essay a full discussion of Herodotus' treatment of Egypt, the Middle East and Scythia would have inflated the volume to unmanageable size (not to mention cost), and in any case lies outside my competence. Nor have I attempted to handle matters of composition. Except where some theological interest is involved, as in Polycrates and the Ring, Herodotus' application of folk motifs to relatively recent history (like The Oath That Went Wrong in the stories of Ariston of Sparta and Xerxes' womenfolk) is one of the topics I have reluctantly passed over. Nor have I dealt with the somewhat speculative question of the order in which the different parts of the *Histories* were composed, a subject that has been thoroughly aired in other works.

Rather I have attempted to focus attention upon what Herodotus actually says at different points of his narrative. The first four chapters bring together material that is scattered throughout the Histories, but deserves to be considered as a whole. The five personalities treated in Chapter 5 include two great figures who make many separate appearances in the *Histories*, Darius and Cleomenes; and three to whom Herodotus accords particularly careful and artistic treatment, Damaratus, Themistocles and Pausanias. Chapter 6 considers the *Histories* against the background of the known facts of Herodotus' life, the various factors that made him the writer that he was, and the impression he made upon other writers of the fifth century, especially Thucydides. There is some overlapping between chapters when the same subject-matter is viewed from a different standpoint. On reflection I have decided to keep it within bounds rather than try to eliminate it altogether.

I have adopted a broadly traditional and conventional spelling for Greek proper names. Consistency is an almost unattainable ideal unless one resorts to such forbidding nomenclature as Korinthos ('Korinth' seems to me pointless) and Themistokleës. My inconsistency is on the conservative side; I retain, however, as an aid to pronunciation, the 'ei' in personal names (Peisistratus, Cleisthenes, Aristeides, etc.) except for the time-honoured 'Darius'; and in deference to the increasing number of holiday-makers who visit it, the pleasant island between Peiraeus and the Peloponnese appears as Aigina. Where Herodotus has Ionicised a familiar proper name, I have used the familiar form – Damaratus and Leonidas, not Demaretos and Leonides.

Unless there is an indication to the contrary, or the context makes it obvious that AD is meant (for instance, references to 1914–18), all dates are BC.

Although this book has had a somewhat prolonged period of gestation, it would probably not have been completed but for the kindness of my headmaster, Martin Rogers, in granting me a term's sabbatical leave, and the generosity of the Goldsmiths' Company in giving me a travelling award. To them go my most sincere thanks. I was thus enabled to live in Greece for three months, basing myself upon the British School of Archaeology in Athens.

I have many other debts of gratitude to pay: to the pupils upon whom some of this material was first tried out; I learned much from their response. To my friends at the British School of Archaeology, with whom I had many profitable discussions on Herodotean topics, especially Graham Shipley, Tina McGeorge, and the Visiting Fellow during my stay there, Mr Peter Fraser of All Souls. To two friends special thanks are due – Desmond Costa of Birmingham University's School of Hellenic and Roman Studies, and my Malvern colleague Richard Penman. Both read the entire work in typescript and by their comments saved me from much that was obscure, inconsistent, inelegant, or simply wrong; neither they nor anyone else but myself is to be blamed for the faults that remain.

It was my wife who encouraged me to begin what turned out to be the enjoyable and satisfying task of writing this book, and her support has sustained me at every stage; to her it is dedicated.

John Hart

PREFACE TO SECOND EDITION

The reissue of this work has had a somewhat chequered history. When the original edition sold out, and the publishers (Croom Helm) were taken over by a conglomerate, it was not reprinted and the copyright reverted to me. Bristol Classical Press took it up and a new edition, fully reset but with no changes other than corrections of the few misprints, had been announced and was nearly ready, but that did not survive their receivership and subsequent take-over. I have now been enabled to make a few small changes and additions to the text and notes, but above all to present the book in the form that I originally wanted – properly type-set, with italics and justified margins; with footnotes in the proper place (at the foot); with some carefully chosen illustrations; and repairing damage done to my text by what Kingsley Amis has called 'boldly illiterate' copy-editing.

For their great help in reading the proofs, and especially in compiling afresh and checking the indexes of this repaginated edition, my sincere thanks go to two students of mine, Edward Clements and Tim Hawkins.

JTH
Malvern

ANCIENT AUTHORS

Herodotus (H): all unattributed citations in the footnotes are from the *Histories*, normally book and paragraph no. only (e.g. ix.27). When mentioned in the footnotes he is always abbreviated to H. I have used K. Hude's Oxford Classical Text with five changes only, each discussed in the appropriate place.

Aristotle (Arist.): in the text the author of *Politics*, *Rhetoric* etc. is referred to as Aristotle, the author of the fourth-century *Athenaion Politeia* as 'Aristotle', and in the footnotes it appears simply as *Ath. Pol.* without author. I do not intend to imply that it does not contain valuable historical information.

Plutarch (Plut.): his *Lives* are cited under the name of the subject; Arist. and Them. are respectively Aristeides and Themistocles. MH: *de Malignitate Herodoti* (On the Meanness, or 'Malice', of Herodotus); cited by *Moralia* paragraph no.; citations from elsewhere in *Moralia* are by paragraph no. only.

Thucydides (Th.): far and away the most important source of parallel, comparative and illustrative material.

Xenophon (X): *Hell.* and *Anab.* are respectively *Hellenica*, and *Anabasis*. In the text the author of the fifth-century *Athenaion Politeia* appears as 'Xenophon', cited in footnotes as Ps.-Xen. *Ath. Pol.* – I do not thereby mean entirely to exclude the possibility that the youthful Xenophon may have written it.

Other authors drawn upon are usually named in full, either in the footnotes or in the text – Sophocles, Aristophanes, the Hippocratic corpus, Plato, Arrian, Quintilian and so on. If not, the abbreviations generally follow the practice of Liddell & Scott.

COLLECTIONS

Hill's *Sources*: G.F. Hill, *Sources for Greek History*, 478-431, revised by R. Meiggs & A. Andrewes (Oxford University Press, 1951).

Kent, OP: Roland G. Kent, *Old Persian* (see bibliography).

M-L: R. Meiggs & D.M. Lewis, *Greek Historical Inscriptions* (Oxford University Press, 1968). Wherever possible I have cited inscriptions from this collection; in the one or two cases where this has not been possible I have given the IG no. (Inscriptiones Graecae).

Moretti: Luigi Moretti, *Olympionikai* (Rome, 1957). This catalogues all Olympic winners so far as they are known.

Page, LGS: *Lyrica Graeca Selecta*, ed. D.L. Page (Oxford Classical Texts, 1968).

PERIODICALS AND REFERENCE WORKS

AJA: *American Journal of Archaeology*

AJP: *American Journal of Philology*

CAH: *Cambridge Ancient History*

CQ: *Classical Quarterly*

CR: *Classical Review*

How & Wells: W.W. How & J. Wells, *A Commentary on Herodotus* (Oxford University Press, 1912); see Bibliography.

JHS: *Journal of Hellenic Studies*

OCT: Oxford Classical Text

RE: Pauly-Wissowa, *Real-Encyclopädie*

TAPA: *Transactions of the American Philological Association*

Other periodicals, e.g. *Hesperia, Historia* etc. are named in full. Numerous proper names, e.g. Cleomenes, Darius, Themistocles etc. are abbreviated in footnotes referring to passages in which they are named in full: these are self-explanatory.

These maps are intended to locate places mentioned in the text and are not maps to Greek history or even to Herdotus' *Histories* as a whole. The maps were drawn by David Plummer.

Map 1: South-west Asia Minor

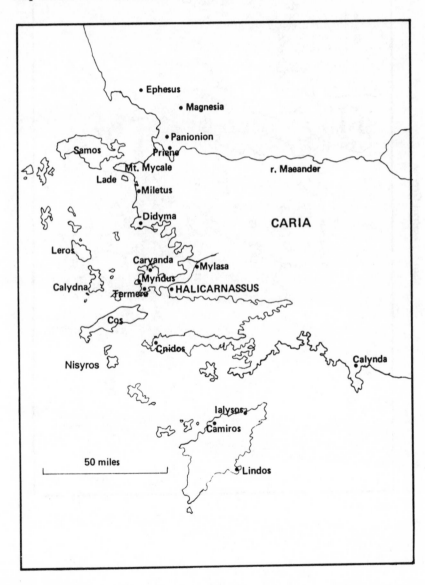

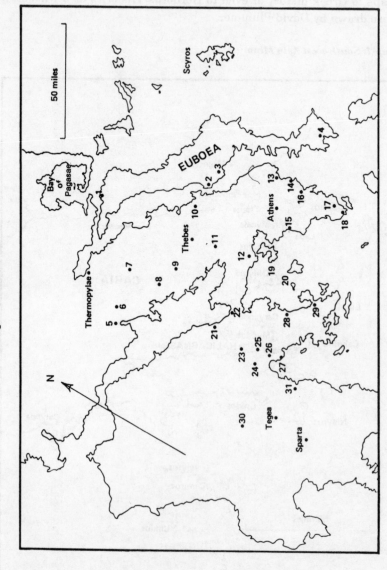

Map 2: Central Greece

Key to Map 2:

A. Euboea

1 Artemisium

2 Chalcis

3 Eretria

4 Carystos

B. Phocis, Boeotia, Attica, Isthmus

5 Crisa

6 Delphi and Mt Parnassus

7 Orchomenus

8 Coronea

9 Thespiae

10 Tanagra

11 Plataea and Mt Cithaeron

12 Megara

13 Marathon

14 Pallene

15 Phaleron

16 Brauron

17 Mt Laurion, site of silver mines

18 Sunion

19 Salamis

C. Peloponnese etc.

20 Aigina

21 Sicyon

22 Corinth

23 Mycenae

24 Argos

25 Argive Heraion

26 Tiryns

27 Nauplia (battle of Sepeia nearby)

28 Epidaurus

29 Troizen

30 Mantinea

31 Thyrea

Map 3: The Greek World

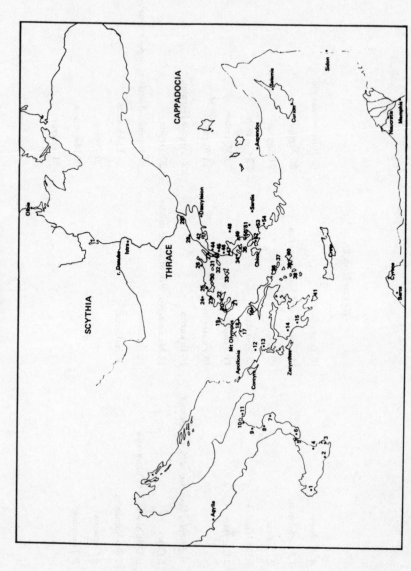

Key to *Map 3:*

A. Sicily and Southern Italy
1 Egesta
2 Gela
3 Syracuse
4 Sicilian Megara
5 Zancle
6 Rhegion
7 Croton
8 Sybaris/Thuria
9 Siris
10 Metapontion
11 Taras

Note: the site of Sicilian Euboea is untraced

B. Mainland Greece and North Aegean
12 Dodona
13 Ambracia
14 Olympia
15 Lepreon
16 Aphetae
17 Larissa
18 Vale of Tempe
19 Therma
20 Poteidaea
21 Scione
22 Acanthus (and site of Xerxes' canal)
23 Eion
24 Myrcinus
25 Abdera
26 Doriscus
27 Chersonese: Sestos and Aigospotamoi
28 Perinthus
29 Byzantium

C. Islands
30 Thasos
31 Samothrace
32 Imbros
33 Lemnos
34 Lesbos: Methymna
35 Lesbos: Mytilene
36 Andros
37 Tenos
38 Siphnos
39 Paros
40 Naxos
41 Cythera
42 Proconnesus

D. Asian Mainland
43 Cyzicus
44 Lampsacus
45 Abydos (site of Xerxes' bridge)
46 Dardanus
47 Sigeum
48 Pergamum
49 Cyme
50 Phocaea
51 Smyrna
52 Clazomenae
53 Teos
54 Colophon

Goodbye, Megacles. See also p.26.
(Deutsches Archäologisches Institut, Athens)

1. The Athenian Nobility

One of the most remarkable features of Athenian history is the long survival, in positions of rank and dignity, of certain noble houses. Even under the developed democracy this continued to be the case, a phenomenon at least partially explained by 'Xenophon': the Athenian commons had no desire to hold such offices as carried responsibility for the public safety; generalships were best left to the magnates. By way of illustration we can think of Cimon's son Lacedaemonius being given a potentially tricky commission in Corcyrean waters before the outbreak of the Peloponnesian War, and Pericles' nephew Hippocrates leading the Athenian hoplites to defeat on the field of Delium; and many other instances.[1]

The two families that displayed the greatest vitality were of course the Alcmeonidae and the Philaidae.[2] Members of each house hold prominent roles in Herodotus' story down to the Persian Wars, and the fact that the families, or their connections, retained high importance during the historian's own lifetime must have added piquancy both to his enquiries into their past history and to his treatment of them.[3] No one doubts that Herodotus drew upon the accumulated traditions of these houses for material; the question that every student of Herodotus must ask himself is whether, and if so to what extent, his account is coloured by them. Do we, in other words, read what the Alcmeonidae and the Philaidae of the middle fifth century wanted us to read and believe, or is the interpretation of their ancestors' conduct Herodotus' own?

We can only answer this question by considering everything that Herodotus tells us about members of the two houses, with any comments or expressions of opinion that he voices, alongside such information as we have from other sources; Herodotus of course tells us more than all the rest put together.

---

[1] Ps.-Xen. Ath. Pol. i.3; Th.i.45 and iv.89 ff.

[2] This term is not in fact used of Miltiades' family by H or any other classical author, but its use is convenient. It is explained on p. 35.

[3] Several of the precise family relationships mentioned in this chapter rest upon inference rather than hard evidence; e.g. it is possible that it was Hippocleides' father Teisander who married the daughter of Cypselus of Corinth, and that Cypselus II was thus Hippocleides' brother; the dates are more difficult to fit around this hypothesis, however. To enter into the detailed arguments is beyond the scope of this work; the evidence is summarised by J.K. Davies, *Athenian Propertied Families* (Oxford University Press, 1971) under Kimon, Megakles, Peisistratos; the work is self-indexing and includes bibliographies with each major entry. Differences of detail may be found in, for instance, A.R. Burn, *Pericles and Athens* (English Universities Press, London, 1948).

THE ALCMEONIDAE

Chronologically the first appearance of the Alcmeonidae is the mention of their role in the suppression of Cylon's attempted coup in c. 630 BC.[4] The full story is not directly relevant to its context in Herodotus, and he omits a number of details for which we are indebted to Thucydides and Plutarch,[5] who evidently draw at least partly on some independent tradition. As the narrative in both these latter writers is intended to serve the same purpose as that of Herodotus – to explain the curse upon the Alcmeonidae – it may be presumed that Thucydides, at least, was consciously filling in details that the curious reader might require, and correcting errors or misconceptions.

Herodotus' account is certainly brief and tantalising. Cylon, an Athenian with an Olympic victory behind him, began to entertain hopes of making himself tyrant of Athens. Aided by friends he attempted to seize the Acropolis but failed, and he and his party fled for sanctuary. The 'Presidents of the Naucrari', who 'in those days were the administrators of Athens', induced them to leave sanctuary and stand trial under promise of safe conduct. This promise was broken, Cylon's party was murdered, and the blame fell upon the Alcmeonidae.

This account obviously leaves a number of questions unanswered. Who were Cylon's 'friends'? What grounds had he for hoping to succeed? What was the constitutional importance of the 'Presidents of the Naucrari', an office extinct in Herodotus' own day? Lastly and most crucially, what was the supposed connection with the Alcmeonidae? To each of these questions Thucydides, with one important detail added by Plutarch, supplies the answer. Cylon was the son-in-law of Theagenes, tyrant of Megara, who had lent him a body of troops. He had been advised by the oracle at Delphi to make his attempt on the Acropolis during the great festival of Zeus. As an Olympic victor, he took that to mean the Olympic Games. In fact, as Thucydides guessed, the oracle obviously meant the Athenian festival of the Diasia, which involved the whole population and took place outside the city – a circumstance strongly favourable to one attempting a coup. (Delphi often made up for its lack of spiritual guidance by an abundance of sound common sense.) Thirdly, as to the responsible authorities, Thucydides bluntly contradicts Herodotus – it was the Nine Archons who held the political power and who conducted the siege of the Acropolis. Finally, Plutarch gives us the name of the Archon[6] for the year – Megacles the Alcmeonid, the then head of the family.

We can pass over the minor inconsistencies: in Thucydides the

---

[4] v.70–1.

[5] Th.i.126; Plut. *Solon*, 12.

[6] 'The Archon' was the senior of the nine and gave his name to the year.

Acropolis was actually seized, and Cylon and his brother contrived to escape; in Herodotus the attempt was a total failure, and all, by implication, were murdered. The question of the responsible authorities however is more serious, and we are bound to agree with Thucydides in rejecting the 'Presidents of the Naucrari'. The Naucrari were officials in charge of the 48 districts into which Attica was divided for the purpose of levying money to pay for ships. The 48 districts (Naucrariae) were superseded by the 'demes' (parishes) under Cleisthenes' reform of 508 BC, with 'demarchs' as the responsible officials,[7] and, beyond Herodotus' statement, there is no reason for supposing that they ever wielded the kind of central political power implied by the story. At the very best they might have been responsible for calling out the local levies to oppose Cylon. The archonship, on the other hand, lay at the very centre of the aristocratic government of Athens at that time, as Thucydides and 'Aristotle' make plain. The passage, therefore, must be considered as an instance of Herodotus either making a false statement in support of his Alcmeonid friends or accepting uncritically a falsehood from the family tradition.

Before we leave the story, there are some points in it that are of general interest to the historian. First, the fact that Cylon, an Athenian nobleman, was married to the daughter of a neighbouring tyrant; we find this paralleled twice in Herodotus. Megacles (II), grandson of the Archon, married Agarista, daughter of Cleisthenes tyrant of Sicyon, after a famous wooing;[8] while the defeated suitor Hippocleides, son of Teisander, he whose ill-timed dancing cost him the bride, was connected with the family of Cypselus tyrant of Corinth,[9] a fact that had commended him to Cleisthenes. A member of the Philaid house, he was probably first cousin to Miltiades the elder, first tyrant of the Chersonese.[10] Such marriages were obviously sought after by both sides – by giving his daughter to an Athenian magnate the tyrant could secure an influential voice in Athenian policy-making, while the Athenian, in his turn, would gain not only a handsome dowry but also prestige and dignity, so long as tyrannies were benevolent and looked upon with favour.

Secondly, it is interesting to speculate on the reasons for Cylon's failure. Tyrannies were, after all, well established in Corinth, Sicyon and Megara, each with a degree of popular support. The most significant fact in Thucydides' account is that the Athenian peasantry rallied in force to the established government of the aristocracy. Evidently, economic conditions in Attica had not yet produced a revolutionary situation, for, unlike

---

[7] Ath. Pol. 21.

[8] vi.130.

[9] vi.128.

[10] Marcellinus' *Life of Thucydides*, 3; for his family tree, see p. 25.

Peisistratus in 561, Cylon did not identify himself with a large and discontented class, nor perhaps did he possess the charisma of the successful military man. It may be, too, that his reliance on foreign troops revealed his personal ambition too nakedly. His mistake was to try 30 years too early.

We pass now to the son of Megacles the Archon, Alcmeon. Megacles himself and those with him immediately involved in the sacrilegious murder of Cylon's party had been forced into exile,[11] and the charge of pollution was to be revived by enemies of the family at least three times over the next two centuries; but if Alcmeon had been obliged to leave Athens then, he was certainly back by the end of the 590s. He worked his passage back with the help of Delphi, serving as general of the Athenians in the First Sacred War,[12] in which the Amphictyonic Council[13] destroyed the Cirrhaeans who had been preying upon Delphi and, by implication, those who travelled there. In this war he fought side by side with Cleisthenes of Sicyon; perhaps the future family alliance was forged at Delphi. The motion to make war was proposed by Solon, and we may conclude that the great reformer and the son of Megacles were not political opponents; they may have been close allies.

None of this is relevant to Herodotus, and he omits it. What we do have is the story of Alcmeon's abrupt enrichment by King Croesus of Lydia as a reward for assistance rendered to the Lydian delegation sent to consult the oracle at Delphi.[14] Even leaving aside the obviously comical exaggeration, the story cannot be pressed in all its details, for chronologically it was no more possible for Alcmeon to visit Croesus than it was for Solon. But while the immortal tale of Solon's visit may be dismissed as a piece of pure fiction, illustrating with historical personalities a principle of popular ethics, this is by no means so with the brief story of Alcmeon. First, there is the connection with Delphi, where Alcmeon must have been a person of influence after the successful conclusion of the Sacred War; this connection was revived to good effect in the time of Alcmeon's grandson Cleisthenes, as we shall see. Secondly, there is the undoubted advance in the family's prominence and wealth. What Herodotus says is this: 'The Alcmeonidae had been distinguished in Athens in earlier times too, but from the time of Alcmeon, and then Megacles [II], they became exceedingly distinguished'; then follows the story of Croesus' generosity, and finally, 'In this way the family became very rich, and Alcmeon was enabled

---

[11] Plut. *Solon*, 12.

[12] Ibid. 11; Aeschines, 3.108.

[13] The governing body of Delphi, composed of delegates sent from the states of central Greece and the Peloponnese.

[14] vi.125.

to carry off the prize for the four-horse chariot-race at the Olympic Games.'

This account is extremely probable. We are not obliged to believe that Alcmeon was the founder of the family's name and fame, for his father Megacles could not have been Archon before Solon's reforms unless the family had been of 'Eupatrid' (i.e. patrician) status. But it was not until the sixth century that the family sprang into real prominence; but for the unlucky coincidence of Cylon's coup with the archonship of Megacles we should not have heard about them earlier. The marriage of Megacles [II] to Agarista of Sicyon, and of their daughter to Peisistratus, show a family that is definitely on the upgrade. Chariot-racing, too, was emphatically a sport for the very rich only.[15] The Philaids were equal to it – the elder Miltiades and his half-brother Cimon both won Olympic victories,[16] as did Cleisthenes of Sicyon and Damaratus, King of Sparta. Outside the pages of Herodotus we find hymned by Pindar Alcmeon's great-grandson Megacles [IV], and millionaire rulers like the Sicilian tyrants and Arcesilas IV of Cyrene. Alcibiades, the most dazzling sportsman of his day, was the son of a man of great wealth, Cleinias, who had footed the entire bill for his trireme and crew at Artemisium; a presumed ancestor, also a Cleinias, was libellously alleged to have made a killing on Solon's debt-reform.[17]

Finally, there is nothing intrinsically improbable about an Athenian magnate lending his good offices to an Eastern king. 'Medism' was not yet a crime. Croesus' father, Alyattes, had consulted Delphi[18] in what would have been Alcmeon's time, and it is surely the case that the story, complete with humorous embellishment, got transferred to the more obviously anecdote-worthy Croesus. This is not particularly important for our purposes: what is highly significant is the placement of the story in Herodotus' text, and that we shall turn to at the conclusion of this sketch.

Alcmeon's son Megacles [II], with his splendid marriage alliance, was a man of the greatest consequence in Athens. When we first meet him in the pages of Herodotus he is an established faction leader, the champion of the men of the 'Coast', at loggerheads with Lycurgus, leader of the men of the 'Plain'. The precise nature of this political feuding is not clear, but what is clear enough is that the 'Coast' party consisted mainly of those who lived in the area south-east of Athens[19] – the country stronghold of the Alcmeonidae – who were near enough to the city to assert themselves in the 'Ecclesia' and reap the benefits of Solon's legislation. The faction may, perhaps, have included some of the newly enfranchised immigrants in the city who were

---

[15] vi.35.

[16] vi.103.

[17] viii.17; Plut. *Solon*, 15.

[18] i.19.

[19] D.M. Lewis, 'Cleisthenes and Attica', *Historia*, 1963.

beginning to contribute so much to Athens' economic growth. The 'Plain' consisted of the landed gentry of the interior, to the north and west of the city; these prosperous folk had not positively gained from Solon's laws and may in some cases have lost money under the debt-reform; they had certainly lost some degree of political privilege. The Philaid family belonged to this 'Tory' element of Attic society, and the traditional rivalry between the two great houses may date from this turbulent period that followed the reforms of Solon. Such was the context of Peisistratus' rise to power at the head of a third group, the men of the 'Hill', or 'Beyond the Hills', the poorer peasantry of eastern Attica who ought to have benefited from Solon's reforms but whose progress was hampered by their relative remoteness from the city, and also, perhaps, by their lack of an effective champion.[20] This certainly explains the statement of Herodotus that the tyrant altered none of the laws:[21] what Solon's legislation required was not amendment but enforcement. However this may be, politically speaking Megacles had a lot more in common with Peisistratus than he had with Lycurgus, and when, as Herodotus says, Megacles and Lycurgus joined forces to throw Peisistratus out, this was doubtless because Megacles considered that his personal position was being undermined rather than because of any real dispute over policies. The unnatural alliance did not last, and Megacles was forced to secure his own position in the state by intriguing with the absent Peisistratus, aiding his return and giving him his daughter in marriage.

The tale of Phye of Paeania being dressed up as Athene to trick the Athenians into accepting the tyrant's return is one of the more diverting in Herodotus. It is certainly true in its essentials: the circumstantial details of the woman's name and deme are there; Herodotus could have spoken to the sons or at least the grandsons of eyewitnesses; and he takes the opportunity to enjoy himself at the Athenians' expense: 'To achieve Peisistratus' return, he and Megacles devised what is (as far as I can see) by far the most silly trick ever: the Greek people has from time immemorial been judged more intelligent than the barbarian world, and further removed from such childish simplicity – and it was among the Athenians, who are reckoned to be the most intelligent of all the Greeks, that they contrived it!'

What he says about Athenian sophistication may very well be true of the educated upper class in the age of Pericles; as for the urban population in general, who enjoyed the plays of Euripides and Aristophanes, they were no doubt a good deal more quick-witted and articulate than most ordinary folk elsewhere in Greece. If the Funeral Speech in Thucydides is a reflection (in matchlessly exalted language) of the sort of things that Pericles and his

---

[20] Note that 'Plain, Coast and Hill' do *not* make up a complete threefold division of Attica, but are the names given to the most prominent semi-organised factions in the state.
[21] i.59.

circle thought and said, and that his audience expected, the Athenians were indeed mighty pleased with themselves. It is unlikely that this sophistication went very deep in the urban poor and extremely so in the case of the peasantry of Attica.

This was all the more true in the middle of the sixth century when the local cults of Attica were as powerful as ever: archaeological discoveries of dedications from the sanctuaries are evidence for this.[22] It has been suggested[23] that Peisistratus, through the father of the statuesque Phye, was able to exploit a local manifestation of the goddess through the cult of Athene Pallenis, the nearest cult to Paeania. In any case it is clear that Peisistratus and Megacles took a gamble by playing upon the superstition of the countrymen of Attica, and that their bluff was not called.

Sober students of history would have preferred Herodotus to discuss what lay behind this bizarre episode; instead he makes a satirical thrust at the intellectual pretensions of the Athenians of his own day: 'Look at the gullibility of your grandfathers!' This treatment of bygone events in such a way as to make a contemporary point is the very type of thing that Thucydides so much disapproved of; we shall meet other examples in the course of this work.[24] Herodotus of course was fully aware of the power of local cults and frequently mentions them: from Attica and Salamis alone, Athene Pallenis, Polias and Sciras, Pan, Demeter Achaiia, Zeus Karios, the Eleusinian Mysteries and the hero-cult of Aias. No less relevantly, in a different context he gives another example of how a tyrant exploited them for a political purpose – Cleisthenes of Sicyon and the cults of Adrastus and Melanippus.[25]

The alliance of Megacles and Peisistratus foundered on the very thing that was intended to cement it. Peisistratus had grown-up sons by an earlier marriage, whom he clearly foresaw as his dynastic successors. The position of any children born to his new and aristocratic wife might well be ambiguous; he may also, as Herodotus suggests, have been influenced by the curse upon the Alcmeonidae. In any event the marriage was unconsummated, and, as one of Megacles' motives had been to secure his own family's future, he realised that the exercise was pointless. Rejoining the tyrant's enemies he succeeded in forcing Peisistratus into a second exile which lasted for ten years. But then Peisistratus returned yet again, this time to stay, and it was the turn of the family to flee into exile, where they remained at least until the tyrant's death.

---

[22] A.M. Snodgrass, *Archaic Greece* (Dent, London, 1980), Ch. 1-3, has much interesting material on cults and (p. 53) some startling figures of objects dedicated down to the end of the seventh century.

[23] By Davies, *Ath. Families*, p. 455; Phye, i.60.

[24] See index of subject matter – attention-catching passages.

[25] Respectively i.62, v.82, viii.94, v.61, vi.105, v.66, viii.65, viii.121 (the last paragraph also implying a reference to Poseidon's cult at Sunion). Cleisthenes v.67, cf. Ch. 3, p. 80.

This is a convenient moment to discuss two shadowy members of the family. Herodotus briefly narrates the battle of Pallene, which sealed Peisistratus' final return; the manuscript texts then continue:[26] 'Some of the Athenians fell in the battle, others fled with Alcmeonides.' The last name has always been emended to read 'with the Alcmeonidae', but the case for this has lapsed with the discovery of independent evidence for an 'Alcmeonides, son of Alcmeon' who was victor at the Great Panathenaea in, needless to say, the four-horse chariot race. As the inscription in question[27] was found in Boeotia, it has been well guessed that his victory was in 546 (the year of Pallene) and that he was forced to flee Attica before he could make his victor's dedication in Athens. Herodotus' text, then, if correct, shows that he was by 546 considered to be head of the family, his brother Megacles [II] having presumably died. Like Megacles, Alcmeonides had a son named Hippocrates. This man is not mentioned by literary sources but well over a hundred ostraka bearing his name have come to light, dating from the later 480s. By then an elderly man, he seems to have caught a share of the popular ill-feeling against the Alcmeonidae which caused the ostracism of his cousin Megacles [IV] in 487/6.

The remaining ghost figure may not be a member of the family at all, but the temptation to entertain at least the possibility is very strong. A magnificent Kouros (standing figure of a young man), found at Anavyssos in south-eastern Attica has been matched with a base bearing a brief epitaph: the youth had been killed in battle, and his name was Kroisos (i.e. Croesus).[28] If any Athenian family were to call one of its sons by that foreign name, who better than the Alcmeonidae? Was he a son or grandson of Alcmeon, killed at Pallene – the date of which is consistent, at least, with the sculptural style? The area of the find falls undoubtedly in the 'Paralia', the 'Coast' area of Megacles [II]; but while it is likely enough that the family owned property in the Anavyssos area, it is only fair to state that 'Anaphlystos' (the classical name) is never found as a deme name in connection with any Alcmeonid, who in all known cases were enrolled in the suburban demes of Alopeke, Xypete and Agryle, at any rate down to the middle 400s.

To father 'Kroisos' upon the Alcmeonidae on the strength of Herodotus VI.125, and then to use the statue as evidence in support of Herodotus' tale, is to argue in a circle. What the statue does show is that a family wealthy enough to afford a grand monument for one of its younger members thought sufficiently highly of the barbarian king to use his name – and that is confirmation, of a sort. The Alcmeonidae looked for support where it was to

---

[26] i.64.3.

[27] IG.i^2, 472.

[28] Now in the National Archaeological Museum, Athens.

be found, and they showed their gratitude to their patrons by the names they adopted. The Sicyonian connection, a very splendid one, produced the names of Cleisthenes (II, the lawgiver), Agarista (mother of Pericles), and Aristonymus (like Hippocrates II, known only from ostraka); Megacles II and his brother Alcmeonides both had sons whom they named Hippocrates: that was the name of Peisistratus' father, and the most likely time for the birth of these cousins would have been in the early 550s, when Megacles II, hard pressed by Lycurgus, was courting Peisistratus' favour.

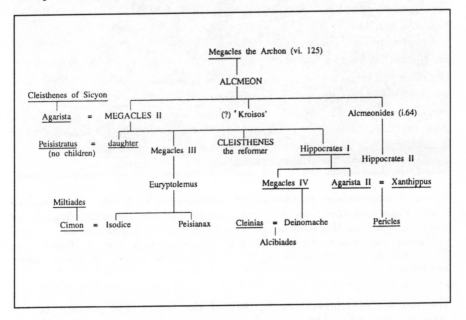

Major personalities within the family in Herodotus' story are in capitals. All others whom Herodotus mentions are underlined.

Of the return of the Alcmeonidae from the exile of 546, Herodotus says nothing. But a fragment of an archon-list on stone, cut in the fifth century, gives the names of Hippias, Cleisthenes and Miltiades in succession.[29] As Miltiades of Marathon is known to have been archon in 524, Cleisthenes had the office in 525 and Hippias in what would have been the first or second full year of his tyranny. It looks exactly as though the new reign was being inaugurated by the chief himself holding the supreme constitutional office, and by such a public display of harmony and conciliation with two of Athens' greatest families. But the Alcmeonidae were in exile again before the end of the tyranny (we cannot determine exactly when) and Miltiades was packed off to a kind of exile-by-employment in the Chersonese.

---

[29] M-L, no. 6; Miltiades' archonship: Dion. Hal. vii.3.1.

The Alcmeonidae confuted. This fragment of the Athenian archon-list (M-L no. 6) inscribed c. 425, shows that Cleisthenes was Archon (in 525) between the tyrant Hippias and Miltiades, disproving Herodotus' statement at vi.123 that the Alcmeonidae were in exile throughout the tyranny. The last name is almost certainly that of Hippias' son, Peisistratus the younger. (American School of Classical Studies at Athens: Agora Excavations)

The murder of Hipparchus, brother of the tyrant and partner in the régime, occurred in 514, and understandably caused the character of Hippias' rule to change. Herodotus and Thucydides agree in all material particulars: Hipparchus was not the reigning tyrant, and as he was the specific target of Harmodius and Aristogeiton, there was no motive of liberation in the murder. If Hippias was to be killed also, that was for the conspirators' own security. It was hardly to be expected that Hippias, who survived, would appreciate the niceties of this, and from being an heir of Peisistratus in his popular and benevolent rule he became sour and repressive.[30] From that moment the days of the tyranny were numbered. The comparable régimes in neighbouring Megara, Corinth and Sicyon had gone under a generation and more earlier; the institution was out of date and could only justify itself by government that was both successful and popular.

Seeking to capitalise on the new discontent the Alcmeonidae and their

---

[30] v.55 ff.; Th.i.20 and vi.53 ff.

fellow exiles began their moves to return. A force was raised and an invasion was launched from Boeotia. They seized and fortified Leipsydrium in the hill-country of northern Attica, but their attempt was put down by Hippias' troops. Cleisthenes, now the head of the family, was forced to try a less direct but more effective approach.

He had put his exile to good use, for the Alcmeonid connection with Delphi was revived – if indeed it had ever lapsed. The temple of Apollo had been destroyed by fire in 548. Money was raised by the Amphictyonic Council, and the contract for completing the rebuilding was awarded to Cleisthenes and his family – an unusual opportunity for him to display his talent as an administrator. The great work was completed to more than general satisfaction, for, as Herodotus says,[31] the Alcmeonidae used their wealth to go beyond the stipulations of the contract in various ways, including the building of the façade in Parian marble rather than tufa. The sum of 300 talents was needed for rebuilding,[32] 75 of which were raised by a collecting-box being passed round the Greek world and Egypt. It may seem odd that a sum far less than imperial Athens received as one year's tribute should take 30-odd years to collect, but that may be no more than a reflection upon Panhellenic as opposed to local piety. (When Athens completed the Parthenon in nine years, the full cost, contributed of course by her allies, lay ready to hand.)

What is not certain is when Cleisthenes took on the contract: Herodotus and 'Aristotle' both say[33] that this took place after the Leipsydrium disaster, but that may be telescoping events somewhat. Be that as it may, Cleisthenes found himself handling large sums of money. That made it all too easy, after the event, for his enemies to say that he had bribed the Delphic priestess to give the answer he desired to all enquirers from Sparta: 'Liberate Athens.' It is not necessary to be a fanatical pro-Alcmeonid to treat the allegation of bribery with scepticism; the splendid work on the temple – partially confirmed by archaeology – may have been bribe enough. Moreover, the Spartan government did have some substantial reasons for intervening. The Peisistratid house may have had 'ties of friendship' with Sparta, but they had even closer ties with Argos, Sparta's hereditary foe; and it now appeared to be settled Spartan policy to put down unpopular tyrannies, reap the credit for so doing and enjoy thereafter the alliance of a docile pro-Spartan oligarchic government. It is difficult to substantiate this statement with firm instances beyond those of Hippias of Athens and Polycrates of Samos – the attack on whom actually failed – but Herodotus, Thucydides and Aristotle independently give Sparta the

---

[31] v.62.
[32] ii.180.
[33] *Ath. Pol.* 19.

principal credit for ending tyranny in Greece.[34]

Bribe or no bribe, it is clear that Cleisthenes and the Alcmeonidae duped the Spartan government, who were sufficiently excited by the prospect of taking Athens under their wing to shrug off the repulse of their first effort and return in force under the vigorous King Cleomenes. A lucky chance enabled him to make a quick end to the siege of the Acropolis, and Hippias left quietly. This was in 510. The exiles now returned, and Cleisthenes found the government of Athens in the hands of a 'Tory' clique headed by Isagoras son of Teisander – a sound pro-Spartan body of men.

Before considering Cleisthenes' appeal for popular support and his reforms, it is worth examining the claim made by Herodotus[35] that the Alcmeonidae were the true liberators of Athens. The claim is emphatically endorsed by Thucydides,[36] whose whole digression on the story of Harmodius and Aristogeiton has the tone of a professor of history correcting a prevalent error. There was after all a statuary group of the two 'Liberators' in Athens, a copy of the original which Xerxes had carried off to Persia; no less potent, there was in popular circulation the romantic drinking song that attributed the liberation of Athens to the famous pair with their swords concealed in branches of myrtle.[37] This can be taken in two ways, not mutually exclusive. There was nothing unreasonable in the memory of Harmodius and Aristogeiton being celebrated in Athens; they had lost their lives in striking a definite blow at the tyranny, whatever their motives may have been, and irrespective of the fact that the tyranny was intensified for a while. But equally we can suppose that the enemies of the Alcmeonidae played up the role of Harmodius and Aristogeiton for all it was worth and a good deal more.

It was two years before Cleisthenes could decisively assert himself in Athenian politics. He had apparently made no headway by 508, for in that year Isagoras himself was Archon. Cleisthenes' bid for power consisted of an appeal to the masses, including a number of unenfranchised immigrants of the first or second generation – who, even if they could not vote, could no doubt make their voices heard. The people of Athens had evidently taken the measure of Isagoras and his supporters – namely that they were reactionaries who would destroy, if they got the chance, the democratic institutions that Solon had created and even the tyrants had not dismantled. This assessment was proved correct when Isagoras, outmanoeuvred, appealed to King Cleomenes to come and bolster his

---

[34] v.92; Th.i.18; Arist. *Politics*, 1312b. A list of shadowy examples, some fictitious, is given by Plut. *MH*, 859D; for Sicyon, however, there is independent evidence.

[35] vi.121.

[36] Th. vi.59.

[37] Page, LGS, nos. 447–50.

position, and at the same time he brought up the old charge of family pollution against Cleisthenes. As the Spartan army approached, the Alcmeonidae left Athens, and many more were banished at a word from Isagoras. But when Cleomenes attempted to destroy the Boulè and replace it by a tame nominated council of 300, the councillors refused to leave and the Athenian people rose. The Spartans were besieged on the Acropolis even as they had besieged Hippias, and left quietly after two days. Cleisthenes and the other exiles promptly returned and the great reform, previously initiated or at least promised, was now carried through to completion .

This is not the place to embark upon a detailed study of Cleisthenes' reform, but rather Herodotus' treatment of it.[38] The historian is of course less than enthralled by constitutional history, but even so his sketch of what Cleisthenes did has given rise to much disappointed criticism. The most apparently extraordinary thing is the way Herodotus compares Cleisthenes' reform of the tribes with the conduct of his grandfather Cleisthenes of Sicyon. The latter, 'in mockery of the Sicyonians', had given opprobrious nicknames to three out of the four tribes at Sicyon; Cleisthenes the younger, 'out of contempt of the Ionians', abolished the four Ionian tribes at Athens and created ten new ones.[39] Herodotus does not go on to explain how each of the tribes was made up of three units from different geographical areas of Attica, nor does he attempt to supply a serious reason for this. Rather, his treatment is light-hearted and cynical.

Why this levity? Cleisthenes may have been a far-sighted statesman who knew, as Aristotle did,[40] that an extension of the franchise is best accompanied by a re-casting of hereditary divisions; who saw the need to break down the power of the local magnates; and who saw the opportunity to unify Attica by the creation of new political and military units that cut across geographical divisions – all of which did actually happen. But at the same time he was a consummate politician with an instinct and a proven flair for survival, and Herodotus clearly saw that his political arrangements were made with a view to securing his personal position and were not merely, nor even mainly, the handiwork of a high-minded legislator. Cleisthenes' supporters were heavily concentrated in and near Athens – the family domains to the south-east of the city, and the newly enfranchised migrants who were mostly tradesmen and artisans – and he could probably count on receiving majority support at an average meeting of the Ecclesia, as well as a strong, possibly dominant voice in the Boulè of 500, which was organised on tribal lines. His reform brought great long-term benefits to

---

[38] For an accessible up-to-date study, see W.G. Forrest, *The Emergence of Greek Democracy* (Weidenfeld & Nicolson, London, 1966).

[39] v.68–9.

[40] *Politics*, 1319b.

Athens, but in inferring his motives we must beware of regarding all the results as having necessarily been willed by Cleisthenes.

Cleisthenes' political future was not in fact to be of long duration. With Athens' new democracy coming under pressure from the Spartans (who mounted two more invasions, both of them abortive) and likely to do so from Boeotia, new allies were needed. Ambassadors were sent to Persia, where they made the traditional gestures of submission to the king and returned home. Their conduct was disowned in Athens – but it is difficult to imagine that the Athenians thought they could get a Persian alliance on any other terms. As we hear no more of Cleisthenes (he simply disappears from history) it is natural to associate him with the public displeasure over this slightly unsavoury episode, which certainly took place during his brief period of pre-eminence. Perhaps he felt, and not unnaturally, that the drawbacks of remote vassalage to King Darius were more bearable than the dangers of defeat by Athens' neighbours. On the other hand, he may simply have died; he was almost certainly in his sixties.

Cleisthenes was the last Alcmeonid of first-rate importance in the male line. In the generation after him we hear of his brother's children, Megacles IV and Agarista, each named after their grandparents. Cleisthenes may have left no son, and Megacles would have been head of the family during the 490s.

One of the most discussed passages in all Herodotus is VI.121 – his defence of the Alcmeonidae against the charge of having raised the shield-signal after the battle of Marathon. In many ways the passage is extraordinary. Herodotus drops the role of the narrator and abruptly assumes, or appears to assume, that of the advocate, with a finely developed argument from probability: the Alcmeonidae had proved themselves the most dedicated foes of tyranny, therefore it was unthinkable that they should support the return of the aged Hippias under the aegis of Persia. But 'Herodotus' attempt to prove Alcmeonid hatred of the barbarian and of the tyrant is illogical and unconvincing.'[41] Indeed it is, if taken purely at face value, but that it is not possible to do. His 'defence' includes one statement that is false on his own showing – that the family was in exile throughout the period of the tyranny. In Book I he showed us the coalition of Megacles II with Peisistratus and their marriage alliance; it was only under Peisistratus' third phase that they were exiled, and again under Hippias after the reconciliation not mentioned by Herodotus. But watch what happens next – look at the placement of this advocacy. To illustrate the distinction of the Alcmeonidae Herodotus singles out two anecdotes that between them confirm precisely the two charges made against the family. Alcmeon got rich by dancing attendance upon an Eastern potentate;

---

[41] How & Wells, ii, p. 115.

Megacles II married the daughter of Greece's most spectacular tyrant. If we can see this, so could Herodotus and so could his audiences. His advocacy, in short, is a dazzling piece of irony – a pure specimen of what Thucydides[42] attacked as 'a showpiece intended for the ears of an immediate public'. Herodotus did not aim to convince, but to ridicule the 'official' defence put forward for the Alcmeonidae.

Bad news for the Alcmeonidae. Ostrakon cast against Megacles (IV) son of Hippocrates (vi.131), ostracized in 487 as a 'friend of the tyrants'. Note the archaic letter-forms. (American School of Classical Studies at Athens: Agora Excavations)

When Herodotus wrote, the archon-list going back to the 500s may or may not have been extant; but every Athenian must have known that Megacles IV – uncle of Pericles, no less – had been ostracised in 487/6 as a friend of the tyrants[43] – that is to say, he had favoured the restoration of Hippias whom his uncle Cleisthenes had done so much to expel. Why should he have taken this line in 490, year of Marathon? The answer is that the Alcmeonid house had been temporarily eclipsed by their hereditary rivals. From his return to Athens in 493 Miltiades had been the dominant figure in public life, emerging scot-free from a prosecution directed at his tyranny in the

---

[42] Th.i.22.
[43] *Ath. Pol.* 22.

Chersonese – a charge for which there was ample evidence. It must have been the prospect of a long spell of Philaid pre-eminence that induced their rivals to contemplate treason; that, plus at least the possibility that Athens would lose the war of 490, and thus it would be as well to take out an insurance policy.

But things seldom work out as they are expected to, and the Alcmeonidae, while unable to save Megacles (who was perhaps more skilful at horse-breeding than politics), were able to be revenged upon Miltiades. After the fiasco of his Aegean expedition following the victory of Marathon, Miltiades was prosecuted; not, indeed, by any of the discredited Alcmeonidae, but by the ablest of their connections, Xanthippus. He pressed the charges home; the verdict and sentence left the Philaid family estates encumbered for many years afterwards.

'While pregnant, Agarista had a dream, and she dreamed that she gave birth to a lion; and a few days later she bore Pericles to Xanthippus.'[44] What did Herodotus really think of Pericles? We must beware of looking at the lion through medieval eyes: it was a decidedly ambiguous symbol, denoting, to some, courage no doubt, but to others perhaps rapacity or violence. How a Greek would have interpreted this omen would have depended on his point of view: a non-Athenian would have felt fear of Athenian power, an Athenian perhaps pride that one of his fellow citizens could strike terror into others. The native of Halicarnassus, but long-term resident in Athens, in Delphic fashion leaves us to decide for ourselves; and on that note he takes his leave of the Alcmeonidae.

What an extraordinary family record! And yet certain constant features occur. The Alcmeonidae always sought power and influence where those commodities were to be found. When the time was not ripe for tyranny, Megacles the Archon ruthlessly suppressed Cylon's coup, with the self-confidence of a ruling oligarch. When reform is in the wind, Alcmeon is publicly associated with Solon. When tyranny is established and prosperous elsewhere, we find Megacles II marrying a tyrant's daughter; at home he leads a vigorous and progressive faction in the state. When things go hard for him in politics, he allies with the tyrant Peisistratus; when the situation alters he helps to throw him out. Cleisthenes serves as archon under Hippias in the early and happier days of his tyranny; when Hippias' rule has turned sour Cleisthenes leads the movement to overthrow him, to some effect; correctly identifying the public feeling against reaction he harnesses it to his own purposes at the expense of the chief elected magistrate, Isagoras. Finally, Megacles IV intrigues for the return of Hippias, moved partly perhaps by hostility towards Miltiades, partly by a not unreasonable

---

[44] vi.131. The passage has been ably discussed by C.W. Fornara, *Herodotus, an Interpretative Essay* (Oxford University Press, 1971), some of whose ideas I follow.

opinion that the Persians would win and that it would be as well to be on the winning side.

The zeal which the Alcmeonidae displayed in seeking support and influence, and in impressing the Greek world with their brilliant and costly racehorses, suggests that they started at some disadvantage as compared with their rivals; and this does in fact seem to be the case. In the seventh and sixth centuries BC, the most effective way of influencing the hearts and minds of men lay through control of the local religious cults of Attica, and these rested with a handful of ancient noble families, such as the Boutadae, to which Lycurgus the leader of the 'Plain' almost certainly belonged. Peisistratus may have had an interest in anything up to three cults;[45] Herodotus was unable to trace the origins of Cleisthenes' rival Isagoras, but he goes out of his way to mention the cult his family controlled, that of Zeus Karios. Neither the Alcmeonidae nor the Philaidae, however, despite their Eupatrid status, and despite their great wealth and estates, are known to have been connected with any cult. The dynastic marriages of both houses, and their tremendous expenditure on horse-racing, seem to be efforts at counteracting this weakness. Peisistratus after all achieved a more solid and permanent success than any of his rivals without, so far as is known, having bred a single racehorse, but by leading a firm and loyal body of supporters and using methods that can best be called direct. The Alcmeonidae do not seem to have been able to count on the *continuing* loyalty of any large group of citizens; even the political capital built up by Cleisthenes in 508 had been dissipated by 490. Megacles [IV], ostracised in 487/6, was ostracised again after 479; a member of a minor branch of the family, Leobotes son of an Alcmeon, appeared as one of Themistocles' prosecutors in the late 470s; but all political initiative had by then passed away from the male line of the Alcmeonidae. They were a spent force.

The story of the family did not of course end there. Herodotus must have known many of its members who were roughly of his own generation: Deinomache, perhaps, mother of Alcibiades, daughter of Megacles IV; her cousin Isodice (to whom it fell to end the family rivalry by marrying Cimon) died before Herodotus is likely to have come to Athens. He could have known Isodice's brother, Peisianax, who built the Stoa Poikile in Athens in about 460, the last major public work in democratic Athens built under private patronage: was he bidding for popularity with this splendid edifice? One of the paintings in it showed the battle of Marathon, with a prominent place going to his sister's father-in-law, Miltiades.[46] Peisianax' son Euryptolemus, almost the last traceable descendant of Megacles the Archon in the male line, was another whom Herodotus would probably have known.

---

[45] Davies, *Ath. Families*, p. 454 f.

[46] Aeschines, iii.186; Paus.i.15.5.

In 406 he showed more moral courage than some of his more celebrated ancestors by standing up to a hostile Ecclesia and demanding a separate trial for the generals accused after the victory of Arginusae; he failed to carry his point and one of those condemned was his kinsman Pericles the younger.[47]

The political careers of Pericles and Alcibiades lie outside the scope of this work, but each can be seen to belong to an Alcmeonid tradition. In his early public career Pericles showed the opportunistic flair that his sixth-century ancestors possessed — the ability to identify the trends of public opinion early and capitalise upon them. This was the Pericles that supported Ephialtes' democratic reform, introduced pay for jurymen and restricted the citizenship — to the advantage of those that survived the review; who advocated the conversion of the Delian League surplus to defraying the cost of the Parthenon and other buildings, brushing aside in the process the moral arguments advanced by Thucydides, son of Melesias. The 'Olympian' Pericles of Thucydides[48] is a mature statesman who has made his way to the top and secured his hold on popular feeling. As for Alcibiades, we can leave aside his opportunistic policies, and need only mention his brilliant success at the 416 Olympics, where his chariot entries finished first, second and fourth. His forebears Alcmeon and Megacles [IV] would have been proud of him.

Herodotus' attitude to the Alcmeonidae varies, but we must acquit him of any undue partiality towards them.[49] We learn more about them from Herodotus than from anyone else, and we learn more to their discredit. Anyone wishing to accuse the family of time-serving and political opportunism can find copious evidence in his pages. While, therefore, Herodotus received information from Alcmeonid sources in Athens (no reason to doubt that), we must give him the credit for assessing and interpreting it himself. Admittedly, he omits Cleisthenes' return from exile under Hippias; possibly he did not know of it.[50] He also fluffs the story of the Cylonian conspiracy: he does not name Megacles the Archon (but neither does Thucydides) and he attributes responsibility to the wrong board of magistrates. But even so he does not play down the matter of family pollution. This was of course very much of a live issue in 432, when Herodotus' work was taking shape: the Spartans attempted to discredit Pericles through it.[51] Not only does Herodotus mention the 'curse' in connection with Cleisthenes' brief expulsion in 508, but also at a point in his

---

[47] X. *Hell.* i.7.16.
[48] Th.ii.65.
[49] A charge repeatedly levelled by, among others, How & Wells.
[50] The archon-list is thought, on epigraphical grounds, to have been engraved c.425.
[51] Th.i.127.

narrative where it was far from indispensable, namely as a possible reason why Peisistratus did not treat Megacles' daughter as his wife.

Equally, no one writing from an Alcmeonid point of view could possibly have portrayed the tergiversations of Megacles [II] as Herodotus did in Book I. The allegation that the Alcmeonidae bribed the Delphic priestess – very possibly unfounded – Herodotus mentions on three separate occasions, once as a virtual statement of fact. Again, while the reform of Cleisthenes brought lasting benefits to Athens, Herodotus does not rhapsodise upon his statesmanship, for he knows, or suspects, too much about his motives. He does not directly name Cleisthenes in connection with the submission to Persia, but the link with the preceding narrative is too close for any reader to miss. The total disappearance of Cleisthenes from the Athenian scene and from Herodotus' narrative is suggestive. It is true that some Alcmeonid connections get a good press: Alcibiades' father Cleinias and his trireme earn their tiny mention in Book VIII, and Pericles' father Xanthippus emerges well from Book IX; but their roles have not been unduly played up and there is no reason to suppose that they were not in any case distinguished and successful men. In the tale of Agarista's wooing – most enjoyable of all Herodotus' stories – one can certainly trace an Alcmeonid source gleefully boasting of a triumph over the Philaid rival; but as the tale as a whole convicts the Alcmeonidae of the very charge they would most evade, that of intimacy with tyranny, we need not assume that Herodotus was unduly influenced. Balance and critical appraisal, not adulation, are the keynotes of his treatment of the Alcmeonidae.

MILTIADES AND HIS FOREBEARS

The family of Miltiades traced its descent from Philaeus, son of Aias. Like the Alcmeonidae, they were of Eupatrid (patrician) status, a fact long assumed but now directly attested by a fragment of the archon-list making Cypselus archon three years before Solon liberalised the qualifications for the office. Again like the Alcmeonidae, and surprisingly in view of their 'heroic' descent, they seem to have had no connection with any traditional cult. However, their antecedents seem more splendid than those of their rivals. The family name of Miltiades crops up in very early archon-lists, but chronologically the first of the Philaidae treated by Herodotus is Hippocleides, son of Teisander. In his archonship the festival of the Panathenaea was founded,[52] and we know that was in 566. It must have been well before then that this glamorous figure paid court to Agarista of Sicyon and won Cleisthenes' favour until, as it were, falling at the last fence: what bad luck to be made the butt of such a diverting story! Proof

---

[52] Marcellinus, *vit.Thuc.* 3; Cypselus' archonship: M-L, no. 6.

that his family had 'arrived' if anything earlier than their rivals is Herodotus' statement that they were already connected with the family of Cypselus, tyrant of Corinth. On the assumption that a grandson would inherit his grandfather's name we can construct a speculative but probable family tree; the main body of it is based directly on information given in Herodotus.[53]

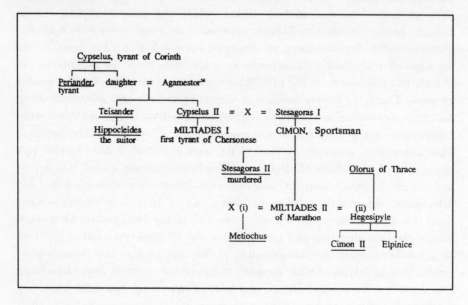

All major personalities within the family in Herodotus' story are in capitals. All others whom Herodotus mentions are underlined.

It has not escaped my notice that attempts are made from time to time[54] to place Cleisthenes' opponent Isagoras, son of Teisander, in this family. Teisander is quite a common name, but only two of those attested definitely were Philaidae, and Herodotus explicitly states that he cannot trace Isagoras' family origin, but does mention the family cult, which we do not hear of anywhere else in a Philaid connection. If Isagoras had been a relation of Miltiades, that would have been a matter of public knowledge, probably aired at one of Miltiades' trials, and we must either accept Herodotus or accuse him of deliberate lying. Though certainly sympathetic to the Philaids, he does not elsewhere suppress information discreditable to them, for example Miltiades' tyrannical rule in the Chersonese and his service under Darius,[55] and there seems no earthly reason why he should do so here.

---

[53] vi.38–9; vi.103.

[54] E.g. recently by P. Bicknell, 'Studies in Greek Genealogy', *Historia*, Einzelschrift 19.

[55] vi.39 and iv.137.

The Athenian Cypselus [II] is little more than a name to us, even with the discovery of his archonship on a fragment of the same huge stone that produced the names of Cleisthenes and Miltiades in the 520s. Miltiades [I] seems to have been the sole survivor of this branch of the family, for he named his heir from the family of his half-brother Cimon, who was by then dead. It has been suggested[57] that when Cypselus' widow married Stesagoras I — another mere name — her new husband was a kinsman of Cypselus, and so she was keeping the family property within the family. This is possible but unproven and probably unprovable.

The Philaid family originally came from Brauron, in the Hyperakria or 'Hill' area of eastern Attica. Philaeus himself was supposed to have settled there, and perhaps for historical reasons under Cleisthenes' reform Brauron was included in the deme named 'Philaidae'.[58] Interestingly, Peisistratus' family also came from Brauron. In the sixth century, however, the family of Cimon lived in the deme Lakiadae to the west of the city — they would have been *Pedieis* or men of the 'Plain'; and it seems most likely that Miltiades I did too: the Dolonci coming from Delphi to Athens[59] would have naturally passed through that district.

It is with this last-mentioned episode that the family enters the main stream of recorded history. The Dolonci, a people living in the Thracian Chersonese (Gallipoli), hard-pressed by their enemies, asked the advice of Delphi on their difficulties. The reply recorded as given to their chiefs was to choose as their *oikistes* (perhaps, here, 'organiser'?) the first man who invited them in; and this man proved to be Miltiades of Athens, their passage through Phocis and Boeotia having proved fruitless.

The story has been tricked out with folk-tale elements for public consumption after the event; in its substance we can be sure it is true. The oracle knew of Athens' abiding interest in the area of the Hellespont. At the beginning of the sixth century Athens had fought a war with Mytilene for the possession of Sigeum, on the Asian side of the narrows. Athens won that round: the poet Alcaeus of Lesbos threw away his shield in the battle, and Periander of Corinth ended hostilities by an arbitration in Athens' favour.[60] At some later time, it is not known in what circumstances, Athens lost Sigeum, but regained it during Peisistratus' tyranny. It was while Athens had no foothold on the straits that Miltiades was approached: this move would have been welcome to all — to the Dolonci, evidently; to Miltiades, as a powerful magnate whose political ambitions were cramped by

---

[57] A.R. Burn, *The Lyric Age of Greece* (Arnold, London, 1960), p. 311.

[58] Other, more cynical explanations are possible.

[59] vi.34–5.

[60] v.95.

Peisistratus' settled government;[61] and to Peisistratus himself, who saw a potential rival honourably removed, and an Athenian presence on the shore of the Hellespont.

The reason for Athens' preoccupation with this area can be stated crisply: corn. When Solon banned the export of corn,[62] Attica could not have been self-supporting; *a fortiori* much less so with the rapid growth of an urban artisan population that followed Solon's reforms. Athens' wise policy was to seek sources of corn from outside the immediate Greek world, where the supply would not be vulnerable to politically-motivated disruption. This policy needs no explaining in an age when the Western world depends for its oil supplies upon some alarmingly unstable regimes. The rich corn-lands of the Black Sea coast were ideal for her purposes, but Athens was never happy unless she had a measure of control over the narrows. After the expulsion of the Persians from Greece in 479, the *very first* place attacked and taken by Athens' forces was Sestos, on the Chersonese;[63] this was the point where Xerxes' host had crossed into Europe[64] and sound strategy demanded its capture, but we can be sure that Athens' own interests were uppermost in the minds of all. Athens in fact held the Chersonese with intermissions until 338, when it was the last of her overseas possessions to be ceded to Philip of Macedon.

Of Miltiades' tenure of the Chersonese little need be said beyond Herodotus' own account. After checking with Delphi he took with him a group of Athenian settlers and ruled as 'tyrant' evidently with the consent of the natives. He did right by the Dolonci by walling off the isthmus; his attack on Lampsacus probably formed part of a scheme to seize a position on the Asian side of the straits. Croesus' intervention on his behalf is interesting in that it shows that the Alcmeonidae did not have a monopoly of his goodwill. If the date which I am assuming is right, the episode belonged to the very moment when Croesus was seriously contemplating an Athenian alliance[65] – though eventually settling for one with Sparta. The feud with Lampsacus dragged on – probably prosecuted with no great vigour – for 30 years or more; Herodotus vaguely links with it the murder of Miltiades' nephew and successor Stesagoras II.[66]

Meanwhile, the head of the family's interests at home was Miltiades' half-brother Cimon. He was known as Coalemos ('Simpleton')[67] and that nickname was probably all too accurate. He is not recorded as having played

---

[61] vi.35.

[62] Plut. *Solon*, 24.

[63] ix.114–20.

[64] vii.33.

[65] i.56; see chronological appendix to Chapter 1, p. 46.

[66] vi.38.

[67] Plut. *Cimon*, 4.

any part in politics or public life, though a man of his wealth and breeding might surely have expected or been expected to. His sole interest was horse-racing, and his success here evidently cost him first his residence in Athens, lastly perhaps his life. To win three consecutive Olympiads with the same team of mares was paralleled only once.[68] Peisistratus exiled him, out of jealousy perhaps of his sporting prowess. Although this occurred before Cimon's first Blue Riband, he no doubt had had several successes in the lesser games and was about to start hot favourite for the 536 Olympics. Anyway, he won that victory when in exile; his second he transferred to the name of Peisistratus, a generous gesture that earned him his recall. His third, 528, was either immediately before or immediately after the old tyrant's death, and it was in the unsettled atmosphere surrounding Hippias' accession that this figure of towering prestige was assassinated. He was a menace to the Peisistratidae not because of anything he did but because of what he was − a symbol of the old nobility, a potential constitutional rallying point for the disaffected. 'Cut down the tallest' was the advice of the old tyrant Thrasybulus to the young tyrant Periander;[69] it is a policy that seems strangely foreign to Athens.

There was evidently enough doubt subsisting about the involvement of the Peisistratidae in Cimon's murder for his younger son Miltiades II to be on tolerable terms with them.[70] He held the archonship in 524, the year after Cleisthenes (who was a considerably older man), and was no doubt being prepared for a career of important public service under Hippias. Whatever plans there may have been for his future, however, had to be revised on the news of Stesagoras' murder. The Peisistratidae promptly despatched Miltiades to the Chersonese with a small military force and, no doubt, strict instructions about what to do. His arrest of the local chieftains by a stratagem, and his employment of a mercenary bodyguard, were a crisp reaction to the events of his brother's murder, and were the sort of behaviour that ranked as 'tyranny' in Athenian eyes. It has often been observed that we know as much about the Chersonese subplot of the Peisistratid period as about any other, and more than most: this is probably due to the recollection or even the record of things said at Miltiades' trial.

The detailed story of Miltiades II in the Chersonese has been bedevilled by an untidy confusion in Herodotus' manuscripts at VI.40, which (if taken at face value) suggests that he was in exile from the Chersonese from 511 to 496. A simple change to the text,[71] removing some repetitive

---

[68] By Evagoras the Spartan—an undatable treble (vi.103); Moretti, *Olympionikai* is the authority for Olympic datings in this chapter.

[69] v.92.

[70] vi.39: Stesagoras II was in the Chersonese being groomed for the succession.

[71] Proposed by Dobree, supported by Powell, 'Notes on Herodotus—II', *CQ*, 1935. It is only fair to point out that this change is not universally accepted; cf. A.R. Burn, *Persia and the Greeks* (Arnold, London, 1962), pp. 218 ff.

words and incidentally making the run of the sentence smoother, makes Miltiades' flight and return all part of the same episode, and belonging to a period much earlier than the Ionian revolt.

The first major episode of his rule was Darius' invasion of Europe. This expedition achieved a solid and durable success in the annexation of Thrace; Herodotus understandably plays down[72] this rather undramatic campaign in favour of the raid into Scythia, which, though in itself unimportant, could have had a sensational conclusion. His picture of the great army lost, wandering through the trackless wastes, is a masterpiece of graphic realism. What concerns us here, however, is the role of Miltiades. Herodotus gives us an interesting list of Greek tyrants serving with their contingents under Darius.[73] Five were from Ionia and Aeolis, including Histiaeus of Miletus, but most were from the Hellespontine and Marmara cities, including Hippoclus of Lampsacus, and, from the European side, Ariston of Byzantium and Miltiades.

Was Miltiades coerced to join, was it his own decision, was it prompted by Hippias? Was the feud with Lampsacus now over and finished? Many questions suggest themselves, but rather fewer answers. Miltiades may have had no effective choice; Darius entered Europe over the Bosporus bridge at Byzantium, but recrossed by ship from Sestos in the heart of Miltiades' domain.[74] Again, we know that Hippias married his daughter Archedice to Aeantides, son of Hippoclus of Lampsacus, in 513. Thucydides – while betraying surprise at an alliance between Athens and Lampsacus, of all places! – regarded this as a frankly Medising move because Hippoclus had influence with Darius, presumably because of services rendered on the Danube.[75] It is possible, therefore, that Hippias was contemplating an indirect Persian alliance a year earlier, though the way Thucydides phrases it makes it seem like a rapidly conceived move. Certainty is unattainable.

What happened on the campaign itself, however, is less disputable. Coës of Mytilene, who accompanied Darius on his march into Scythia, advised him to leave the naval force on the Danube in order to keep their bridge in being; the other Greek officers stayed behind. When Darius had been gone for the agreed two months, a force of Scythian cavalry urged them to break up the bridge, depart, and strand Darius in the wasteland to be destroyed at leisure. According to Herodotus, Miltiades spoke up in favour of this blow for freedom, but in the ensuing discussion was overruled by

---

[72] v.1–2.

[73] iv.138.

[74] iv.87; iv.143.

[75] Th.vi.59.

Histiaèus and the majority, who pointed out that they, as Persian appointees, would lose their positions if Darius fell. Consequently a stratagem was adopted to deceive the Scythians, and when Darius and his attenuated army duly reappeared, they were able to cross to safety.

The account of Miltiades' role almost certainly comes from his defence when on trial, but there are good grounds for believing it. He was in fact one of the few, perhaps even the only one of the Greek tyrants there, who was not a Persian appointee. He had been ruler of an independent principality long enough to acquire the taste for it; and being in Europe, he had less to fear from the long arm of Persian vengeance; for all Persia's interests in Europe would surely collapse if Darius and the army were lost. And as, unlike Histiaeus and the rest, he did not depend on Persian power in reserve to maintain his position, he had the less reason to fear a democratic revolution.

Further evidence comes from the sequel. Darius handed out rewards to his loyal servants: Coës, an officer with no position, was installed as tyrant of Mytilene; Histiaeus was given a site for a colony in Thrace – incidentally in an area of interest to Athens; and Hippoclus of Lampsacus had 'great influence' with the king. Miltiades got nothing, perhaps because rumour had got out about his disloyal attitude. If so, Hippias must have been both annoyed and alarmed. Along with the marriage alliance with Lampsacus. it is possible that the Athenian outpost at Sigeum was given to Lampsacus.[76] Certainly Hippias lived at Sigeum for some years,[77] unmolested, after his expulsion from Athens.

Shortly after Darius' withdrawal the Scythians (who obviously could have known nothing of the debate among the officers at the Danube) launched a reprisal raid into the Chersonese, forcing Miltiades to flee; but this was a brief interlude.[78] He was evidently able to mend his fences with Darius. It is about now that he remarried, his new wife being Hegesipyle, daughter of a Thracian prince, Olorus.[79] This marriage produced two of Miltiades' recorded children, Cimon II and Elpinice; he had a son, Metiochus, by his first wife, who was captured by the Persians in the closing stages of the Ionian revolt[80] and lived the life of a Persian gentleman thereafter.

Nothing is recorded of Miltiades for a decade or more. His capture of Lemnos and Imbros[81] – acquisitions of lasting value to Athens – are not

---

[76] H.T. Wade-Gery,'Miltiades' in *Essays in Greek History* (Blackwell, Oxford, 1958), p. 160.

[77] v.94–6.

[78] See above, p. 39 f. for chronology.

[79] The parents of Thucydides the historian were named Olorus and Hegesipyle, probably first cousins, grandchildren of Miltiades.

[80] vi.41.

[81] Lemnos: vi.140; Imbros (vi.41) evidently was Miltiades' by 493.

dated by Herodotus and are difficult to date by any other evidence. The most probable context is in the opening stage of the Ionian revolt, when the eyes of Persia and the Greek world were focused elsewhere; for both islands had been seized by Persian forces[82] and governed by Lycaretus, brother of the Samian Maeandrius. The occupation had, it seems, lapsed with Lycaretus' death, but Persia never relinquished a claim to territory she had once occupied.

At what stage Miltiades definitely threw in his lot with the rebels, we cannot say. He was, however, active until the very end, after the fall of Miletus, and escaped to Athens when Hellespontine Asia was reduced by the Phoenician fleet. He was immediately brought to trial on the charge of 'tyranny' by his enemies – we may guess who they were – and no doubt all the facts given in Herodotus were aired for all they were worth: by the prosecution, his commission from the Peisistratidae, his arrest of the chiefs, his bodyguard of 500, his service under Darius, his undignified flight from the Scythians, and (to excite general prejudice) his marriage to a barbarian wife; by the defence, his proposal to destroy the Danube bridge, his acquisition of Lemnos for Athens, and, no doubt, his future value to the city.

Miltiades was fortunate in his timing. Athens had begun by giving the Ionian revolt modest but solid and practical support. She had fairly soon thought better of this and had withdrawn her forces,[83] underlining this new spirit of 'appeasement' by electing Hipparchus son of Charmus, a kinsman of the Peisistratidae, to the archonship of 496.[84] Early in the year 493 the tragic playwright Phrynichus was tried and convicted, perhaps on some technical charge of impiety, perhaps simply for inciting a public disturbance, after the production of his drama *The Capture of Miletus*.[85] This evidently dealt in harrowing terms with the events of the previous year, and, perhaps, castigated the Athenian authorities for pusillanimity in failing to give Ionia proper support. But that conviction was appeasement's last throw. A new archon came into office: Themistocles. He saw both the menace of Persia and the value of Miltiades. Legally of course Miltiades was entirely guilty of the charges, but political trials at Athens were decided on political grounds[86] and he was acquitted. He was elected general at the earliest opportunity, an office he held every year until his death.

This is not the place to discuss Marathon in full, but only such aspects of the battle as concern Miltiades. It is ironical that the first and arguably greatest triumph of Athens' democracy should have been achieved under a

---

[82] v.28.

[83] v.103.

[84] Dion. Hal.vi.1.

[85] vi.21. The play has not of course survived.

[86] E.g. in the *cause célèbre* of 330, Ctesiphon was manifestly guilty of the charges on the indictment, but Demosthenes' popularity and advocacy ensured Aeschines' defeat.

man whose experience of democracy was barely more than minimal, and who probably thought very little of it. Still, Miltiades and the Athenians needed each other: he knew he was a marked man in Persian eyes and could never go back; they knew that he was the one man with the expertise to give them a chance against Persia.

The name of Miltiades is imperishably associated with Marathon; he was not, however, the Athenians' commander, but the general of his tribal contingent (Oeneis). The supreme commander was Callimachus of Aphidnae, by virtue of the office of Polemarch (War Archon),[87] who, says Herodotus, was chosen not by vote but by lot. This looks like an error of fact, as the change from vote to lot in the archon's elections was made in 488/7.[88] Whether, as is at least possible, Herodotus did not know the date of the reform, or even if he went in for a little deliberate distortion, there is obvious dramatic value in making the fate of Athens hinge, as it were, upon a name drawn from a hat. But any distortion is more apparent than real. The reform of the archonship may have been less dramatic in its effects than has sometimes been supposed: since the reform of 501/0, whereby the board of ten generals was elected by popular vote,[89] the generals had assumed increasing importance, and as an office the generalship had the great advantage (from an ambitious politician's point of view) of permitting repeated re-election; the archonship could not be held more than once, and after one's year one was merely an elder statesman on the Council of Areopagus.[90] For most of the rest of the fifth century nearly all political figures held the generalship, be they great soldiers like Cimon, good ones like Pericles, or novices like Cleon. But before 487 the position of the Polemarch was unsatisfactory. There could be no guarantee that to meet a military emergency the official commander-in-chief would be the best general available, if only because that individual might have held an archonship already (as Miltiades had). While Callimachus held the traditional post of honour on the right – and all honour to him for personal courage and for listening to good advice[91] – the credit for the strategy of the campaign and the tactics of the battle must go to Miltiades. This is not only

---

[87] vi.109.

[88] *Ath. Pol.* 22.5: H's error, if error it is, was suspected long before this papyrus was placed before the public in 1891. The possibility is at least worth considering, however, that H was right: could it have been the practice that the man who topped the poll was always *the* (eponymous) archon, but the other elected 8 drew lots for the subordinate positions? Something like this is suggested by J.L. Myres, *Herodotus, Father of History* (Oxford U.P., 1953), p.208.

[89] *Ath. Pol.* 22.2.

[90] *Ath. Pol.* 62.3, and Heliastic oath ap.Dem.xxiv.150: generals were exempt from re-election disabilities because they were not magistrates of the whole people, but only of their respective tribes.

[91] C.W. Fornara, 'The Athenian Board of Generals, 501-404', *Historia*, Einzelschrift 16, pp. 6 and 72 ff., well argues that between 501 and 487 the Polemarch was still supreme in fact as well as title, but could be overruled by a majority of the (now democratically elected) generals; hence the importance of Callimachus' casting vote at Marathon.

because of the overwhelming literary evidence, and the place of Miltiades in the pictures in the Stoa Poikile, but the fact that the following year Miltiades was able to secure for himself an extraordinary commission from the people on the strength of his achievement.

The crowning deliverance of Marathon set the seal on Miltiades' fame. But what followed is a fascinating example of the mutability of fortune: Herodotus, who is so interested in this historical theme,[92] is too much of an artist to underline this instance, for it speaks clearly for itself. Miltiades' plan was to conduct a seaborne campaign round the Cyclades and take measures unspecified to prevent the Persians returning by the same way; and this was strategically sound. Herodotus also attributes to him a personal motive: he wanted to punish Lysagoras of Paros 'for denouncing him to Hydarnes the Persian'. What lies behind this (if anything does) we cannot say. Miltiades, no doubt for respectable reasons of elementary security, did not spell out to the Athenian people what his exact aims were; but when the expedition did not prosper, and finally had to be called off when Miltiades was wounded at Paros, their anger was all the greater. He was tried and condemned – not to death, for he was dying already, but to a fine of 50 talents. The rich Athenians of the fifth century were as nothing when compared with Roman magnates of later ages, but, to put the sum into perspective, it was nearly double the largest single annual payments of tribute to imperial Athens – 30 talents each from the rich islands of Thasos and Aigina. And yet, the fine was paid, not without difficulty, by his son Cimon, who by the 460s was again in the forefront of the Athenian rich.

So ends the story, as far as Herodotus tells it. He only mentions Cimon twice – his payment of the fine and, in passing, his capture of Eion in 477/6.[93] His brilliant exploits for the Delian League against Persia occupied the years of Herodotus' young manhood, and may have influenced his attitude to the Philaidae; but Cimon died abroad soon after the expiry of his ostracism and it is doubtful whether Herodotus ever met him. He may well have known his sons, including Lacedaemonius, general in 433. But we do not get from Herodotus an anecdotal picture of the Philaid house such as he gives of their rivals, and this suggests a lesser degree of family intimacy. The picture is, however, impressive: it is balanced, with elements of triumph and failure; both sides at Miltiades' trial have made their voices heard; but the dominant note seems to be one of admiring sympathy. This seems only right. For all their brilliance the Alcmeonidae could not show any achievement as glorious as Marathon, nor as enduringly valuable as Lemnos; and it is a fine artistic touch on Herodotus' part to end the narrative of Book VI, not with Miltiades' miserable failure and death, but

---

[92] i.5.

[93] vi.136 and vii.107.

44

with his capture of Lemnos, which he introduces out of sequence with effortless skill.

Miltiades' Helmet, Olympia. Inscribed 'Miltiades dedicated me'. (Deutsches Archäolgisches Institut, Athens)

APPROXIMATE CHRONOLOGY ASSUMED IN THIS CHAPTER

Much of this dating is necessarily speculative and sometimes controversial. Some of the approximations involve a margin of error of not more than a year either way, for instance Leipsydrium, c. 513. Others, especially the marriages, may be five years or more out. All sporting victories are in the four-horse chariot race.

659	A Miltiades is archon.
c. 655	Cypselus becomes tyrant at Corinth.
c. 630	Megacles archon: Cylon's attempted coup. Marriage of Cypselus' daughter with Philaid Agamestor.
c. 625	Periander succeeds Cypselus at Corinth.
c. 600-570	Cleisthenes is tyrant of Sicyon.
597	Cypselus II archon at Athens.
c. 595	Alcmeon serves in the Sacred War for Delphi, alongside Cleisthenes of Sicyon. Alcmeon is enriched by Alyattes of Lydia.
594	Solon's archonship and reforms.
592	Alcmeon wins at Olympia.

c. 590	Miltiades I, son of Cypselus, born.
c. 585	Cypselus II dies; his widow marries Stesagoras I.
c. 584	Cimon I born.
c. 575	'Trial of the Suitors': Megacles II wins the hand of Agarista of Sicyon.
566	Archonship of Hippocleides. Cleisthenes II born about this time.
561	Peisistratus' first tyranny; it is of brief duration.
556	Peisistratus' coalition with Megacles II and marriage to his daughter. His second tyranny, also of brief duration. His exile.
c. 554	Miltiades II, son of Cimon, born.
548(prob.)	Miltiades I wins at Olympia. Temple at Delphi burnt down.
546	Alcmeonides' victory at the Great Panathenaea. Battle of Pallene; Peisistratus returns as tyrant. Exile of the Alcmeonidae.
546/5	Miltiades I takes possession of the Chersonese. He wins the favour of Croesus.
544	Fall of Croesus.
In 530s	Peisistratus' forces seize Sigeum in the Troad from Mytilene .
536	Cimon in exile. He wins at Olympia.
532	Cimon's second win, ceded to Peisistratus. His recall to Athens.
528	Cimon's third win.
528/7	Peisistratus dies; Hippias succeeds to his position. Cimon murdered, perhaps at the instigation of Hippias.
In 520s	The Alcmeonidae recalled from exile.
525/4	Cleisthenes II is archon.
524/3	Miltiades II is archon.
In 520s	Miltiades I dies, succeeded as tyrant of Chersonese by Stesagoras II.
c. 515	Stesagoras murdered in the Chersonese. The Peisistratidae despatch Miltiades II to succeed him.
514	Hipparchus murdered by Harmodius and Aristogeiton. Hippias' tyranny becomes oppressive. Probably now the Alcmeonidae exiled again. Darius' invasion of Europe. Miltiades II serves with him at the Danube.
c. 513	Alcmeonid attempt to remove Hippias defeated at Leipsydrium. Scythian reprisal raid into the Chersonese. Miltiades forced to flee, but returns.
513	Hippias adopts Medising policy: marriage alliance with Lampsacus. Cleisthenes II intrigues at Delphi.
512	Spartan invasion of Athens, under Anchimolius, defeated.
c. 512	Miltiades takes as his second wife the daughter of Olorus of Thrace.
510	Second Spartan invasion of Athens, under Cleomenes. Hippias forced to withdraw to Sigeum. The exiled Alcmeonidae return, under Cleisthenes.

c. 509   Cimon II born.

508   Isagoras is archon, Cleisthenes opposes him. Third Spartan invasion, under Cleomenes, is defeated. Cleisthenes' reform of the tribes.

507/6   Fourth Spartan invasion: army breaks up when the kings disagree. Athens fends off attacks from Chalcis and Boeotia; seeks alliance with Persia, then evokes it.

c. 503   Spartans fail to carry a proposal to restore Hippias. He wins the support of the satrap Artaphernes. Athens rebuffs Artaphernes.

499/8   Outbreak of Ionian revolt. (Prob.) Miltiades captures Lemnos and Imbros.

496   Hipparchus son of Charmus is archon. Athens disengages herself from Ionian revolt.

c. 494   Birth of Pericles.

493   End of Ionian revolt. Miltiades' flight from the Chersonese. Themistocles is archon. Trials of Phrynichus and Miltiades.

490   Marathon.

489   Miltiades fails at Paros. His conviction and death.

488/7   Ostracism of Hipparchus, son of Charmus.

487/6   Ostracism of Megacles IV.

2. RELIGIOUS BELIEFS, FATE AND ORACLES

Outside the walls of Troy Patroclus, clad in the armour of Achilles, is dealing death among the Trojan ranks, and is about to engage Sarpedon, son of Zeus, King of the Lycians and Hector's noblest ally. Above the battle, Zeus addresses his consort:[1]

> Alas! Sarpedon, the dearest of mortals to me, is fated to fall to Patroclus. My heart is torn two ways – shall I snatch him up alive from the battle, and set him down in Lycia's rich land, or shall I slay him, at the hands of Menoetius' son?

Hera will have none of it.

> August son of Cronos – what a thing to say! He is a mortal man, whose fate is long settled: are you wanting to rescue him from grim death? Go on and do so, but you do so without the approval of the rest of us gods. And here is another thing for you to ponder: if you do send Sarpedon home alive, consider whether some other one of the gods may want to remove his dear son from the battle; for there are many fighting around Priam's great city who are sons of immortals, and the gods will strongly resent such conduct.

She advises Zeus to let him fall, then transport his corpse home to Lycia for honourable burial. Zeus has little choice but to comply, and 50 lines later Sarpedon duly falls.

There in a few lines of Homer is the Authorised Version matchlessly expressed. Zeus knows full well what is fated to happen to Sarpedon; he vaguely thinks aloud about the possibility of interfering with this, but Hera sharply reminds him that this is impossible. She skilfully deploys two arguments: that the decision about Sarpedon is made and cannot be changed on a whim; secondly, that if it *were* changed, other gods would seek to do the same, and then where would we be?

Hundreds of books have been written on Greek religion This chapter must confine itself to Herodotus' treatment of religious themes and how religious ideas affect his attitude to history. His view of life is fundamentally conditioned by his view of fate and destiny, though he goes

---

[1] Homer, *Iliad*, xvi.431 ff.

further than Homer and sometimes seems to leave out the Olympian gods altogether. He correctly states,[2] not that Homer and Hesiod invented the gods, but that they gave the Olympians their fixed durable forms, roles and so on. For a believer, as he demonstrably is,[3] his own interest in the roles of gods is really quite slight, and, except where he refers to shrines or quotes oracles, he far more often than not simply speaks of 'God' or 'The Gods' as being responsible for whatever phenomenon is under discussion. This attitude is entirely consistent with the Homeric passage quoted. 'Fate' and 'Zeus' will' and 'The will of the Gods' are identical. Neither Zeus nor, *a fortiori*, any other divinity has any real room for manoeuvre once the broad decisions have been taken. That being so, there is little point in laying stress on them.

Small instances of the hand of fate are casually dropped throughout the work: 'The Naxians were not destined to fall to this expedition'; 'Candaules was destined to come to a bad end'; 'Artaynte was doomed to a bad end, with all her house',[4] and others. In Thucydides, things happen because the protagonists are the sort of men they are – Cleon, Brasidas, Nicias and so on – or else they 'just happen'.[5] In Herodotus things happen because they are going to happen. But it does not follow that the decisions of fate are arbitrary or random, nor that the gods are (in effect) malignant practical jokers at the expense of innocent mortals.[6] Each of the acts of 'fulfilment' stands at the end of a chain of causation. Sometimes this is clearly visible, sometimes it is visible only in parts, sometimes it can be plausibly inferred, sometimes it is quite obscure. Naxos is not captured because Aristagoras, an unheroic boaster, has undertaken the scheme from entirely selfish motives and has lied to Artaphernes. Candaules loses his wits and pays the price for his grossly improper suggestion to Gyges. Here the beginning of the 'chain' lies out of sight: why, we ask, does Candaules become infatuated? Herodotus may not have known the answer, but he would have been sure that there was an answer.

The grim story of Amestris, Masistes and Artaynte lies, perhaps, in the middle of a 'chain': like Croesus, Xerxes is punished by domestic tragedy as well as public disaster; what Herodotus does not need to underline, for it would have been well known to many of his public, is that a decade and a half later Xerxes was himself murdered by his son Darius, who was promptly murdered by his younger brother Artaxerxes.

Above all, there is the figure of Croesus. For all his piety, and his

---

[2] ii.53.

[3] E.g. viii.129—he endorses the Poteidaeans' belief that Poseidon sent the flood that saved their city.

[4] v.33; i.8; ix.109.

[5] E.g. Th.iv.3.1, iv.9.1, etc.

[6] A note struck in, for instance, Euripides' *Hippolytus*.

benefactions to Apollo, Croesus expiates the sin of his ancestor Gyges: the three-year stay of execution that Apollo procures for him shows just how little room for manoeuvre the gods were conceived to have.[7] Croesus is introduced almost at the very beginning of Herodotus' story – not because he was 'the first barbarian to have dealings with Greeks, subduing some and making them pay tribute, forming alliances with others': that was not strictly true, on Herodotus' own showing. His ancestors Gyges and Ardys took Colophon and Priene; his father Alyattes took and destroyed Smyrna, and made war on Miletus.[8] Rather it is because Croesus in his person and life was a perfect illustration of what was to Herodotus a cardinal truth about the world.

There are three great 'theological' passages in Herodotus: the story of Solon and Croesus, the tale of Polycrates and the Ring, and the account of Xerxes' cabinet meeting and consequent dreams before the great invasion. All are unhistorical. Herodotus had no informant with an ear at Xerxes' keyhole; the rediscovered ring is one of the most widely attested folk-tales (though the lessons to be drawn from it may vary no less widely); and accepted chronology prevents Solon and Croesus from meeting.[9] None of this matters. Each of the tales contains what were to Herodotus and his public profound truths. We can say 'his public' with some confidence, because a fundamentally similar note is sounded quite frequently in the dramas of Herodotus' contemporary and friend Sophocles, and he was the most popular playwright of his age.[10]

Their message is not an optimistic one: man is a weak creature who may delude himself with visions of power and prosperity, but is utterly under the power of God, and utterly unable to prevail against it. In the last paragraph of his preface Herodotus says 'Cities that were great of old have become, many of them, small; those that were great in my day were insignificant before. I shall therefore treat of both impartially, because I know that human prosperity never stays long in the same place.'[11] He then continues, 'Croesus was a Lydian . . . '

There is no need to repeat the story of Solon's visit. It is enough to discuss a few of the points that arise from it. The text of Solon's sermon is 'Call no man happy till he be dead'. Human prosperity is a fleeting, transient thing and one cannot know the mind of God; any judgement of a

---

[7] i.91

[8] i.6; i.16.

[9] This tale was recognised as unhistorical in antiquity (Plut. Solon, 27). From time to time attempts are made to adjust the traditional datings, but pointlessly; to H the important thing is not the meeting, but the content of Solon's discourse, which might have been delivered by any sage to any potentate.

[10] Friendship of H and S suggested by Plut. *Mor.* 785. S's popularity: more than three-quarters of his productions won first prize.

[11] i.5.4.

man's life, therefore, must be suspended until that life can be seen as a whole. Solon's two examples, Tellus the Athenian and the brothers Cleobis and Biton, have more than one thing in common. They are ordinary folk who live their ordinary lives rather well; they are not so rich or prosperous that they get to think themselves independent of God; they belong to happy, united families; and finally they are fortunate in both the manner and the timing of their deaths. In each case death overtakes them when they are at the pinnacle of their public esteem. Croesus' sin here is his presumption, and for it he suffers swift punishment in the death of his elder son.

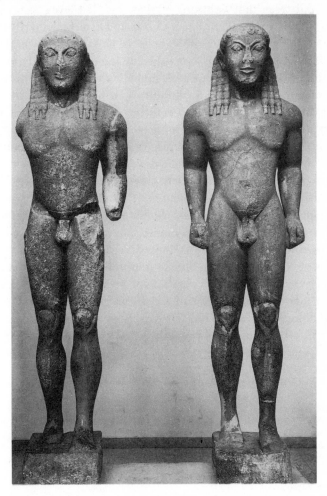

'Cleobis and Biton', Delphi. The assumption that these are the statues referred to at i.31 rests on no hard evidence, but stylistically they certainly belong to the age of Solon. (Deutsches Archäologisches Institut, Athens)

It is perhaps a finer artistic touch on Herodotus' part to follow the Solon episode with Atys' death rather than the fall of the Lydian kingdom. The domestic tragedy, a folk-tale finely narrated, touches Croesus more closely; however it is after the fall that he calls upon the name of Solon, and realises that he had spoken all too truly.

'I know that the power of God is jealous, and likes to trouble us', says Solon; 'Among living things', says Uncle Artabanus to Xerxes, 'you see that God blasts the great with his thunderbolt, and allows them not to make a show of themselves; the small vex him not at all. It is always the tallest buildings and trees that lightning strikes, for God loves to bring the lofty down . . .'; 'It is pleasant to learn of a friend's success', writes Amasis to Polycrates, 'but your great good fortune is no joy to me, for I know how envious God is.'[12] What exactly was this 'divine envy'? Surely the gods, who have all things, know all things and, under Fate, control all things, are not 'envious' of mortal frailty and fallibility? To ask the question thus is to answer it – the idea is almost self-refuting.[13] The truth is that wealth and prosperity *per se* are not offensive to the gods. The trouble is that possession of these things to a greater than ordinary degree is liable to induce feelings of 'hubris' in the subject: he becomes over-confident,[14] imagines himself insulated against failure,[15] restlessly insatiable[16] – that is the sin, familiar from so many tragedies. Agamemnon walks on the purple tapestries. Oedipus' solving of the sphinx's riddle puts him beyond the reach of prophets. Achilles in the *Iliad* demands far more than his due portion of recompense and pays dearly for it.[17]

Croesus is to Herodotus a largely admirable character, a philhellene in sentiment (even if not in political practice), seemingly likeable and of course pious. Not only does he offer a stupendous sacrifice to Apollo – many of the wonderful things Herodotus himself saw[18] – but in the smaller yet crucial matter of treating suppliants properly he did not put a foot wrong, as the

---

[12] Respectively i.32; vii.10e; iii.40. H. Lloyd-Jones, *The Justice of Zeus* (University of California Press, Berkeley, 1971), ch. iii, is a good modern discussion of this topic.

[13] Almost, but not quite: cf. E.R. Dodds, *The Greeks and the Irrational* (University of California Press, Berkeley, 1951), Ch. 2, where he cites Artabanus' speech as an example of belief in divine envy ('phthonos') leading to punishment without the moral link of hubris. I think that though the actual word is not used, some of Artabanus' vocabulary does seem to imply hubris. Dodds also points out, rightly, that the concept of divine envy was not felt by the irrepressibly boastful heroes in Homer.

[14] E.g. Croesus, i.54.

[15] E.g. Xerxes, vii.48.

[16] E.g. Polycrates, iii.123 f.

[17] For a kindred idea, cf. iv.205: Pheretime was punished by dying a revolting death, because the *excessiveness* of her revenge on the Barcaeans had incurred God's wrath. The interpretation of the *Iliad* implied here is the one that I would imagine was prevalent in the age of Herodotus and the tragedians, when interpretations were often put upon traditional stories; I doubt whether Homer's immediate audience saw Achilles in this light.

[18] i.51.

tragic tale of Adrastus and Atys shows.[19] There was one black spot on the family's record, the crime of Gyges' usurpation; and one on his own, the torture and killing of a man who supported Croesus' brother as a claimant for the throne, whose confiscated property helped Croesus to make some of his dedications. The latter, perhaps, was of no great consequence; the former – his ancestor's crime, now due to be expiated – ensured that Croesus was the last of his line, by a process of cyclical justice. But the real fault was Croesus' own. Apollo sought to warn him of impending doom,[20] but Croesus had in the heat of over-confidence, in other words hubris, construed the oracle as he wished without further enquiry.

It is entirely characteristic that, after Croesus' life is miraculously spared, Herodotus makes him admit that the blunder was his, and allows him to learn from his errors and be a trusted counsellor of Cyrus thereafter.

Polycrates of Samos is a less agreeable personage than Croesus. Herodotus has some admiration for his successful buccaneering, and quotes without overt disapproval his cynical dictum about keeping friends by robbing them and then restoring the spoils. But he was sole tyrant of Samos by virtue of having murdered one brother and banished another.[21] For that crime, retribution would very surely come, sooner or later. The longer it was delayed, the more terrible might it be, all the more so as Polycrates' prosperity knew no bounds. Like Midas, everything he touched turned to gold. On the advice of his friend and ally Amasis of Egypt, he attempts to disarm the forces of fate by a costly sacrifice, the famous ring; but the sacrifice is not accepted, and Amasis, recognising that a fearful fate is in store for him, breaks off the alliance. That fate duly befalls him at the hands of the Persian satrap Oroetes, an even less admirable figure than Polycrates. Playing upon his victim's proven greed he lures him to his court at Magnesia and impales him.[22] Herodotus is not sure of the motive for this piece of brutality, but knows that it was inadequate; Oroetes was soon punished in his turn for this and other crimes.

In the story of Xerxes and the dreams, the theme is similar but the treatment is different again. The scene is set in Xerxes' cabinet room, and the king opens with an address that begins in moderate terms, but grows more grandiloquent, with hints of hubris: 'Thus we shall see both the guilty and the innocent bearing the yoke of servitude', ending with a slightly unconvincing profession of belief in free discussion. Mardonius takes up the theme in a brash shoot-from-the-hip style, padded out with some forceful

---

[19] i.34–45.

[20] i.91.4. For another example of cyclical justice, cf. the story of Sperthias and Bulis (vii.134 ff.), see Ch. 5 p. 184 and note 73.

[21] iii.39.

[22] iii.125.

rhetoric. He boasts of his previous achievements in Greece and belittles the 'Ionians in Europe' in quite entertaining fashion. Plainly we are being prepared for his eventual downfall in Book IX. Artabanus then makes his speech urging caution, on both military and theological grounds, and receives for his pains a ferocious wigging from the king. That evening, however, Xerxes thinks over his uncle's words and concludes that he was, after all, right, and, forgetting an admonitory dream that night, apologises handsomely to him in the morning. Then follows the further sequence of dreams that visit both the king and Uncle Artabanus, convincing them that the Greek expedition must go ahead as planned.

What are we to make of all this? When both Xerxes and his senior adviser are wanting to back out of the great invasion, the supernatural forces are brought to bear upon them: they are forced to reconsider their position and are, in effect, driven towards a disaster that their mature judgement would have avoided. This is how Xerxes' case differs from Croesus': Xerxes is not deluding himself, he is being deluded. But the forces of destiny have prepared the defeat in Greece for Xerxes as a punishment for his arrogance and cruelty. We have seen a taste of these in his opening speech and his initial reaction to Artabanus; we see more of it once the campaign is under way in his flogging of the Hellespont, an act of gross impiety, and his burning of the temples of Athens,[23] not to mention acts of cruelty like the punishment of Pythius the Lydian[24] and the mutilation of Leonidas' corpse, the latter a flagrant violation of Persian honour.[25] Xerxes, in other words, is punished for being the sort of man he is – only the most impious and presumptuous man would aspire to dominion over both Asia and Europe[26] – and the Greeks are the instruments chosen by Fate to accomplish this.

There is a Sophoclean quality in all of this. As *Oedipus Tyrannus* opens, Oedipus is prosperous, successful, revered as the father of his people. At the prompting of an oracle he embarks on a course of action that leads to disaster; he misconstrues a warning given to him to desist,[27] and forges ahead in the confidence that he is invulnerable. The reversal of fortune he suffers is shattering in its swiftness and decisiveness. And yet (in *Oedipus Coloneus*) he had emerged from his torrid past as a mature person, reconciled to his lot, and he comes to a tranquil end under the gods' protection. This is the story of Croesus, even to the extent that both are in some measure the victims of cyclical justice that demands satisfaction for

---

[23] vii.35; viii.53 f.

[24] vii.39: son of Atys, presumably grandson of Croesus, named in honour of Apollo.

[25] vii.238.

[26] viii.109 (put into the mouth of Themistocles).

[27] By Teiresias, who seeks to evade Oedipus' cross-examination.

Religious Beliefs, Fate and Oracles

the offences of an earlier generation. Then consider the case of Polycrates: he tries to avert his probable destiny by an offering, but the offering is thrown back at him and the course of destiny rolls on unchecked. Oedipus, as he narrates his story to Iocaste,[28] tells how he evaded his prophesied destiny of parricide and incest by keeping away from his home city of Corinth: as the drama unfolds it becomes apparent that by the very act of avoiding Corinth he has run head-on into the fulfilment of his destiny. And in the chorus that immediately follows that scene, we read 'Tyranny breeds Pride [hubris]. Pride, if it is vainly sated with such wealth as is neither fitting nor beneficial to it, . . . rushes headlong to doom':[29] a poetical summary of the Herodotean Xerxes.

'Who then can be saved?' Very few of the great ones: such are the perils of their position, moral or political, that they come to grief more often than not: Croesus and Xerxes, Cyrus and Cambyses too. But most people are not like Croesus and Xerxes. Herodotus' view of history is not grimly determinist, and he does not rule out the chance of an individual fashioning, within limits, his own destiny. First and foremost, one must regard the laws of the gods as transcending any considerations of political or financial advantage. In the excellent story put into the mouth of King Leotychidas, Glaucus the Spartan sounded out Delphi before definitely committing himself to an act of perjury and embezzlement. He was punished for putting God to the test by seeking approval for a contemplated sin.[30] Aristodicus of Cyme and his fellow citizens were threatened by the oracle at Branchidae with swift destruction. This was for their impiety, again, not in *doing* anything, but in merely contemplating the surrender of the suppliant Pactyes to Persia, an act which would have been politically convenient.[31] For this conflict of divine law and political interest, Sophocles again provides a parallel, in the plot of *Antigone*, where King Creon is punished for placing the deterrence of treason higher than the requirements of proper burial.

Secondly, Herodotus does not suggest that a man should passively accept whatever God sends; rather he should strive to make the best use of what gifts he has, and so may be honoured among his fellow men. It was that which put Tellus and Cleobis and Biton, into the ranks of the 'happy'; and through these examples Herodotus put 'happiness' within the reach of any man who was willing to listen and learn.

---

[28] S. *OT*, 789–99.

[29] S. *OT* 873 ff.; 'hubris' is the word used. The text translated here is that of R.D. Dawe's edition of the play (Cambridge U.P., 1982) – see his note *ad loc.* where he argues the case convincingly for this reading.

[30] vi.86: the story is not very appropriate to its context, as the Athenians did not deny that they were holding the Aiginetan hostages; but it remains a superb illustration of ethical thought.

[31] i.159.

PREMONITIONS AND ORACLES

Belief in the power of destiny or 'necessity' (*anankaie* in Herodotus) is the foundation for a belief in the efficacy of oracles. If the course of the future is within certain limits mapped out, it must be known by someone, somewhere, if not on earth, then by the gods. Sometimes the gods send, unbidden, a premonition of the future; more often they are reluctantly persuaded to distil some of their secrets through the medium of the oracles.

There is an apparent illogicality about this, in so far as one of the purposes of learning the future, as it relates to oneself, must be to enable one to take action to avert or evade what is unpleasant – in which case, the future will have been changed in some measure. This difficulty was not of course unperceived by intelligent thinkers; neither in Herodotus nor in Sophocles do we actually find examples of premonitions or 'predictive' oracles given to individuals being successfully acted upon. As we have seen, it is in his attempt to take evasive action that Oedipus, in the drama, actually ensures his doom. On the other hand, when a military disaster was predicted for a community or town it was perfectly possible for individuals to extricate themselves in advance; and when men abandon a seemingly lost cause, such a prophecy can be almost self-fulfilling. Perhaps the intimidating first oracle given to Athens in 480 was intended to achieve that.[32] (The great majority of oracles quoted or paraphrased by Herodotus are of course not predictive but 'prescriptive', advising a certain course of action.)

Croesus – how hard to escape from him! – has a clear premonition in a dream of the nature of his son's death.[33] His elaborate attempts to obviate the tragedy are frustrated by what was to all appearances an accident. The Chians had warnings of disaster before the battle of Lade (in which they suffered crippling casualties), but, by implication, they were not recognised as such. Polycrates' daughter foresaw her father's gruesome death in a dream, but he brushed her warnings aside.[34] The logical position was put most clearly in the finely told anecdote of Thersander the Orchomenian. His Persian fellow guest at dinner weeps copiously and tells Thersander of his premonition that most of the Persians in Greece would soon be destroyed. 'Shouldn't you tell Mardonius?' cries Thersander in amazement; but no, he would not be believed. 'What God has enjoined, it is not in man's power to avert . . . Many of us Persians know the truth, but we continue to follow as we are constrained by necessity [*anankaie*]: the cruellest pain is to know much, but have no power to act.'[35]

---

[32] vii.140. Cf. also the prediction of the fall of Miletus, vi.19.

[33] i.34.

[34] vi.27; iii.124.

[35] ix.16.

'Oracle' is a word used confusingly in English to denote both the shrine that is the seat of the prophecy and the text of the prophecy itself. Before we turn to Delphi, the greatest Greek oracle and far and away the most important to Herodotus, it will be convenient to deal briefly with a minor class of prophecy that crops up from time to time in his pages. This is the written oracle that forms part of a collection, to be brought out at the appropriate time. The 'Sibylline Books' of Rome was the best known example of this sort of thing in antiquity. In Herodotus' day there was a veritable ragbag of assembled prophecies passing under names of ancient mythical seers like Musaeus and Bacis.[36] This type was of doubtful utility because it was only likely to be noticed after the event and had little or no predictive value. This was to earn Thucydides' well-justified scorn when the plague of 430 was discovered to have been predicted: 'A Dorian war shall come, and with it pestilence';[37] but there was an alternative version, with a difference of one letter (and probably pronounced almost indistinguishably) meaning ' . . . and with it famine'. As Thucydides cynically observed, the dust would be brushed off the latter version when a future Peloponnesian War was accompanied by a famine. This form of collected oracle was peculiarly vulnerable to forgery, or rather interpolation after the event,[38] and Herodotus rather unwisely quotes one such with warm approval, regarding its unambiguous 'prophecy' as proof of the reliability of oracles.[39]

With Delphi we are on quite different ground, for here we are dealing with responses given to specific enquiries that arise from the contemporary situation. The large and fascinating body we find in Herodotus, public and private, political and ethical, include some that are the responses genuinely given, some that were forged after the event (and here forgery is the word), and some in the middle ground that preserve the essential message of the original but have been touched up subsequently for public consumption. Of those that are quoted verbatim in verse (usually hexameter, occasionally iambic) some reach a high sub-Homeric standard of expression with Homeric elements of vocabulary and phrasing; others are little better than hack work.

PRIVATE ENQUIRIES

We may assume that nine-tenths or more of the enquiries at Delphi were of a purely personal and private nature, relating to such things as marriage,

---

[36] vii.6; viii.20.

[37] Th.ii.54.

[38] Cf. vii.6 again.

[39] viii. 77 (Bacis).

wills, travel and so on. This small change of oracular business was most probably done through a simple process of 'lot', involving two differently coloured beans indicating yes and no,[40] and has left very little mark in history. What fascinated the ancient authors were the oral answers given by the Pythia herself, especially when these were on subjects relating to state policy.

(In the rest of this chapter verse oracles quoted verbatim by Herodotus are denoted by an asterisk – *.)

Private responses are not numerous in Herodotus. There is that given to Glaucus* in the excellent moralising story already referred to. Another extremely interesting one is that given to Teisamenus of Elis[41] – not a very helpful answer to one enquiring about having children, but let that pass. He was told that he would carry off the 'five greatest contests'. Now the oracle had plainly sized Teisamenus up and had recognised him as a sportsman of great potential, and obviously meant what Teisamenus thought it meant, namely that he would win the Olympic pentathlon. He went into training – but only came second. The oracle somehow came to the notice of the Spartan government, and they, thinking that some sterner contests were intended, bid for his services as diviner on their military campaigns (he came from a noble priestly family in Elis). Teisamenus played his cards shrewdly and succeeded in extorting Spartan citizenship both for himself and for his brother; and the Spartiates were the most notoriously exclusive citizen body in the Greek world. The prophecy was deemed to have been fulfilled when Teisamenus' first five campaigns ended in victory, beginning with Plataea.

The other two private replies of note were given to Miltiades I, who checked on the advisability of going to the Chersonese[42] – hardly surprising that the answer was favourable when in all probability the oracle had pointed the Dolonci to him in the first place – and to Eëtion of Corinth, who put the same question as Teisamenus, namely about his prospects of parenthood.[43]

Eëtion's oracle will be considered below among the political examples. There seems no reason to doubt the authenticity of the other three. King Leotychidas spoke with what seemed like personal knowledge of Glaucus' story, and there seems to be no motive for inventing it. Teisamenus' oracle *ex hypothesi* cannot have been given after the event, and it was only by cheating slightly and including a trivial skirmish in the Helot Revolt that the Spartans considered the 'five victories' fulfilled. What Miltiades did was no more than any averagely pious Greek would have done before an

[40] See H.W. Parke & D.E.W. Wormell, *A History of the Delphic Oracle* (Blackwell, Oxford, 1956), p. 18 f.
[41] ix.33.
[42] see Ch. 1 p. 38
[43] v.92b

undertaking involving overseas travel and the prospect of a long absence from home.

ORACLES RELATING TO CULTS

Delphi was in the sixth century the recognised authority on purification. In that age the belief prevailed that a sacrilegious act committed by a citizen or group of citizens could incur the pollution of the entire state. This theme has received matchless poetical treatment in Book I of the *Iliad*, where the seer Calchas shows how Apollo's anger on behalf of his priest is to be stayed; and, more relevantly to Delphi, in *Oedipus Tyrannus*, where at the play's opening Oedipus has already sent to the oracle to find a way of checking the plague that has fallen on Thebes. Possible evidence of the fear of pollution even in the late fifth century comes from Thucydides. The mutilation of the Hermae in 415 was construed both as a bad omen for the Sicilian expedition and as part of a conspiracy to overthrow the democracy. That is to say the enemies of democracy who thought the expedition would bring a great access of tribute to Athens, thereby rendering the democracy lastingly secure, tried to stop it, or at least impair its morale, by incurring some public pollution with an act of gross impiety.[44]

There are four purification oracles referred to by Herodotus, three from the sixth century:[45] one given to the men of Agylla (later Caere, in southern Etruria) after their massacre of some Phocaeans, one prescribing compensation after the murder of Aesop the fable writer, the last to the Apolloniates after the blinding of Evenius. In each case the motive for consultation was a run of bad harvests or the like,[46] and the oracle was appreciably more specific than in *Oedipus Tyrannus*, spelling out what compensation to pay or, in the case of Agylla, what cult to establish in honour of the dead. The exception is that given to the Pelasgians of Lemnos, which must be mythical, belonging as it does to an epoch centuries before Delphi was of any great account.[47]

Rather similar to the Evenius oracle is that given to the Parians concerning the priestess Timo, who was alleged to have tried to betray Paros to Miltiades. The oracle forbad any punishment, as Timo was merely an instrument of fate to help bring Miltiades down; just as Evenius' negligence in letting the wolves attack the sacred flock was itself heaven-

---

[44] Well argued by K.J. Dover on Th.vi.27 in A.W. Gomme, *A Commentary on Thucydides* (Oxford University Press, 1970), vol. iv, p. 284.

[45] Respectively i.167; ii.134; ix.93.

[46] For the Aesop story, this detail comes from sources much later than H but is obviously probable.

[47] vi.139.

sent. It seems that Delphi did not judge the priestly class over-strictly. Still on a religious theme is the entertaining story of Aristeas of Proconnesus and his 'reappearance'. Here the oracle plays safe by commanding the men of Metapontion to set up a cult statue in his honour; Herodotus' wording suggests that Delphi was, perhaps momentarily, nonplussed by this phenomenon. 'Do what the vision said' seems rather lame by Delphic standards.

Our last 'cult' example comes from Herodotus' own lifetime: after Salamis the victorious allies sent their several offerings to Delphi. The god expressed full satisfaction with all save the contribution of Aigina, whose contingent had earned the highest award for valour. Herodotus describes their (evidently satisfactory) second offering, three golden stars mounted on a bronze mast.[48]

POLITICAL ORACLES, GENUINE AND OTHERWISE

And so we come to the public, political oracles. There are over 30 of these, 19 of which are given verbatim, and there is no need to consider them all. How is it that Delphi was able to give value for money for so long? Or, to put it differently, how did Delphi continue to command the confidence of the Greek states in its efficacy? And not just Greek, but barbarian as well, for we read of consultations by Gyges and Alyattes of Lydia;[49] the purification of Agylla already quoted; the interest of Amasis of Egypt, who contributed generously to the rebuilding programme;[50] and of course the supreme example of Croesus. Greek belief held Delphi to be the centre of the world, that tricky question having been determined by a controlled experiment conducted by Zeus. And so it was, in a real sense. Delphi lies almost on the north-south and east-west axes of the Greek world. It was accessible equally easily from Thessaly and northern Greece, from Boeotia and Attica, and from the Peloponnese, for there was a convenient harbour below it. That same harbour could serve travellers from Italy and Sicily, and from Asia Minor via the Isthmus.

This cut both ways. Not only was Delphi easier to visit than, say, Dodona or some of those in Asia Minor, but the priestly staff had better opportunities to gather up-to-date intelligence about political developments in and around the Greek world. The oracle had no hot line to the secrets of fate. But what it lacked in supernatural guidance it strove to make up for in well-informed common sense. It followed, of course, that if there were any sudden upset in the balance of world power, the oracle was liable to be

---

[48] vi.135; iv.15; viii.122.

[49] i.13, 19.

[50] ii.180.

caught out. Ways were found of minimising or even explaining away such embarrassments, as we shall see. By and large we can guess that the oracle gave as general satisfaction to states as it did to private individuals.

Most frequently, this means giving (or withholding) approval to a project already conceived, rather than initiating an idea. States contemplating war or a colonising venture would consult the oracle as a matter of course. As we have seen,[51] the oracle pointed the Dolonci of the Chersonese towards Miltiades, and he checked with Delphi before leaving; Dorieus of Sparta failed to consult the oracle before his attempt to settle in North Africa, and his enterprise did not prosper. He did not repeat the error when he planned to colonise western Sicily, and the oracle prophesied success for him – wrongly, as it turned out.[52]

Sometimes the oracle could be called in as a kind of Royal Commission to solve a governmental problem with an authority that transcended party quarrels. There is a neat example of this from Cyrene. This community was advised to call in an arbitrator from Mantinea, and Demonax, the one chosen, reorganised the tribes to take account of immigration patterns, and curbed the king's powers. Another 'Royal Commission' example is the oracle that adjudicated King Damaratus of Sparta illegitimate.[53] To produce this desired result the other king, Cleomenes, had bribed the Pythia through a Delphian intermediary. Unfortunately for the reputation of the oracle, the truth came out later and in the ensuing scandal the priestess was unseated.

Much has been made of the ambiguity of the Delphic oracle or of individual utterances of it. Obviously it was prudent for the oracle to insure itself against failure, but we can be sure that the ambiguities were not of the puerile type supposedly delivered to Croesus.[54] The actual oracle that related to his invasion of Cappadocia is lost; Herodotus' brief summary was padded out into a hexameter line by the fourth century, but incomplete even so, for it leaves out the matter of his alliance with a Greek state. It is possible that quite often the ambiguity hinged on the small print, as it were. Cylon's attempted coup failed because he chose the wrong festival of Zeus.[55]

An entertaining and surely authentic example of this occurs in Book V.[56] In 507/6 Athens' nervous neighbours had made a concerted attempt to strangle the Cleisthenic democracy at birth. But the invading Spartan army broke up, owing to the differences between the kings Cleomenes and Damaratus, and Athens was left free to beat Thebes and Chalcis soundly.

---

[51] see Ch. 1 and p. 58 above.

[52] v.43 ff.

[53] iv.161; vi.66.

[54] i.53. For a discussion of a modern defence of this oracle, however, see Appx. 2, p. 236 n. 11.

[55] Th.i.126, see Ch. 1, p. 18.

[56] v.79.

The Thebans, endeavouring to return to the charge, were advised by Delphi to seek the aid of their 'nearest' after referring the question to 'the many-voiced one': they could not succeed alone. Assuming that a public assembly was intended, they discussed the question, and were puzzled by 'the nearest': the men of Thespiae, Tanagra and Coronea had always helped them loyally anyway! Then a speaker from the floor suggested that it be interpreted mythologically – trying, as it were, to beat the oracle at its own game – and that Aigina be approached: Aigina and Thebe were the two daughters of the river-god Asopus. This was eagerly seized upon: and we must award the Aiginetans full marks for humour when they countered this symbolic interpretation by sending symbolic aid – the images of their native heroes the Aeacidae. Needless to say the Thebans did no better than before.[57]

A different type of ambiguity is the 'oracular' utterance that is traditionally almost incomprehensible but possesses a certain mystical impressiveness. A splendid specimen of this, again surely authentic, is the oracle given to Argos at some time in the 490s, probably at the opening of the Ionian revolt,* when a war with Sparta was on the horizon. It looks as though Aristagoras. rebuffed by Sparta, went next to her hereditary foe Argos, who consulted the oracle and received the response. The full text of the oracle is split into two (Herodotus explains why) but should be analysed as a whole.[58]

> But when the female defeats the male,
> drives him out, and wins glory among the Argives,
> then shall she make many Argive women tear their cheeks.
> Thus will it be said, in future generations,
> 'The dread, thrice-coiled snake was slain, subdued by the spear.'
> And then, indeed, Miletus, doer of wicked deeds,
> thou shalt be a feast for many, a glittering prize;
> thy wives shall wash the feet of many long-haired ones,
> and the care of our temple at Didyma shall fall to others.

No doubt about the second half – 'Didyma' was the site of Apollo's oracular shrine that Herodotus usually refers to as 'Branchidae', in Milesian territory; the long-haired ones can only be the Persians. But the fall of Miletus so confidently prophesied is actually conditional on the first half; and what on earth does that mean? To try to solve it is utterly pointless. More for amusement than anything else, here are some theories that have

---

[57] I wonder whether the oracle meant 'You won't succeed unless you detach Plataea from the Athenian alliance', Plataea being the nearest city on the southern side of Thebes, only fractionally more distant than Thespiae and appreciably nearer than Tanagra and Coronea.

[58] vi.77 and vi.19—to be taken in that order.

been discussed in the past: Sparta (a feminine noun) will defeat Argos (a male mythological figure); Hera (patroness of Argos) will prevail over Heracles (ancestor of the Spartan kings); more generally 'subtlety will prevail over brute force', or even 'the natural- order of things will be reversed', and so on. But bearing in mind the somewhat menacing tone, it is small wonder the Argives left the Ionian revolt severely alone and thereby contributed to the fulfilment of the second half.

In international affairs the oracle tended to play safe as far as possible by backing the likely winners, and some of the less creditable passages in Delphi's history were the result of this. Let us look first at Croesus and the group of oracles associated with him. The story of Croesus' trial of the oracular world need not delay us long; apart from the theological unlikelihood of Delphi allowing itself to be tested in the way described, the list of oracles allegedly put to the test is highly suspect. There are the Big Four – Delphi and Dodona from the mainland, Didyma from Ionia and, rather bizarrely, the oracle of Ammon in Libya – but also three puny shrines in central Greece. These last were Delphi's domestic competitors in the fifth century; a genuine list from the middle of the sixth century could hardly have omitted Apollo's oracle at Claros near Colophon, nor the Lycian Telmessi (whom Croesus actually consulted on a separate occasion). Then again, there is the fact of Croesus' benefactions to other shrines which Herodotus narrates out of sequence.[59] The rumour he reports that Branchidae did as well as Delphi out of Croesus may or may not be true (that shrine had of course been sacked long before Herodotus' time) but it seems as though Croesus made offerings to Greek oracular shrines in proportion to the weight they carried in the Greek world – in the case of Thebes' temple of Ismenian Apollo, evidently not much! Croesus' predecessors had contacts with Delphi, but the main thrust of Lydian patronage came when Croesus was seeking allies from the Greek world; obviously he had a healthy regard for the Greek fighting man. He knew that no state would serve alongside him without prior consultation of the oracle, which could now be relied upon for an encouraging reply; equally his Ionian Greek subjects would be discouraged from contemplating rebellion. Though the full text of Delphi's reply on the matter of the Persian invasion is lost beyond recovery, we can be quite sure that it was definitely encouraging. Why should it not have been? To Delphi Croesus was a king of boundless resources, while Persia was an unproven force. All rational calculation must have pointed to a Lydian victory.

The oracle relating to the 'mule' may be genuine or an explanatory invention after Croesus' fall; it matters little.* That warning Croesus not to desire a cure for his son's dumbness* might be genuine: if so, it suggests an

----

[59] i.92; Telmessi, i.78, cf. i.84.

awareness – likely enough at that time – of the medical fact that certain types of dumbness are psychological in origin and can be unlocked by a violent shock or trauma.[60]

The fall of Croesus not only removed the shrine's main benefactor, but must have damaged the self-confidence of the oracle. The power of Persia was plainly unstoppable. When the men of Cnidos, on the end of the Triopian peninsula, had difficulty in cutting through the isthmus and consulted Delphi, they were bluntly told to desist.* The Persians later walked in unopposed.[61] During the long years of Persian occupation Delphi did nothing for Ionia, nor did it lend any aid or comfort to the Ionian revolt, if the interpretation of the Argos oracle, above, is correct.

When Xerxes' invasion was imminent, Delphi seems to have done a roaring trade in public enquiries, and her attitude was quite consistent – Persia will win. Argos received a dignified utterance* which plainly recommended neutrality. Crete was urged to abstain on mythological grounds. Both states complied.[62] The Delphians themselves were advised to 'pray to the winds' – fair enough, but hardly a ringing call to arms – and when they expressed anxiety about the temple treasures, the god assured them that he would look after his own:[63] he knew that the Persians would not risk losing Delphi's support for the sake of the plunder there.

But the most spectacular are the two given to Athens* and the one given to Sparta*. The first of the two Athenian oracles is an utterly blood-chilling prophecy of doom. It was all very well for the oracle to speak with dignified calm to Argos, who everyone knew wanted to be neutral anyway; but Athens wanted to resist, and the first oracle, had it got about early, might have had a disastrous effect on public morale. 'Miserable wretches! Why do ye sit here? Flee to the ends of the earth!' it begins; 11 lines later it ends 'but away with you from the sanctuary: steep your soul in woe'. It is the blackest utterance quoted by Herodotus, and the Athenian delegates to the oracle refused to take it back with them. They supplicated the god for a second, less menacing response. The reply they got, equally long (they are the longest in Herodotus),[64] is a good deal lighter in tone. It does here seem as if the oracle is at least attempting to mention Athens' plans: for no doubt the Athenians had not said 'Lord Apollo, what shall we do?' but something like 'We are planning resistance by sea at Salamis – what does Lord Apollo

---

[60] Respectively i.55 and 85.

[61] i.174. H states all this on the authority of the Cnidians themselves (therefore presumably not Delphi) and the oracle might be a forgery; see below, p. 66. On the other hand, it seems perfectly reasonable for the oracle to ban such digging on the grounds given, namely that 'Zeus would have made an island, had he wished.'

[62] Respectively vii.148 and 169.

[63] vii.178; viii.36.

[64] vii.140-1.

think of that?' Lord Apollo was non-committal. 'Pallas cannot propitiate Olympian Zeus, though she pray mightily . . . but Zeus grants that the wooden wall alone remain untaken . . . but do not await the coming of the mighty host' – and ended with a prophecy that, yes, there would be a battle at Salamis, but when, and with what result, he declined to say. This was much more palatable to public opinion, but examination shows that it makes no promises and really has little or nothing of substance for Athens. It was a public relations exercise. As Athens was putting her shirt (as it were) on resistance at sea and was not now going to adopt any alternative strategy, oracle or no oracle, the ambiguity of the 'wooden wall' was valuable. If, as Delphi clearly expected, Athens lost, then obviously she would have put her trust in the wrong wooden wall.[65]

The oracle given to Sparta is no less interesting.[66] 'Either your glorious city will be ravaged by the sons of Perseus, or . . . the boundary of Lacedaemon shall grieve for a slain king of Heracles' line . . . ' This oracle was triumphantly fulfilled. Leonidas fell at Thermopylae and earned his posthumous fame by the fact that Sparta did not succumb. But the oracle's intention was surely otherwise. In Xerxes' entourage, as courtier and trusted adviser, was the former King of Sparta, Damaratus, he who had been dethroned by the intrigues of Cleomenes with Delphi. Xerxes was surely going to use Damaratus as Darius would have used Hippias in 490, had Marathon gone the other way: namely as the head of a tame collaborationist 'Vichy' regime in Sparta. The oracle meant: 'Kill the usurper Leotychidas and take Damaratus back – or else!'

With that, Herodotus closes his long list of major consultations; fittingly, for Delphi again lost some prestige for its misjudgements in the Persian War. Surprisingly, they were not fatal: the institution possessed amazing vitality.

It remains to discuss the question of forged oracles. Obviously there is far more likelihood of forgery in state oracles than in private responses, and from the numerous examples given by Herodotus probably no two critics would agree completely on lists of authentic and spurious ones. We can, however, list a few principles to help decide individual cases. Most will accept that oracles which do not come true are likely to be authentic. The first oracle to the Athenians in 480 is the leading example of that. Secondly, anything expressed with 'oracular' obscurity is worth considering, like the Argos one from the 490s. Any responses which fall within an ascertainable policy on Delphi's part deserve attention – witness the various oracles

---

[65] Alternatively, it could have meant 'trust to your ships to escape'.

[66] vii.220. Parke & Wormell (*Delphi*, vol. I, p. 167, vol. II, p. 44) regard this as a forgery after the event, composed with Delphic help, to restore Spartan morale. (The phrasing has a genuinely Delphic ring.) But this view fails to explain why the oracle, which had backed Persia before, should now, at Greece's apparently blackest hour, change sides.

counselling non-resistance to Persia.

It is even easier to think of motives for forgery. The oracle itself may bend the record of its utterances, if the originals are disproved by events. It may invent responses completely. The oracle urging Croesus to invade Persia has been doctored; the response to Croesus' alleged 'trial' is wholly fictitious, but served to raise Delphi's prestige in the fifth century. Sometimes the doctoring was relatively harmless. The fundamentally authentic episode of Miltiades and the Dolonci has had some folk-tale elements added for appearances' sake. The oracles relating to the foundation of Cyrene* cannot be genuine, two of them in fact are mutually inconsistent;[67] but the connection between Cyrene and Delphi was solid and real, and most of the subsequent oracles look genuine – one where the priestess sarcastically praises the settlers who had occupied a puny island off the North African coast instead of the mainland itself,* another advertising land to be distributed in Libya,* and that concerning Demonax of Mantinea already referred to. It looks as if Delphi had supplied an oracular background for a state that became one of its best clients.

Equally, 'utterances' could just as well be faked by 'recipients' in order to justify some action taken or policy adopted. The oracles relating to Cypselus,* first tyrant of Corinth, belong in this class. Cypselus seized power and bore heavily down upon the narrow aristocracy that had formed the governing circle. The first two oracles quoted, with some very accurate circumstantial detail and some loaded phraseology, look like creations, the first to justify Cypselus' usurpation, the second to justify resistance to him.[68] It is also possible that the oracle (already referred to) given to Cnidos was in fact a forgery put about by members of a pro-Persian party in the town who hoped for favour by preventing a hopeless resistance. The mythical oracle given to the Pelasgians of Lemnos may have been invented to give Athens a claim on Lemnos in advance, or to justify Miltiades' seizure of it after the event.

In general, however, Delphi was good at its job. Had it not been, neither Herodotus nor any other intelligent Greek would have taken notice of it. We shall end with two examples that belong under no particular classification, but which serve simply to illustrate its sheer competence. In the early 500s Sparta was going through a strongly expansionist phase and the government conceived the idea of conquering Arcadia – a preposterously ambitious enterprise.[69] Delphi instead gave Sparta a realistic and manageable programme, the reduction of Tegea, the nearest Arcadian city to Spartan soil.* 'You ask me for Arcadia? a big request, I shall not grant it

---

[67] All the Cyrenian oracles are between iv.150 and 161.

[68] v.92.

[69] i.66.

. . . but I do not begrudge you: I shall give you Tegea to stamp your feet upon in the dance, and her lovely plain for you to measure out with the rope.' The pointed phrasing suggests the dance of victory, followed by the congenial job of surveying and dividing up the conquered land. But, alas! the Spartans lost. They were chained together and worked as labourers in the fields of Tegea, fulfilling the prophecy in no anticipated way.

Our last example is the oracle given to the islanders of Siphnos.* Enriched beyond their hopes by the yield of their mines, they had just refaced their public buildings with Parian marble, and they asked the oracle whether their present prosperity could be of long duration.[70] 'But when the town-hall of Siphnos shines white . . . then must the thoughtful man be on his guard against a wooden ambush and a scarlet herald.' Shortly afterwards a small fleet of Samian exiles arrived with their ships painted, in the fashion of the 520s, scarlet. In the ensuing scuffles and raids the Samians succeeded in levying 100 talents, no less, from the Siphnians. What a coup for the oracle! The odd thing is that while everyone from Herodotus downwards plainly regarded the prophecy as having been fulfilled, actually it was not – at least, not in the terms of the question that was put. This raid did not bring the prosperity of Siphnos to an end; it paid high tributes to the Delian League in the next century. In short, the oracle used its common sense to predict, correctly, what was the most likely immediate threat to the well-being of the Siphnians. That was good value for money.

CONCLUSION

Herodotus is a believer, and the Delphic oracles, and even other less respectable ones, formed part of the body of his faith. He accepts the oracle's explanations of its own failures, its doctoring of responses and so on. Sometimes he does not notice that an oracle has not been literally fulfilled; once or twice he allows his head to prevail over his heart, as when he commends the Athenians for not being intimidated by that awful first oracle given to them by Delphi.

It is easy to laugh at his uncritical acceptance of material that is obviously (to us) not authentic. Born and brought up in an age when religious fundamentalism was all but universal, and a cosmological thinker like Anaxagoras was regarded as a dangerous heretic, it is difficult to see how he could have taken any other line. He was almost contemporary with the pioneer sophists: Protagoras, greatest of them all, and Gorgias were probably born c.490, and Herodotus' opinions and attitudes would have been moulded by the time that their influence could have been brought to bear.

---

[70] iii.57.

Herodotus was as much of a pioneer in the field of literary composition as they were in thought and rhetoric, and it is hardly to be expected that he would break fresh ground on every front. What contacts he had with the sophists we cannot say: Protagoras is said to have drafted the code of laws (444 BC) for the new colony of Thuria where Herodotus went to live; he was probably in Athens during the historian's second period of residence there.[71] There are in fact a few passages in the *Histories* that seem to show sophistic influence. For example in Book III Darius uses a remarkable argument from expediency to justify lying (the substitution of 'advantage' for 'right' which was a sophist's commonplace) and Darius' theoretical arguments for monarchy suggest a similar provenance.[72] Herodotus' satirical defence of the Alcmeonidae is made to hinge upon an argument from probability, and that was a development of the Sicilian rhetoricians whose pupil Gorgias was.[73]

But on matters of religion Herodotus was fully a man of his age. We have already considered briefly his closeness to Sophocles in questions of beliefs and ethics. There are several other hints of his traditionalist outlook to be found in the *Histories*: one is his acceptance of myth in historical narrative. He gives us an almost entirely folk-tale version of Cyrus' birth, preservation, upbringing and recognition, with minimal attempt to relate it to the realities (whatever they may have been); the mythical prototypes of, or rather parallels for, the different parts of the story include such familiar tales as the exposure of the infant Oedipus, the banquet of Thyestes, and others.[74] This suggests that Herodotus regarded the traditional body of Greek myth as an acceptable substitute for history when hard information was lacking.

The Odes of Pindar, who was roughly a generation older than Herodotus, are shot through and through with myth, either in narrative or sometimes in fleeting allusion – testimony to the hold that such material still possessed upon the minds of men in the fifth century. Perhaps even more interesting evidence is the use of myth by Plato (or Socrates himself – who can say?) to reinforce his not always adequate arguments. The best known are probably the story of Er the Pamphylian with which the *Republic* closes and the glowing picture of life in the next world near the end of *Phaedo*.[75]

---

[71] DL. ix.8.50 (in Hill's *Sources*); on H's life, see Ch. 6 p. 210 ff.

[72] iii.72, 82.

[73] vi.124; cf. W.K.C. Guthrie, *The Sophists* (Cambridge University Press, 1971), p. 178 f.

[74] i.108–22; other examples include Atys and the Boar-Hunt and Polycrates and the Ring, already discussed.

[75] A point made by G.S. Kirk, *The Nature of Greek Myths* (Penguin Books, Harmondsworth, 1974), p. 108. He adds 'Some may feel . . . that Plato might have done better to work a bit harder on the philosophical arguments before resorting to the traditional device of the persuasive myth; but . . . he

In this as in some other respects, Herodotus has suffered by comparison with his rationalist successor Thucydides. It is perhaps bad luck on Herodotus that the 30 years that separated the composition of their respective histories was the period of Greece's most rapid development in the field of thought: the condemnation of Socrates in 399 was almost the last protest by the traditionalists. As Socrates is made to say in the *Apology*, Anaxagoras' revolutionary book on cosmology – by implication, once banned – could now be bought openly in Athens for a drachma.[76] Thucydides, a most highly educated Athenian, is fully abreast of sophistic thought and techniques, a fact most evident from his speeches. But religious scepticism informs his entire work. Historical events that have some religious motivation he treats with detachment, as a kind of sociological phenomenon;[77] oracles and observances he seldom mentions except in order to sneer at them.[78] He thereby does us a disservice by underplaying the importance of religion and its power over the hearts and minds of men. When the Athenian troops were dismayed by the eclipse in Syracuse, their commander Nicias was in touch with their feelings; Thucydides was not. Herodotus would have understood.

What Thucydides was to history, so, in a sense, was Euripides to drama. In some of his plays he introduces representations of the gods that are ambiguous or downright unflattering – in *Hippolytus*, *Ion* and *The Bacchae*, for example. It is not readily conceivable that such treatment could have come from Sophocles or Herodotus. To sum up, Herodotus' religious attitudes are those of his time: he believes in his gods and he accepts a well-established view of man's relationship with them. Ordinary folk no doubt continued to cherish these beliefs for centuries; but in educated circles, the changing intellectual climate of Greece was soon to make such a view appear terribly old-fashioned.[79]

---

was thereby succumbing to an almost irresistible force in Greek culture.'

[76] Plato, *Apology*, 26D.

[77] E.g. the purification of Delos (Th.iii.104) and the mutilation of the Hermae (Th.vi.27).

[78] E.g. Th.ii.54 (already quoted), vii.50, viii.1; and cf. Th.v.104 f (Melian Dialogue).

[79] Such generalisations are hazardous, and Xenophon's *Anabasis* shows that for that author at least the old pieties retained much of their power.

3. HERODOTUS ON POLITICS AND POLITICIANS

No one could claim for Herodotus a burning interest in constitutional detail. We have seen the cavalier way in which he handled the reform of Cleisthenes,[1] and his (perhaps deliberate) mistake over the archonship reform of 488/7. Again and again we are tantalised by him. In his fascinating picture of Spartan usages, for example, we would have welcomed a little more than the muddled remark on the kings' right to have proxies in the Gerousia.[2] And yet on the attaining and exercising of political power – the reality rather than the forms – he has a very great deal to say. He tells us far more about the early 'tyrants' than any other source. He gives us an insight into the way the men of his age thought and talked about political ideas. And from the standpoint of one who lived much of his life under a developed democracy he has some valuable things to say about Athenian democracy's early days.

In the course of this chapter we shall consider the passages where political themes and personalities are discussed and attempt to assess Herodotus' own position. The importance of this for the study of ancient historians can be simply shown by an example, namely Thucydides' treatment of Cleon. In each of the three major episodes in which Cleon appears, and once posthumously, Thucydides either belittles him or jeers at him;[3] these passages, coupled with stray remarks on the fecklessness of democracy,[4] enable us to evaluate more confidently Thucydides' other remarks on men in politics and to make allowances where necessary.

Does Herodotus' work possess any such 'tendency'? It used to be customary to begin the hunt for Herodotus' own views in the famous Debate of the Three Conspirators,[5] for the historicity of which Herodotus (not very convincingly) vouches with his hand on his heart. In fact this is, as an example of method, quite fallacious. The facts demanded that Darius, who advocated monarchy, should win the argument. We can no more tell which of the three views expressed represents Herodotus' own (if any one does) than we can gauge a tragedian's religious viewpoint from lines spoken by

---

[1] Ch. 1, p. 29.

[2] vi.51–60.

[3] Th.iii.36.6, iv.28.2–3, v.10.9, v.16.1.

[4] E.g. Th.viii.1.

[5] iii.80–2.

individual characters in his plays.[6] What we can legitimately do is to see, in the speeches given to Otanes, Megabyzus and Darius, a reflection of practical political questions as discussed by the busy man in the Athenian equivalent of club and pub. One notable feature is the shortage of political philosophy; the three *appear* to be talking theoretically – there are only two examples quoted, those of Cambyses and the Magus (bad) with which Otanes prefaces his argument, and Cyrus (good) with which Darius ends his – but in fact it is clear that they, or rather Herodotus, have concrete examples in mind for many of their assertions.

Otanes, who advocated democracy, does indeed begin with some genuine political philosophy when he attacks monarchy for being irresponsible (*aneuthunos*), an argument of great force in democratic Athens; but he moves from there to some layman's psychology – the usual vices of men raised to exalted station, arrogance and envy; and thence to some commonplaces on royal behaviour – willingness to listen to tale-telling, and ambivalent attitude to flattery; then some specific charges, doubtless with a particular example in mind – abuse of women and putting of men to death untried. In his much shorter defence of democracy there are two points to note. One is his use of the word *isonomia*,[7] 'fairest of names', to denote his ideal. The other is the mention of election by lot, among the other advantages of democracy like accountability of officials and public control of decision-making. The terminology we shall discuss later; as regards 'lot', we note that no arguments are advanced as to why election by lot is thought to be either democratic or satisfactory: it was entirely taken for granted by fifth-century Athenian democrats that it was both, and Otanes treats it as a self-evident truth.

Megabyzus upholds oligarchy more tersely, but again in largely commonplace terms. Like Otanes, he attributes 'hubris' to monarchs, but he also points out that an unbridled mob may be just as guilty of it. The ignorant multitude plunge into public affairs like a river in spate – just the government for Persia's enemies! Rather, let power be put into the hands of the best citizens, and the best policies will surely emerge. Megabyzus began by using the neutral[8] descriptive term *oligarchia*, 'rule of the few'; but the real point of an oligarchy is not the fewness of its members but their excellence, and sure enough it is the *aristoi* ('including, of course, ourselves')

---

[6] Well argued by K.H. Waters, 'Herodotos on Tyrants and Despots', *Historia*, Einzelschrift 15, p. 12. For a notorious example, Hippolytus (E.*Hipp.* 612) says 'It is my tongue that has sworn the oath, my heart is not bound by it,' a quotation that was often turned against Euripides, quite unfairly—doubly so, as Hippolytus actually kept the oath!

[7] In this chapter I transliterate from the more familiar Attic forms. For the word-counts in this chapter I am indebted to J. Enoch Powell, *A Lexicon to Herodotus* (Cambidge U.P, 1939).

[8] So used by a supporter of the institution, Ps.-Xen. *Ath. Pol.* Depending on context, 'oligarchy' could bear invidious overtones, like 'minority rule'.

whom Megabyzus would invest with authority. The 'good', 'better' or 'best' citizens was how Greek oligarchs normally referred to one another.[9] Megabyzus has only got one real argument (as he is agreeing with Otanes' anti-monarchical points) and that is that the common people have no *knowledge* of what is right. That this 'ignorance' formed the main burden of criticism that democracy had to bear comes from two works from the opposite ends of the anti-democratic spectrum: Plato's *Republic* and the *Athenian Constitution* of 'Xenophon'.[10] We may wonder whether Herodotus had any specific occasions in mind when he composed this passage: one possible example from his text we shall discuss later;[11] Thucydides would have had no difficulty in producing instances.[12]

Darius, conveniently accepting Megabyzus' attack on democracy, makes a strong and impressive case for monarchy – deservedly, as it had to win the argument. His whole plea rests upon the assumption that the king will himself be 'the best' man (*aristos* again) and, once more, this has dramatic fitness, because of all the sovereigns treated by Herodotus Darius is the most successful: a reign not without setbacks – Scythia, Marathon – but marked by solid progress abroad and consolidation at home, and not coming to grief at the finish. His arguments are a mixture of the theoretical and the practical, the latter including the indubitable fact that kings find it easier to organise secret repressive measures against the disaffected. His sketch of how feuds and rivalries among the great oligarchic families lead to faction strife and monarchy is an accurate forecast of the death of the Roman republic and the principate of Augustus; Herodotus probably had in mind something like the squabbles of 'Plain, Coast and Hill', out of which emerged the Peisistratid tyranny. Darius' next argument, that corruption among democratic politicians leads, by a series of stages, to the same result, could not have been substantiated by example in Herodotus' own day, and looks like a speculative argument drawn from a sophist's debating school. But Darius keeps his trump card to the end – the example of Cyrus, who had done more for Persia than anyone else. No theoretical argument could prevail against that.

All sides, then, get a fair hearing, and we must look elsewhere for evidence of political 'tendencies' in Herodotus.

HERODOTUS' POLITICAL VOCABULARY

The Greek language had a wide vocabulary of words denoting 'liberty' in its various aspects, rather fewer denoting the loss of liberty. Thucydides, for

---

[9] E.g. Ps.-Xen. *Ath. Pol.* i.4–5.

[10] Ibid. The theme of the *Republic* is that government is a task for the educated expert.

[11] v.97.

[12] E.g. Th.vi.1.

instance, narrates the revolt of Naxos from the Delian League,[13] c. 470 BC; the Naxians were reduced by siege, and 'this was the first allied city that was enslaved [*edoulothē*] contrary to the established rules'. We would be wrong to suppose that the slave markets were filled with Naxians. All Thucydides is doing is to give us the stock rhetorician's contrast between freedom and unfreedom: if you're not 'free' you are *ex hypothesi* a slave. This is familiar in Latin, and with more excuse, for its resources of vocabulary are less, and the influence of rhetoric is stronger. (The antithesis of *libertas* and *servitus* is very marked, for instance, throughout Tacitus' *Agricola* and at several points of his *Annals*.) Herodotus likewise uses derivatives of *doulos* (slave)[14] far more often to denote subjection than actual servitude.[15]

On 'freedom', however, Herodotus gives us full value. His commonest choice is the most general word *eleutheria*, which can mean personal freedom, internal political freedom or external political independence. An example of it meaning 'constitutional government' comes in the narrative of Peisistratus' return from exile: Peisistratus was welcomed back by 'those who preferred tyranny to freedom' – a seemingly 'loaded' remark.[16] Maeandrius of Samos, having proclaimed *isonomia* after the death of the tyrant Polycrates, went on to offer the Samians *eleutheria*, a commodity which, as Herodotus sadly remarks, they evidently did not want.[17] *Eleutheria* in its external sense (again contrasted with 'slavery') was the word used by Bias of Priene when he proposed a mass emigration from Ionia.[18]

Now clearly *eleutheria* is something desirable for its own sake, but it has little or nothing to do with democracy. Ex-King Damaratus of Sparta praises to Xerxes the 'freedom under the law' that all Spartans enjoy;[19] and Sparta was never a democracy.

A few other words can be rapidly disposed of. *Eunomia* (good government) he uses only twice in a Greek context, both referring to Sparta[20] after the reforms of Lycurgus; *autonomia* only once, though in the age of the Delian League, Herodotus' lifetime, the question of 'enjoying one's own laws' was a living one. When Alexander of Macedon transmitted Xerxes' message promising *autonomia* to Athens if she changed sides in 479,[21] presumably this meant that within the Persian empire Athens could

---

[13] Th.i.98.

[14] Throughout this chapter I treat cognate words together like *tyrannos, tyrannis, tyranneuo*.

[15] Too many examples to quote.

[16] i.62.

[17] iii.142 f.

[18] i.170.

[19] vii.104.

[20] i.65 f.

[21] viii.140.

continue to enjoy a town-council democracy deliberating such matters as festivals, drains and market regulations. *Isokratia* also occurs once, when Sosicles the Corinthian says how topsy-turvy the world will have become if the Spartans are going to abolish *isokratias* and re-establish tyrannies in Greece.[22] The word is probably best rendered as 'republic' or 'common-wealth', again without any specifically democratic flavour, although it is in fact democracy in Athens that Sparta was then proposing to do away with. Sparta was no lover of democracy, and it has dramatic fitness that Sosicles should avoid using the word in his advocacy of Athenian interests.

Demokratia is a neutral, descriptive word, and the relatively few occurrences in Herodotus require no discussion.[23] More interesting are the words *isonomia* and *isegoria*. The former means 'equality of political rights' or 'equality under the law', and evidently has some emotive value. Otanes, as we have seen, said that popular government had 'the fairest of names, *isonomia*'; Maeandrius of Samos, in his well-meaning (or hypocritical) speech after Polycrates' death, said 'I proclaim *isonomia* to you'; and, the only time the word occurs in narrative, Aristagoras resigned his tyranny and gave the Milesians *isonomia*, to set off the Ionian revolt.[24] A similar note is struck in the well-known drinking song commemorating Harmodius and Aristogeiton,[25] in which it is claimed (falsely) that the tyrannicides brought *isonomia* to Athens. It is notable that in each of these examples there is a contrast, actual or implied, between 'equality of rights' and some antecedent state of tyranny – in Otanes' argument, the reigns of Cambyses and the Magus. Better still is *isegoria*, 'equal rights to speak'. This can only really refer to a fully democratic state like Athens where any citizen from the floor could address the Ecclesia. 'Who wishes to speak?' cried the herald[26] – that was democracy in practice. In Sparta (whose citizens being *homoioi* or 'peers', did enjoy literal *isonomia*) this was not the case; it was speeches from the platform only, the citizen body merely attending in order to vote yes or no.[27] In his most celebrated political comment Herodotus says '*Isegoria* proved, not only in one respect but in all, what a noble thing it is, seeing that under the tyrants the Athenians were no better than any of their neighbours; after getting shot of the tyrants, they were second to none.' His next sentence roughly repeats the idea in different words.[28]

---

[22] v.92a.

[23] E.g. iv.137 (speech of Histiaeus), vi.131. ('Cleisthenes, who set up the tribes and the democracy at Athens') and a few others.

[24] Respectively iii.80, 83; iii.142; v.37.

[25] Page, LGS, no. 449.

[26] Dem. xviii.170.

[27] In Th.iii.62, in a somewhat emotive context, a Theban speaker uses the term 'isonomous oligarchy'. See p. 97.

[28] v.78.

Little need be said of vocabulary on the opposing side. Herodotus often uses *tyrannos* and its derivatives loosely to denote oriental sovereigns, but these will not be considered here.[29] He most often uses the word descriptively, without necessarily implying 'tyranny' in the modern sense of cruel or despotic rule, of Greek usurpers who exercise extra-constitutional power in their cities such as Peisistratus and Periander; and of Greeks appointed by Persia to head collaborationist régimes in Ionia and elsewhere such as Histiaeus and Coës, again of course strictly 'unconstitutional' but not necessarily oppressive. He sometimes uses *monarchia* in the same sort of way, especially of the Sicilian tyrants; but the word also appears, interestingly, in the first oracle relating to Cypselus of Corinth, describing the undoubtedly *oligarchic* rule of the Bacchiadae.[30] *Tyrannis* (tyranny) is, however, once used emotively in contrast to *eleutheria*, as we have seen – those who joined Peisistratus were men who preferred tyranny to liberty. As liberty was a self-evident 'good', does it follow that Herodotus is an enemy of tyranny? And does his famous comment on Athens imply unqualified admiration for democratic freedom? On the face of it, yes, to both questions.

It would be surprising if it were not so. Tyranny in Herodotus' lifetime was both outdated and discredited. Outdated, in the sense that the contribution made by the tyrants to the political and economic growth of cities like Athens and Corinth lay far in the past, and it was not to be conceived that any return to tyranny could, in the vastly changed social conditions, produce any comparable benefit, or indeed any benefit at all. (Herodotus does seem at least intuitively aware of the valuable part played by the tyrants in Athens' evolution.) It was discredited, because of the association between tyranny and Persia, not just by Hippias at Marathon in 490. For Persia, having allowed the Ionian cities to have their own town-council democracies in 492,[31] later reverted to the old system of collaborationist tyrannies. We read of Strattis of Chios and Theomestor of Samos in 480; Themistocles in Magnesia in the 460s; Damaratus of Sparta and Gongylus of Eretria, and their descendants, in various cities of western Asia Minor; the system was enduring up to Xenophon's day.[32]

---

[29] H's treatment of these monarchies is intensely interesting but lies outside the scope of this chapter. (The theme is discussed in Waters, 'Herodotos on Tyrants and Despots', pp. 45–85.) The differences between the Persian kings and the Greek tyrants are profound, and the disparity in size between a city-state and the Persian Empire is such as to make comparisons meaningless — which is one of the reasons why the 'debate of the three conspirators' has at times an unconvincing ring. To make but one point, the mainland Greek tyrants represented successful factions or classes in a social and political revolution; if their sons inherited their position, they also inherited in some degree their supporters and their enemies. Darius and Xerxes, on the other hand, would regard themselves as being undoubted king of all their subjects. H's treatment of Darius as an historical personality will be dealt with in Chapter 5.

[30] For this oracle (v.92b) see Ch. 2, p. 66.

[31] vi.43.

[32] Respectively viii.85 and 132; Th.i.138; X. *Anab.* ii.1.3 and vii.8.8. H does not necessarily imply that the *islands* received democracies in 492.

On the other hand, it was democratic Athens that offered Herodotus a home for much of his life and gave him an unmatchable opportunity to win a name. As an imperial capital, Athens in the age of Pericles was a tremendous magnet for genius and talent. Pericles' citizenship law introduced in 451, besides disqualifying many existing citizens, sent a clear signal to the citizens of the allied states that Athens was determined to erect barriers of privilege between herself and them: anyone with idealistic notions of Greek unity could forget them. Even so, life for the well-connected 'metic' could be both comfortable and in some measure privileged. To Athens in this age came, among others, Anaxagoras of Clazomenae, the thinker and cosmologist, Protagoras of Abdera, greatest of the sophists, Hippodamus of Miletus, planner of the Peiraeus, the versatile poet Ion of Chios, and Herodotus. Athens under Pericles was an incredibly successful state for a while, and it was natural that Herodotus should feel some admiration for the system that produced this result. (He will also have had reservations, of which more later.)

TYRANTS AND TYRANNY

When we examine Herodotus' narrative treatment of tyranny and democracy, however, we do not find these impressions consistently borne out. Herodotus names a total of 55 tyrants of Greek states in the course of his work; 20 of these are Persian appointees or at any rate those who enjoy Persian support; of these 20 only six are mentioned more than thrice, the rest figuring in mere lists. Of the remainder, only 12 receive any substantial mention.[33] The six 'Medisers' are Histiaeus and Aristagoras of Miletus, Syloson and Aeaces of Samos, Miltiades (II) of the Chersonese and Coës of Mytilene. The dozen others are Cypselus and Periander of Corinth, Thrasybulus of Miletus, Peisistratus and his two sons in Athens, Polycrates and Maeandrius of Samos, Cleisthenes of Sicyon, Miltiades (I) of the Chersonese, Hippocrates of Gela and Gelon of Syracuse. Some of the figures he mentions in passing are men of whom we would gladly know more: Lygdamis of Naxos, for instance, the military adventurer who helped and was helped by Peisistratus, may have been, very probably was, a great man in his island's history: Naxos by the end of the sixth century was a major 'small' power.[34] Pittacus of Mytilene, another extremely interesting personality, evidently lies outside Herodotus' chronological framework;[35] nor does he have occasion later to discourse upon the history of Mytilene, as he does on Samos, Corinth and the Chersonese.

---

[33] These statistics are from Waters, 'Herodotos on Tyrants and Despots', p. 42 ff.

[34] v.28, 30; Lygdamis, i.61, 64.

[35] i.27. H rightly refuses to take responsibility for making Pittacus a contemporary of Croesus.

For the rest, we shall discuss the most salient examples. Chronologically the earliest tyrants whom he handles are Cypselus and his dynasty in Corinth, and Thrasybulus of Miletus. The tale of Cypselus is told by Sosicles of Corinth[36] in Herodotus' longest speech. In about 503 the Spartan government, having failed to install a docile oligarchy in Athens after expelling the tyrant Hippias, conceived the idea of restoring him. He had been on good enough terms with Sparta, who in turn considered she had been misled by Delphi on the question. But the Corinthians, who earlier had been instrumental in causing a Spartan invading force to break up,[37] again showed that they were good friends to Athens. Tradition preserved the name of the speaker who put their case and carried the majority of Sparta's allies with them, but the arguments used were more a matter for speculation. Sosicles may very well have begun as he is pictured as doing – vividly pointing up the inconsistency of Sparta in proposing to restore a tyrant to Athens, while continuing to take rigorous measures to safeguard against tyranny at home. But we would then expect him to continue with a slashing attack on the record of the Corinthian tyrants, culminating in a ringing account of how, and why, Sparta put down the Cypselid dynasty. He does not in fact end so, and this seems to me a very weighty argument from silence,[38] next door to proof, that Sparta had no hand in bringing the Corinthian tyranny to an end.

But it is what comes between that is most curious. 'The government of Corinth used to be an oligarchy consisting of one clan, the Bacchiadae, who intermarried amongst themselves.' On the speaker's own showing this oligarchy was a most selfish, narrow, inward-looking body with some whiff of the police state about it. On learning of the prophecy that Eëtion's son will overthrow them they seek to kill the new-born child, but – in a charmingly told tale – he is saved, survives and grows up. For over two pages the story continues, almost everything in it contriving to *win* our sympathy for Cypselus, this being by no means offset by the little remark inserted to the effect that 'evils were destined to arise for Corinth from Eëtion's son'. Then comes another oracle, 'prophesying' the duration of his dynasty.[39] We are told nothing of his seizure of power (a pity!) and his 30-year reign is actually dealt with in five lines. He banished many Corinthians, expropriated many, put many more to death, but 'wove life's web well to the end'. That is all: there is no specific information about who, precisely, were his victims (presumably, the members of the oligarchy); not

---

[36] v.92. In some MSS he appears as Socles; it matters little as he is otherwise unknown to history.

[37] v.75.

[38] Considerably weightier than the statement in Plut. *MH*, 859D, that she did; Plut.'s list of Spartan 'expulsions' is fictitious at more than one point.

[39] I regard all three 'Cypselus' oracles as *post eventum* fakes; see Ch. 2, p. 66.

a word about Cypselus' successful colonising enterprises that gave Corinth a long-standing interest in north-west Greece. The general prosperity of his long reign is hinted at, and earlier Herodotus has mentioned the splendid treasury he dedicated at Delphi; after the fall of the Cypselid dynasty the Corinthians rather meanly sought and gained permission to alter the dedication, but Herodotus will not let that pass without a fair-minded comment.[40]

On balance, then, Cypselus emerges in a more sympathetic light than the Bacchiadae, whom 'posterity never rehabilitated',[41] despite memories of Periander's cruelty in later years. Periander did in later times come to be regarded as the type or specimen of a 'tyrant' in the modern sense, suspicious and oppressive.[42] What does Herodotus say? Periander was 'milder than his father' at the start of his reign, but soon he became 'even more bloodthirsty than Cypselus': this as a result of his celebrated consultation of Thrasybulus of Miletus. Periander, evidently a young man (he reigned for 40 years), seeks advice from an acknowledged master of the craft and is urged, by an action more eloquent than any verbal message, to 'cut down the tallest'. He acts upon this at once, 'subjecting the Corinthians to every outrage, killing or banishing such as Cypselus had left untouched'; it is after this self-evidently wild exaggeration that Sosicles produces his example, the tale, partly gruesome, partly pathetic, of Periander's necromancy, and the sacrificial offering of the clothes of the women of Corinth. 'There's tyranny for you, men of Sparta' he concludes: an anticlimax indeed![43]

As in the case of Cypselus, we get no steady picture of Periander's reign, his vigorous foreign policy and military power, which put Corinth in the very front rank of Greek states. But elsewhere Herodotus does give us some glimpses. His patronage of the lyric poet Arion of Lesbos[44] anticipates the interest of Polycrates and the Peisistratidae in Anacreon, Simonides and others; he is recorded as having in his turn tipped Thrasybulus off about the content of a Delphic oracle given to his enemy Alyattes of Lydia. To be forewarned was to be forearmed, needless to say.[45] His great standing in the Greek world, and his reputation as a sage, is shown by his selection as arbitrator[46] between Athens and Mytilene, whose hostilities he concluded

---

[40] i.14.

[41] A. Andrewes, *The Greek Tyrants* (Hutchinson, London, 1956), p. 43.

[42] Arist. *Pol.* 1313, one of Aristotle's less impressive passages: 'tyrants keep their citizens hard at work on building projects to prevent them conspiring', forgetting that the projects he quotes were dwarfed by Pericles' 'democratic' building policy.

[43] So Waters, 'Herodotos on Tyrants and Despots', p. 14.

[44] i.23.

[45] i.20.

[46] v.95.

on the classic basis of *uti possidetis*, which meant that Athens kept Sigeum. His reputation for cruelty perhaps stems from the last days of his life, whence comes the tragic tale of his alleged responsibility (in some way) for the death of his wife Melissa; the quarrel with his favourite son Lycophron; the successful attack on his father-in-law Procles of Epidaurus; the murder of Lycophron in Corcyra, and the embittered old tyrant's vindictive reprisal, the rounding-up of 300 Corcyrean boys of noble family, to be sent to Lydia for castration and slavery – mercifully frustrated.[47]

In fact, apart from the arbitration episode and the war with Epidaurus, every piece of information about Periander is a *logos*, a popular tale of the type that tends to attach itself to powerful personalities of the moderately recent past, and cannot be taken as evidence of Herodotus' political views. The fact that he does not make Sosicles' speech into a burning indictment of tyranny, but rather a vehicle for the transmission of some excellent tales that he has not previously had an opportunity of including, suggests no doctrinaire attitude of mind on the author's part.[48]

As for Thrasybulus, he makes only the two appearances already referred to, the first in the tale of Periander's tip-off about a Delphic utterance, enabling his friend to outwit Alyattes; and the (evidently earlier) tale of his 'hints on tyranny' to Periander. The first of these, in so far as it is historical at all, is definitely pro-tyrannical; Thrasybulus plays his hand with masterly skill. The second is so much a part of the stuff of 'tales' that Aristotle reverses the roles of the protagonists, making Periander the giver of the advice; and Livy implausibly switches the whole tale to a Roman context.[49]

A similar undoctrinaire approach is evident in his handling of Cleisthenes of Sicyon. The part played by this city in the war against Xerxes was solid and valuable, but small – 15 ships at Salamis, 3,000 men at Plataea, and a distinguished showing at Mycale;[50] the days of Sicyonian greatness lay far back in the past, and Herodotus has no occasion for a grand digression on Sicyonian history. Instead we have Cleisthenes' régime featured in two digressions on Athenian history, and Herodotus is too much of an artist to hang one substantial digression upon another.[51] Consequently we find Cleisthenes appearing in Herodotus' story at the height of his fame and prosperity; there is nothing on the origin of the tyranny and nothing on

---

[47] All this in iii.48–53.

[48] As well argued by Waters, 'Herodotos on Tyrants and Despots'.

[49] Arist. *Pol.* 1284a; Liv. i.54.

[50] viii.43, ix.28 and 105.

[51] In fact the first appearance of Cleisthenes of Sicyon is as a digression within a larger one, the history of Athens antecedent to Aristagoras' visit. Close inspection will, I think, show that in this and other 'two-tier' digressions some careful attention is paid to scale and architecture by the historian. For another example, cf. the Gephyraioi, v.57–61.

its duration – traditionally a century, by some way the most durable of all Greek tyrant dynasties. A few shadowy names, from before and after Cleisthenes, and some even more shadowy facts, are preserved in Aristotle and other later writers. There is no need to discuss them here; put them all together and they do not come near the picture we have in Herodotus of a glamorous grandee and successful sportsman, holding court like a Renaissance prince.

Cleisthenes fought a war with Argos, we do not know why, nor with what result. As part and parcel of this Cleisthenes sought to whip up hatred of Argos and the Argives in Sicyon. Some of his measures resemble the refusal of certain English orchestras to play Beethoven and Wagner during the Great War. He put a stop to the rhapsodic contests in Sicyon because the Homeric epics sing the praises of Argos and the Argives.[52] In Chapter 1,[53] we considered the importance of traditional local cults in the lives of ordinary folk, and Cleisthenes did everything he could, short of abolition, to minimise the importance of the cult of the legendary Argive hero Adrastus (upon whom had devolved the throne of Sicyon in the days of the 'Seven against Thebes'); his cult was evidently the most popular in Sicyon. Delphi, in cheerfully insolent fashion, would not let him banish Adrastus entirely – 'Adrastus is King of Sicyon: you are a mere stone-thrower' – but his importation of the new cult of Melanippus, complete with the supposed bones of that Theban hero, shows ingenuity and manipulative skill.[54] (It was Melanippus who slew two close kinsmen of Adrastus at Thebes, and was his bitterest foe.)

Most important was his reform of the tribes at Sicyon. His family was evidently of the non-Dorian stock[55] (just as at Corinth Cypselus' father Eëtion had been) and the rise of the Sicyonian tyranny under Orthagoras represented an upsurge of the non-Dorian majority against the ruling aristocracy. In any event the tribes at Sicyon had had the same names as in Argos; the three Dorian tribes Cleisthenes renamed with insulting titles – 'pigmen, ass-men, swine-men'; his own tribe, presumably a majority of the citizen body, became Archelaoi, 'rulers of the folk'. True, false or a grim joke[56] by Cleisthenes (as the original name of his tribe was Aigiales, 'goat-men')? There does seem to have been a genuine tradition that Herodotus knew, however, and if the insulting names did indeed persist for 60 years after Cleisthenes' death, which on most judgements would be well after the

---

[52] These details are based on v.67 f.

[53] pp. 23, 33.

[54] Cleisthenes was later able to mend his fences with Delphi in the First Sacred War (see Ch. 1, p. 20.) and dedicated a splendid treasury there. For the talismanic properties of heroic bones, cf. i.67 f. (Sparta and the bones of Orestes); and Plut. *Cimon*, 8 (Cimon recovers the bones of Theseus from Scyros).

[55] Implied by v.68.1.

[56] See J.B. Bury, *HG*[3], p. 156.

suppression of his dynasty, it suggests that the non-Dorians were strong enough to go on humiliating their erstwhile better.[57] 'Childish as this is, it must be taken as seriously as the modern campaigns of propaganda of which it is the ancient counterpart.'[58] But, to return to Herodotus, we find no note of disapproval or even of moralising in his narrative. Because of the superficial similarity of a tribal reform, and the family relationship, he (with splendid inconsequence) calls in Cleisthenes of Sicyon as a precedent and example for Cleisthenes of Athens.[59]

Cleisthenes' other appearance is also in connection with the Alcmeonidae, the tale of the wooing of Agarista already discussed in Chapter 1. Here we need do no more than comment on the general impression of wealth and splendour, and the tyrant's spheres of influence. The list of suitors,[60] though it does raise certain problems, is realistic in so far as the gentlemen concerned come from areas where Cleisthenes' influence would have been felt, the Peloponnese, Athens, Thessaly (through Delphi), north-west Greece, Sicily and southern Italy – Sicyon was a minor sea power in Cleisthenes' time as in 480 – but none from Ionia, the islands other than Euboea nor the Hellespontine area. Herodotus, at the end of the excellent tale, leaves us with an abiding impression of Cleisthenes as a man of courtesy and generosity.

Tyranny came late to Athens. Why this was so has been much discussed but need not detain us here for long. As we saw in Chapter 1, Cylon failed to install himself at a time when Athens' three nearest neighbours to the south all had flourishing tyrannies – Corinth under Cypselus, Megara under Theagenes and Sicyon under Cleisthenes' predecessors. Athens was not troubled by 'racial' conflict between Dorian and non-Dorian, nor, probably, was the rule of the aristocracy particularly oppressive. Changing economic circumstances, which bore more heavily upon the poor, might have created enough discontent to fuel a revolutionary tyranny, but that threat was averted by the marvellous body of laws passed by Solon, and when the tyranny finally did arrive, 30 and more years after Solon's reform, it was in the person of one who had been a friend of Solon and who shared many of his political ideals.[61]

As so often with Herodotus' tyrants, Peisistratus is introduced by way

---

[57] Waters, 'Herodotus on Tyrants and Despots', suggests that the insulting names can't have outlasted the tyranny and that they belong to one of Cleisthenes' predecessors. Possible, but not what Herodotus says.

[58] Andrewes, *Tyrants*, p. 59.

[59] Herodotus' treatment of the Athenian Cleisthenes' reforms is discussed in Ch. 1, pp. 29 f.

[60] vi.126 ff., e.g. 'Leocedes son of Pheidon of Argos' looks anachronistic; no need to discuss the point here.

[61] Plut. *Solon*, 29, 31.

of a digression.[62] Croesus, limbering up for his great invasion of Cappadocia, has received the excellent advice from Delphi to discover the strongest state in Greece and seek its support. His researches narrow the field down to Athens and Sparta, then follows a model digression on the recent history of the two cities, each part containing a solid body of irreplaceable[63] information, enlivened by a 'tale'. Peisistratus' birth was presaged by a warning sign to his father, interpreted by Chilon the Spartan.[64] As we have seen, such warnings and premonitions cannot logically be acted upon or at least never are acted upon. The picture of the faction struggles of 'Plain, Coast and Hill' does not answer all the questions we would like to ask about post-Solonian politics in Attica, but it is the foundation of all subsequent discussion of the period and a good, believable foundation at that. Peisistratus, 'with a tyranny in mind', assembled his Hill faction, presumably hoping to be *tertius gaudens* as Lycurgus and Megacles concentrated upon damaging one another.[65] Whether or not we accept the motivation attributed to Peisistratus, it is only fair to point out that his faction were men from the area of eastern Attica where his family possessed estates and great influence to match.

Peisistratus is presented as an Odysseus of his age[66] or, perhaps, an anticipation of Themistocles.[67] Three times Peisistratus took power in Athens, each time either by means of, or with the help of, a trick. He already had a fine military reputation; he was probably not the first, and certainly not the last man to seize power with the aid of a bodyguard officially voted to him.[68] He ruled well, not tampering with the existing magistracies and laws (Solon's), presumably therefore exercising a kind of 'principate'. Proof came when Megacles and Lycurgus formed an unnatural coalition strong enough to force Peisistratus out – his tyranny 'not yet having put down firm roots' – and Athens promptly reverted to factional strife. The pliant Megacles then did a deal with Peisistratus, and back he came, bluffing the superstitious Attic peasants in the manner discussed in Chapter 1. The story of Peisistratus' marriage alliance and its breakdown, the revival of the coalition against him, and his withdrawal, is told in straightforward terms. The brisk narrative of his ten-year exile leaves us

---

[62] i.59–64.

[63] As much of the narrative content of *Ath. Pol.* 14 f. is a straightforward reworking of Herodotus' narrative; the Spartan portion is unduplicated.

[64] Waters, 'Herodotos on Tyrants and Despots', p. 21 n., amusingly argues that probably 'every . . . tyrant and Roman emperor was *post eventum* invested with preliminary omens . . . ; Herodotos, not being Suetonius, gives us only a selection, [but] includes one for Pericles' (vi.131).

[65] Discussed from the Alcmeonid point of view in Ch. 1 pp. 21 f.

[66] Remark attributed to Solon, Plut. *Solon*, 30.

[67] Not only the Herodotean Themistocles: cf. Th.i.90 f. for his bluffing of the Spartans in 479/8.

[68] A similar pattern could be traced in several twentieth-century coups.

with an impression of a man of drive, resourcefulness, and an ability to win friends and make use of them. When he made his final comeback, his stratagems to win the battle of Pallene and minimise bloodshed are entirely to his credit.

Finally we have a crisp account of how Peisistratus at last 'caused his tyranny to strike root' with a number of conventional techniques – hiring a mercenary guard, taxation at home, taking hostages from among the sons of his remaining opponents and winning divine favour by the first 'purification' of Delos. There were some Athenian casualties in the battle and some fled into exile.[69] Peisistratus, according to the chronology assumed here,[70] would have newly achieved undisputed power at the time when Croesus made his enquiries, and that explains Herodotus' seemingly unfair but surely truthful remark, in the very first sentence of his digression, that 'Attica had been torn by feuds, and was now held down by Peisistratus'; this is not a value judgement by the historian, but an accurate summary of Peisistratus' rule at the outset of his third tyranny: having tried and failed to achieve his aims by consent, he now had to employ measures to muzzle the opposition. Throughout the whole digression there is no word of overt censure of Peisistratus, nor mention of any specific acts of cruelty or oppression. It is his aristocratic opponents who are made to look time-serving and opportunist. There is just the one seemingly critical remark, that has been discussed already, about his supporters preferring tyranny to liberty.

Athenian affairs pass out of Herodotus' frame of reference for many years. Croesus plumped for Sparta, but too late for them to be able to render material aid. The advance of Persia to the Aegean brought Samos into the forefront, but on the mainland the remarkable record of Peisistratus in fostering the growth of Athenian prosperity, and his almost uniquely successful foreign policy, kept Athens out of any entanglements that might make her history a matter of relevance to Herodotus. The spotlight returns to Athens[71] in 499, in the now familiar manner: allies are being sought from overseas.

Aristagoras of Miletus has given the signal for the Ionian revolt to break out, and visits first Sparta, then Athens. The digression on Sparta is of medium length, and is mainly concerned with how Cleomenes became king at the expense of his supposedly better-qualified brother Dorieus. After narrating Aristagoras' failure at Sparta, Herodotus embarks on a colossal[72] and intensely valuable digression on Athenian history from 514 up to the moment of Aristagoras' arrival. The opening paragraphs deal with the last

---

[69] '. . . with Alcmeonides', see Ch. 1, p. 24.

[70] See chronological appendix to Ch. 3, p. 102.

[71] v.55.

[72] Twenty-five printed pages in Hude's text (OCT).

years of the Peisistratid tyranny, beginning with the murder of Hipparchus, complete with internal digression on the Gephyraioi, and a third-tier digression on Phoenician writing. Then come the efforts to expel Hippias, the third attempt succeeding; the struggle for power between Isagoras and Cleisthenes, the democratic reforms (including the sketch of Cleisthenes of Sicyon); the Spartan attempts to overthrow the new constitution; Athens' wars with her neighbours and with Aigina (and an internal digression on Aiginetan history); the abortive Spartan proposal to restore Hippias; and finally Hippias' residence in Asia, winning the ear of Artaphernes the satrap – with which Herodotus neatly leads us back to the Persian Question and Aristagoras' appeal for aid. Herodotus has skilfully made the bad relations that subsisted between Athens and Artaphernes follow by a natural process from the fall of the Peisistratidae; and that helps to explain why Athens took what Herodotus thought was the mistaken course of listening to Aristagoras.

To begin with Hipparchus' murder: at no point is Herodotus contradicted by Thucydides, and he is well aware of the relative status of Hippias and Hipparchus.[73] We may register surprise that if Herodotus knew the story of Aristogeiton's motivation as narrated by Thucydides, he did not tell it, for it has a very Herodotean quality. Be that as it may, the murder left Hippias still in power and 'embittered against the Athenians';[74] interestingly Herodotus does not specify what this meant in practice, so that the impression of general sympathy with, or at least understanding of, the Peisistratid régime is barely damaged. He switches directly to the moves to unseat Hippias, logically enough: he intuitively realises that tyrannies could last indefinitely if they remained rooted in popular feeling; as soon as that was forfeited, a régime's days were numbered. Though Harmodius and Aristogeiton did not liberate Athens, they did set in train a process that led inexorably to the tyrant's fall. The Leipsydrium enterprise failed, Anchimolius of Sparta failed, but King Cleomenes succeeded – just. Herodotus conveys to us that Hippias evidently continued his father's sage foreign policy, for the Spartans launched Anchimolius' expedition 'despite the fact that the Peisistratidae were on very good terms with them', in order to satisfy the pressures of Delphi;[75] to counter this, Hippias called up a powerful force of auxiliary cavalry from his Thessalian friends which effectively won the battle of Phaleron for him. Against Cleomenes they were less effective, perhaps because the king did not attempt the hazardous task of making a seaborne assault and forcing a landing against opposition. But

---

[73] Th.vi.53. Th.'s version has gained general acceptance, owing largely to the *auctoritas* of the historian. For a sceptical view see Mabel Lang, 'The Murder of Hipparchus', *Historia*, 1955.

[74] A remark echoed at vi.123.

[75] In Ch. 1, pp. 27 f., I have argued that Spartan policy in fact was undergoing a change and swinging against tyranny; here I am concerned with H's treatment of Hippias.

his actual achievement of the objective was due almost entirely to luck, as Herodotus goes out of his way to stress;[76] the Spartans were as good as abandoning the siege of the Acropolis, where Hippias' party were well supplied, when the tyrant's children were fortuitously intercepted while being smuggled out of Attica. A bloodless capitulation followed, there were no reprisals, Hippias was given five days to tidy up his affairs, and quit Athens with dignity. For all the 'increased harshness' of Hippias' later days, they cannot have been too terrible.

Hippias lived for some time at Sigeum,[77] intriguing with Artaphernes and even, seemingly, coming within an ace of restoration by Sparta until Sosicles of Corinth stopped all that. Hippias is made to utter prophetic words on that occasion: 'One day Corinth will long to have the Peisistratidae back!' In fact, despite Herodotus' stories of dissension at Salamis, relations between Athens and Corinth do not seem to have taken a turn for the worse until c. 461.[78] Finally Hippias returned with the Persians to Marathon, apparently advising their high command on the topography of Attica and, presumably, as viceroy designate. He cuts a slightly pathetic figure with his deceitful dream and his loose teeth; he must have been well into his 70s by then.[79] Apart from one remark in Miltiades' speech to Callimachus the Polemarch, suggesting what Athens will suffer if entrusted to Hippias, Herodotus allows him to fade out of history quietly and without rancour.

To the sequence of tyrannies in Samos Herodotus devotes many pages, on the face of it a disproportionate amount; but he had a store of high-grade information which is generally agreed to be the result of a prolonged stay on the island in the earlier part of his life. This is suggested by his detailed and obviously first-hand knowledge of dedications in the temple of Hera,[80] his considerable knowledge of and interest in Samian artists and their work,[81] and the fact that he is very much at home with Samian names and genealogies;[82] he also carefully records the stone set up in the *agora* of Samos commemorating (at least 15 years after the event) the eleven Samian captains who did not desert the line at the battle of Lade.[83]

There is another reason for the extended treatment of Samian history

---

[76] v.65.

[77] Evidently he was well enough liked in the Greek world to be offered residences in Thessaly and Macedonia also—v.93.

[78] Th. i.103.

[79] Having been an aide-de-camp to his father in and before 546 (i.61, 63).

[80] E.g. ii.182, Amasis dedicates two wooden statues 'out of friendship for Polycrates son of Aeaces'; iv.88, Mandrocles the engineer dedicates a tithe of his reward from Darius.

[81] E.g. Theodorus: i.51, Croesus' giant bowl at Delphi; iii.41, Polycrates' ring.

[82] E.g. ix.90, four names and parentage.

[83] vi.14.

in Book III, however.[84] The relentless march of events had brought Samos into the main stream of history. Croesus had contemplated a naval campaign against the islands after polishing off Ionia, but a witticism of Bias of Priene made him pause, and more serious affairs on the eastern frontier supervened.[85] The fall of Lydia in c. 544, and the efficient reduction of Ionia by Harpagus the Mede, brought Persia to the Aegean. Once again, however, any interest Cyrus may have had in further progress westward was overtaken by pressing requirements to the east, and Lesbos, Chios and Samos survived.

The advent of Cambyses and the acquisition by Persia of Phoenician seapower[86] changed the entire situation. The great project of Cambyses' reign was the conquest of Egypt, which was then under the Pharaoh Amasis, who as we have seen was a friend of Polycrates son of Aeaces, tyrant of Samos. He is not named as tyrant at that first incidental mention; he makes his full-dress appearance in Book III as an established ruler of extraordinary success and prosperity.[87] It is quite possible that Samos had been under a tyranny in the previous generation, perhaps under Aeaces, when Polycratean piratical practices were evidently well established.[88] (Herodotus records two such, the Samians' interception of a great bronze bowl, sent as a gift from Sparta to Croesus before his fall, and of a valuable ornamental corslet being sent by Amasis to Sparta.[89]) If that is so, the tyranny of Polycrates and his brothers Pantagnotus and Syloson would have been achieved by the displacement of their father – perfectly conceivable seeing that later we are told that the coup was pulled off with just 15 men-at-arms.[90] In any event, Polycrates soon had Pantagnotus killed and Syloson banished, and his story opens with him at the height of his power.

Herodotus has a matchless tale to fix upon Polycrates, for what made his seemingly unbroken run of success so amazing was the fact that he pursued a 'high-risk' foreign policy. He does not seem to have shrunk from incurring local enmities, and his indiscriminate plundering, for all that he sometimes returned the spoils, makes a marked contrast with the tranquil policies of peace on all fronts pursued by his senior contemporary Peisistratus. According to the tale, Amasis, alarmed by Polycrates' infallibly good luck, broke off the alliance in order not to be on Polycrates' side when

---

[84] iii.39–47, 54–9, 120–5, 139–49. B.M. Mitchell, 'Herodotus and Samos', *JHS*, 1975 is of much interest on this.

[85] i.27.

[86] iii.19, 34.

[87] He probably became sole tyrant c. 538, well before Cambyses' accession, though Thucydides i.13 properly makes him an effective contemporary of Cambyses.

[88] As argued by Mitchell, 'Herodotus and Samos', p. 78.

[89] i.70 and iii.47 f.

[90] iii.120.

the inevitable disaster struck.[91] Herodotus however goes on to record that when Cambyses was projecting his Egyptian campaign, Polycrates hinted to him that he would be willing to participate against his former friend and ally – so we draw our own conclusions. Thus the long series of digressions on Samos turns out to be a variant on the familiar theme of a search for allies.

The Herodotean Polycrates is by no means a wholly admirable character. Though Herodotus as usual refrains from overt condemnation, and indeed has some admiration for the sheer panache of the man, the factual content of what he has to say contains more to the tyrant's discredit than do his accounts of the Athenian and Corinthian tyrannies.[92] Having seized sole power as described and engaged in successful wars, he used his Greek captives as slave labour in public works; his aid to Cambyses consisted of a fleet manned by political suspects whom he was aiming to be permanently rid of. The last tactic failed, for once, as the crews made their way back to Samos and made a determined but unsuccessful attempt to oust Polycrates. The tyrant ensured against any home support for these returning malcontents by rounding up the wives and children of other citizens still in Samos – presumably of the aristocratic families – putting them in the shipyards and threatening to burn them alive if their menfolk came out against him. This was the sort of conduct more traditionally typical of a 'tyrant' than anything recorded of Peisistratus.

The Samian exiles appealed for help from Sparta; their opening plea was insufficiently 'laconic' – an amusing tale, this – but help they got, and one of Sparta's tyrant-suppressing enterprises was launched. It did not succeed. Herodotus had some good-quality information on this little campaign and gives a brisk account of it, concluding with the Spartan withdrawal after 40 days. He records a 'rather silly story' that circulated to the effect that Polycrates bought them off with Samian currency in gilded lead. We may commend his scepticism, but also be glad that he reported the story, for, unlikely as it sounds, half-a-dozen such coins have been found.[93]

After tracing the further fortunes of the Samian exiles, Herodotus forgets the 'search for allies' theme and justifies his digression on Samos by remarking on the importance of three great public works, the temple of Hera (Heraion) designed by Rhoecus, the great harbour works and the

---

[91] The tale is fully discussed from the theological point of view in Ch. 2. It fitted the facts of Polycrates' life and there is no need to assume that Herodotus distorted history to fit the tale, except perhaps over the question of who broke off the alliance. Mitchell, 'Herodotus and Samos', argues convincingly that Herodotus drew on 'aristocratic' sources in Samos who may have been tempted to put a gloss on some of the more disreputable passages of Polycrates' reign, such as this Medism.

[92] This may in part be due to H's aristocratic informants (see above, note 91), but the whole picture of Polycrates is consistent.

[93] J.P. Barron, *The Silver Coins of Samos* (Athlone Press, London, 1966), p. 17.

tunnel big enough for a man to walk through. These he does not attribute to Polycrates, but there are good grounds for assigning the latter two to his reign,[94] not least the fact that we know how he could exploit slave labour. These two works were vital for defence purposes, given the kind of adventurous foreign policy that Polycrates pursued, and the tunnel no doubt helped him to sustain the 40-day siege without undue discomfort.

The tunnel and watercourse designed by Eupalinus of Megara (iii.60) on Samos in the age of Polycrates. (Deutsches Archäologisches Institut, Athens)

When Polycrates is drawn to his end Herodotus does not withhold sympathy. The detestable Oroetes, satrap of Sardis, had held office throughout Cambyses' reign, and Herodotus carefully times the episode to the confused period around Cambyses' death (c. 522),[95] which suggests that Oroetes was seeking to take advantage of events to build up a private

---

[94] E.g. Arist. *Politics*, 1313b.
[95] iii.120.

power-base for himself. Herodotus gives two possible motives for his wanting to murder Polycrates. The less generally accepted one (that Polycrates, relaxing with Anacreon, slighted a messenger from Oroetes) is mainly of interest as yet more evidence of the way tyrants patronised the lyric poets.[96] The other story, that Oroetes had a bitter quarrel with his neighbour Mitrobates, satrap of Dascyleion, is quite believable when we recall the jealousy of Tissaphernes and Pharnabazus in the late fifth century, which so hindered the development of an effective western policy by Persia from 412.[97] (Oroetes later had him, too, murdered.)

In any event Oroetes, having first duped Polycrates' secretary Maeandrius (or having done a deal with him – see below), enticed the tyrant to Magnesia with the prospect of wealth. The trick for which Polycrates fell was an old one but still a good one; it was good enough in 416 when Athenian envoys were tricked by the Egestaeans.[98] The story also characterises Polycrates neatly. He was a bold buccaneer, a prince of splendour and a healthy cynic; but when compared with such as Periander, Thrasybulus and Peisistratus, he seems lacking in sagacity.[99] Never was he a candidate for a chair among the 'Seven Sages'. The horrible Oroetes had clearly sized his man up as one whose cupidity could be safely played upon; Polycrates for his part had got out of so many tight corners in the past that he did not imagine that there was anything here that he could not handle. Disregarding (of course) the premonition of his daughter he pressed ahead to his brutal murder. This death was 'unworthy of himself and of his ambitions', for 'only the Syracusan tyrants are fit to be compared with Polycrates in magnificence'.

Oroetes survived the interregnum of the Magus, but was removed and executed in an early cleaning-up operation of Darius' reign – for Polycrates had been an ally of Persia.

Maeandrius, Polycrates' former secretary, had been left in charge, and he at least went through the motions of 'restoring the republic'. Herodotus takes his proclamation of *isonomia* at face value: 'he wanted to be the justest of men, but this proved impossible'.[100] The Samians looked the gift horse in the mouth, as it were, and Maeandrius was obliged to safeguard his

---

[96] Anacreon is recorded as having sung Polycrates' praises, but, disappointingly, none of his surviving fragments contains the name of Polycrates.

[97] See (e.g.) Th.viii.109.

[98] Th.vi.46: Th. had high-grade contemporary information on Sicily.

[99] *Contra* Waters, 'Herodotos on Tyrants and Despots', p. 28 f.: 'It is hard to imagine the wily Polycrates falling for this ancient ruse'—but was he 'wily'?

[100] iii.142. Mitchell, 'Herodotus and Samos', p. 86, suggests that an over-favourable view of Maeandrius comes from an aristocratic source: we are not obliged to believe the taunt of low birth thrown at M in iii.142.5, for such things are the small change of Greek political argument. Apart from the opening commendation of M's motives, however, I question that H's portrait of M is over-favourable; he comes out as a total failure.

position by turning it into a tyranny. In view of his previous visit to Oroetes we are entitled to wonder, at least, whether he came to some arrangement with the satrap to betray Polycrates and so assumed power with Oroetes' support. If so, the discreditable fact was suppressed by Herodotus' informants, or perhaps never even leaked out at all. It is possible that Maeandrius did make a speech on the lines stated, intending it to be a sham (like Augustus[101] in 27BC) or intending to provoke the reaction that he did. But if Maeandrius really did rule with the connivance of the disloyal Oroetes, that would explain why Darius was quite prompt to unseat him in favour of the dispossessed Syloson.

Maeandrius ruled Samos with none of the flair of his predecessor and seems to have been unable to rely on any kind of support. He arrested and imprisoned his potential political enemies early on, and when he fell ill his brother Lycaretus, hoping to succeed, put them to death. Like the Peisistratidae, Maeandrius and his brothers worked as a team, for the mentally unstable Charilaus may have had some military responsibility before being locked up, and it was under the cover of his violent intervention that the unheroic Maeandrius made his escape. Lycaretus was evidently able to do some private deal with the Persian authorities, for he later turns up as tyrant of Lemnos after its conquest by Otanes, son of Sisamnes;[102] he died in office.

The charming story of Syloson, Darius and the flame-coloured cloak is one of those felicitous tales that reflect equal credit on both protagonists. However, if the Persians really were intending to avenge the murder of their late ally Polycrates, they had in his brother Syloson a ready-made candidate for the tyranny, cloak or no cloak. Syloson had hoped to take over the island painlessly, but was spitefully prevented from doing so by Maeandrius and Charilaus, who provoked a massacre. Herodotus was given what must have been grossly exaggerated accounts of the reprisals taken by the other Otanes (son of Pharnaspes), for a Samian contingent was serving under Darius on the Danube only about four years later under Syloson's son Aeaces.[103]

Maeandrius, who is one of the most steadily unsuccessful rulers recorded by Herodotus, attempted to secure aid from Cleomenes of Sparta to overthrow the restored Persian-backed tyranny. His attempt to 'influence' him with a show of wealth is reminiscent of the bait Oroetes set for Polycrates. In the previous reign the Spartans had, after all, unsuccessfully attempted to unseat Polycrates on behalf of Samos' aristocracy, as we have

---

[101] This is no place to justify such a comment! See Gibbon, *Decline and Fall* Ch. 3, or R. Syme, *The Roman Revolution* (Oxford, 1939) Ch. 22, if desired.
[102] v.27.
[103] iv.138.

seen; and it was not entirely unreasonable for Maeandrius to repeat the appeal. But Cleomenes had either learnt from that failure, or else he had simply taken the measure of Maeandrius and recognised a loser when he saw one. He 'showed himself a man of the highest principles' and had him sent packing.[104] With that he fades from history.

The rest of the story of the Samian tyranny need not detain us long. Herodotus tells us nothing of Syloson's brief reign (three or four years at the most); Aeaces is merely mentioned in the interesting list of tyrants on the Danube, fell from power when Aristagoras got the Ionian revolt off the ground, but was the only ex-tyrant who was successful in his overtures to the members of the Greek fleet before Lade.[105] Forty-nine out of Samos' contingent of 60 ships deserted the line at the outset of the battle. Evidently his rule had not been too frightful, though Herodotus records[106] that the Samian aristocracy did not welcome this development at all, and they sailed off on a colonising adventure in Sicily. Those that remained evidently settled down well enough and the Samians gave a good account of themselves fighting for Xerxes at Salamis.[107]

Gelon of Syracuse deserves attention. His incidentally is the only important tyranny which Herodotus treats in one sitting; it is noteworthy how all other substantial references to tyrannies are split into two units, each with its own criteria of relevance, but neatly cross-referenced.[108] Gelon appears, needless to say by now, in the context of allies being sought – this time by Athens and Sparta in 480. Gelon learned his trade under Hippocrates of Gela, a tremendous warrior who fell in battle after seven years as tyrant; Gelon served with great distinction as his Master of Horse, having started as a member of the tyrant's guard. What followed was interesting: there was a popular rising against Hippocrates' sons, Gelon took up the cudgels seemingly on their behalf, crushed the insurgents and then seized power himself. No people's champion he! He likewise befriended a body of propertied citizens who had been thrown out of Syracuse, and with their aid (and presumably his own faithful cavalry) he took Syracuse without resistance from the common people. He ceded Gela to his brother Hiero and concentrated on Syracuse thereafter: under him it rose to stupendous heights. He went in for large-scale population transfers; his treatment of defeated enemies was, to say the least, unorthodox. He had overcome Sicilian Megara in a war instigated by the wealthy of that city; he brought them into Syracuse and gave them citizen rights. The commons,

---

[104] iii.148.

[105] vi.10, 13, 14.

[106] vi.22.

[107] viii.85.

[108] E.g. the two 'Periander' passages are linked by his wife's death; the two 'Miltiades' ones by the Philaid family tree.

who had no share of responsibility, he sold into slavery. Similar treatment was handed out to Sicilian Euboea. Gelon (whose political sympathies seem perfectly consistent) 'found the common people unpleasant to share a house with'.[109] 'Such was the way in which Gelon had become a great tyrant,' concludes Herodotus drily.

Then follows the group of speeches, and a finely composed, dramatic set they are. Gelon is excellently and rather sympathetically portrayed by Herodotus as realistic, courteous and humorous. 'But now that the tide of war has shifted and has reached you, you remember Gelon!' – a splendid thrust – but he generously offers colossal forces and provisions, on the sole condition that he is made supreme commander. The touchy reactions of the Spartan and Athenian envoys are amusingly portrayed, and Gelon lets them go with a last witticism – again surely authentic, the characterisation is so consistent – 'it seems that you've got the generals, but you won't have any men for them to command'.[110] Herodotus then briefly mentions how Gelon took modest precautions against the event of a Persian victory. His agent in this, Cadmus of Cos, was the son of Scythes of Zancle, a man who had stood high in Darius' esteem,[111] and therefore a good choice as envoy to Xerxes – if required. From there Herodotus goes on to record Gelon's great war with Hamilcar of Carthage, which 'according to a story current among the Sicilians' was the real reason for Gelon not aiding the homeland, whether as supremo or not. It is impossible to say whether this belief is well-founded or false; what is certain is that Gelon could not in the event, have sent any aid. The Himera campaign, with its brilliantly successful result, settled that.

It remains to discuss briefly some representatives of the tyrants who held positions under Persia. Now Herodotus with his familiar distaste for technicalities lumps these tyrants together under the same name as Periander and the rest. In a sense this is fair, because there are real similarities: they hold a monarchical position; they are not *isonomoi*, that is to say they cannot be reached by the processes of law that affect all other citizens. The mainland tyrannies however mostly began as usurpations; those in Persia's interest were generally appointed and were presumably not 'irresponsible' in the way that Periander was;[112] they must have had to render some account of their stewardship to the satrap and, as we have seen, they were liable to be required to furnish contingents for military expeditions. The career of Miltiades (II) in Persian service has been fully discussed in Chapter 1 and needs no further mention here. Aristagoras of

---

[109] vii.156 – this remark has the ring of an authentic *mot*.

[110] Doubts have been cast on the authenticity of the whole Gelon episode. It is (in my opinion) satisfactorily vindicated by P.A. Brunt, 'The Hellenic League Against Persia', *Historia*, 1954, p. 158 ff.

[111] vi.24.

[112] Usurpers who Medised could of course carry on, as Polycrates did.

Miletus will be considered in connection with the Ionian Revolt in Chapter 4; instead we shall look briefly at Coës and Histiaeus.

Coës' career stands as a warning to those who would entrust political power to those who simply want it. An officer of no position, he commanded the contingent from Mytilene on Darius' Scythian campaign.[113] Darius had conveyed his army to the north bank of the Danube by way of the pontoon bridge and was about to begin his famous raid into Scythia. Presumably in order to maximise the forces he had with him, or perhaps to guard against treachery, he gave orders that the bridge be broken up and the naval force follow him. Coës, having first taken soundings as to how Darius would listen to a candid expression of opinion, advanced a cogent argument for the bridge being left in situ, adding, however, that he would continue to serve with Darius on the march into the interior. Darius was delighted with the advice and promised to reward Coës at the conclusion of affairs.[114]

The reward was what Coës asked for, the position of tyrant of Mytilene,[115] presumably displacing some similar regime. Herodotus gives us no details of Coës' rule in the dozen or so years that he held the position, except to imply that he assisted Otanes in the conquest of Lemnos and Imbros;[116] but he was evidently an abler staff officer than tyrant. When Aristagoras of Miletus brought out Ionia into revolt, the suppression of the tyrannies was achieved bloodlessly, with the sole exception of Coës. The Mytilenians stoned him to death.[117]

We know too little of Coës to discuss him in particular, but the sequence of events illustrates something that goes some way to explaining why Persian overlordship was resented, even though it was not necessarily, nor even usually, oppressive: the way that Persian kings sometimes used the Greek cities in their empire as pieces of personal property, to hand out as tips to their servants and supporters. It would be interesting to know the nature and popularity of the regime that Coës supplanted.

Our final example is Histiaeus of Miletus, one of the most fascinating and controversial of all the minor figures in Herodotus. He was firmly installed as tyrant in Persia's interests by the time of Darius' Scythian expedition. No connection can be traced between him and Thrasybulus, tyrant in the days of Alyattes of Lydia; we have next to no information on the internal affairs of Miletus in the long period that separates them, apart

---

[113] iv.97.

[114] 'Delight' (*hēdomai* and its compounds) is a Herodotean characteristic of Persian kings, especially when receiving advice: e.g. i.90 and 156, Cyrus is delighted by hints passed to him by Croesus; viii.69 and 103, Xerxes is delighted by Artemisia's contributions to debate. More general examples, especially of Xerxes, are too numerous to list, but cf. Th.i.129.

[115] v.11.

[116] v.26.

[117] v.37 f.

from the tantalising snippet referring to 'two generations of civil disorder' which was terminated by an arbitration, in favour of the propertied class, by a commission from Paros.[118] This must have fallen between the end of Thrasybulus' dynasty (if he had one) and the establishment of Histiaeus,

The dramatic events at the Danube crossing[119] have been fully discussed from Miltiades' point of view in Chapter 1. The picture that emerges of Histiaeus there is of a cool-headed, realistic politician able to see behind the surface of events. Miltiades had argued that Darius' seemingly imminent catastrophe gave his Greek subjects a heaven-sent chance to escape from Persian sovereignty. This must have been justified as far as it went, for had the Persian army become stranded in Scythia and been totally destroyed (with Darius among them, and no obvious successor to him yet in sight) it is hard to see how Persia could have maintained any firm grip on western Asia. Histiaeus countered this by a straightforward argument from self-interest: all Persian appointees would be thrown out of their cities. His position, and that of all others except perhaps Miltiades himself, depended squarely upon the reserve power of Persia. The assembled tyrants had at first wavered, but Histiaeus brought them back into line. Then, while the work of demolishing the north end of the pontoon was begun, to convince the Scythians of their good faith, it was Histiaeus who explained to them what was going on: fortunately they believed him and left, so the sham destruction of the bridge could be halted. When the Persians eventually arrived, after suffering great privations, it was pitch dark. No bridge! But Darius knew his man. A stentorian Egyptian was bidden to call the name of 'Histiaeus of Miletus!', Histiaeus was on the alert, no second shout was required, and the army was conveyed to safety.

Such loyalty deserved and received its reward. Darius seems genuinely to have admired the native talents of his Greek supporters, who also had the advantage (from his point of view) of standing outside the court intrigues and rivalries of the Persian noble families. Histiaeus chose (or perhaps was offered, and accepted) Myrcinus, a position on the river Strymon in western Thrace. This was quite close to the spot which the Athenian people, at the second attempt, successfully colonised as Amphipolis in 437. For Persia this had great advantages. Being on the edge of Megabazus' newly conquered Thracian province, it offered a forward base for expansion into the Greek world, in a position of strategic strength with road and river communications. For Histiaeus, too, it offered scope for his talents of leadership and organisation.

But none of this was proof against the hostility of Megabazus himself. This officer is represented by Herodotus as exercising prudent foresight in

---

[118] v.28 f.
[119] iv.136–9.

Persia's interests, and arguments put into his mouth, when warning Darius against Histiaeus' project, are the sort of things he would plausibly have said.[120] But there may have been other motives at work. It was all too common for Persian grandees to envy the influence of Greeks with successive Persian kings,[121] and the later attitude of Artaphernes to Histiaeus bears this out.[122] Darius evidently liked Histiaeus and when he summons him to Susa we need not question his sincerity quite as overtly as Herodotus does;[123] certainly if the king required an expert confidential adviser on Greek affairs, and he surely must have done, it is hard to think that he could have had a better man than Histiaeus. He had a healthy respect for Persian power, and was probably close to the truth when he told Darius that had he been left in charge of Miletus the Ionian revolt would never have happened. (Statements made in the pluperfect subjunctive are not susceptible of proof, but this at least sounds plausible.) His involvement in the revolt itself will be discussed separately; all that need be said here is that Herodotus treats this ambiguous figure with scepticism, but without hostility. He nowhere suggests that his régime in Miletus was harsh or oppressive, and at the end, when Histiaeus is trapped and put to death by Artaphernes, he takes his leave of him in such a way as to arouse our sympathy.[124]

OLIGARCHY AND DEMOCRACY

Enough has been said to show that Herodotus has no doctrinaire attitude towards tyranny as such. He treats rulers on their merits and lets their successes and failures speak for themselves. We must now turn to what he has to say about other political systems in Greece. We must remember that in Herodotus' lifetime the normal government in the 'average' city-state was a moderate oligarchy; we know so much about Athenian democracy, and rightly recognise its transcendant importance, that it is easy to forget how untypical Athens was. Democracy in the Athenian mould needed a large urban population, a relatively high level of literacy and education, an economy that included some slave labour, and sea power. This is not the place to argue these points at length. Briefly, the citizens living in the country districts of Attica would think it worth their while to come in to vote at meetings of the Ecclesia, if only to prevent their interests being overlooked by the urban residents, while such things as the staffing of the

---

[120] I am not, of course, meaning to imply that H had any firm information as to this!

[121] Two other examples (there are more): Achaemenes and Damaratus, vii.236 f., Epixyes and Themistocles, Plut. *Them.* 30.

[122] vi.1 f., 30.

[123] v.24.

[124] vi.30.

jury courts would largely have fallen to the latter. Democratic control meant, among other things, publication of decrees and treaties, and strict accounts being kept of public expenditure. Athens is unusually rich in inscriptions because all these things were engraved for public scrutiny. It would be wise to assume that citizens with an interest in politics (which meant most citizens)[125] made it their business to study these things. In Athens free men, 'metics' and slaves might work side by side, and the economic life of the community did not come to a halt every time there was a meeting of the Ecclesia; and the connection between sea power and democracy, well grasped by 'Xenophon',[126] was founded upon the sound Greek principle of an equation between civic rights and public service. Athens' rowing benches were manned by men of the *thetes* or labouring class, unpropertied or virtually so, and both policy and common fairness demanded that this service be paid for by full franchise. (A state that had no navy would confine membership of its Ecclesia to members of the moderately propertied hoplite class.) Very few cities in the Greek world, apart from Athens, actually had these features in combination; one that had was Syracuse, which did indeed enjoy a democratic constitution for several decades after the end of the tyranny there.

Herodotus' great interest in tyranny is at least partly due to the fact that tyranny was virtually extinct in the Greek world that he knew outside the Persian empire; the institution had curiosity value both for him and his audience. This of course was not so with oligarchy and democracy, and Herodotus very seldom feels any occasion to comment either on these forms of government or on particular decisions made by them. We have already seen how the Bacchiadae of Corinth received something of a bad press. They were of course one of the old-fashioned oligarchies that were truly aristocratic, a closely knit group of patricians whose authority was based on immemorial tradition. The oligarchies that were closer to his own day were not like this. Herodotus speaks (without comment) of the *pacheës* (rich citizens, literally 'the fat') of Chalcis – where this class was styled *hippobotai* (horse-rearers): they were the ruling oligarchy of Chalcis dispossessed by the Athenians after their victory in c. 506.[127] The same word *pacheës* he uses of the exiled oligarchs from Naxos whom Aristagoras attempted to restore (with Persian help) as a curtain-raiser to the Ionian revolt;[128] and of the ruling oligarchy of Aigina which put down the Athenian-backed revolt of Nicodromus.[129] Their act of sacrilege following

---

[125] Implied by Pericles' Funeral Speech, Th.ii.40.2.

[126] Ps.-Xen. *Ath. Pol.* i.2 etc.

[127] v.77.

[128] v.30.

[129] vi.91.

this success recalls that of Megacles the Archon after the suppression of Cylon's conspiracy.[130] Oligarchies were now, by implication, timocratic organisations, with office-holding based on criteria of wealth rather than patrician birth.

One undoubted oligarchy that Herodotus does not actually name as such is that holding office at Thebes in 480/79.[131] A speaker in Thucydides, defending his city's conduct in the Persian War, says that Thebes did not then enjoy democracy nor even *isonomia* under an oligarchy, but was in the hands of a narrow oligarchic clique. We are not obliged to believe this wholly, for the speaker is concerned to put his city in the most favourable light possible compared with Plataea (whose record in the Persian War was honourable). But we may assume that it was near enough the truth to be plausible: Thebes must have had one of the less open oligarchic governments of the age. Oligarchic governments down the ages displayed a regrettable readiness to betray their city to the national enemy in order to secure their own position – not that the oligarchs would have considered it betrayal. Aristagoras' Naxian friends fall into this category. Examples from outside Herodotus include the oligarchs of Samos in 440 making an agreement with Pissuthnes, satrap of Sardis, and the newly installed 'Four Hundred' of Athens making overtures to Agis of Sparta in 411.[132]

The typical Greek oligarchy, so far as it is legitimate to generalise, resembled Athenian democracy in having two-chamber government, Council (Boulè) and Assembly (Ecclesia), with the former framing the policies and the latter voting upon them. The difference would lie in the importance attached to each, and their membership. In Athens the Council of 500 was a representative cross-sectional body of the whole people and was regarded as the handmaid of the Assembly; all free citizens could turn up to the periodical meetings of the latter and not just vote on the business placed before them by the Council, but speak from the floor as well. The oligarchic council, by contrast, would be of membership limited to noble or propertied classes – as the Council of Areopagus had been in archaic Athens – and was the body where effective decisions were taken; these would then be placed before the Ecclesia, however that may have been composed.[133] This merely had the power to accept or reject – no speeches from the floor, in other words; *isegoria*, as we have seen, was a phenomenon peculiar to Athens. It follows, however, that oligarchy was not necessarily an oppressive form of government, as the citizen body was not utterly bound by the decisions of

---

[130] Ch. 1, p. 18.

[131] ix.86, cf. Th.iii.62.

[132] Th.i.115 and viii.70.

[133] The moderate oligarchy of the 'Five Thousand' effectively restricted full franchise to the hoplite class (Th.viii.97). This may have been typical.

the council, but it could become one in the hands of a selfish clique.[134]

Sparta had an uniquely mixed constitution, which was however closer to oligarchy than to any other single type. Of course the kings had great influence (rather than power): in a state that was so strongly oriented towards the military virtues, hereditary generals (which is what the kings in effect were) would carry great weight; while on the civil side they were ex-officio members of the Council of Thirty (Gerousia, literally 'body of elders' or senate). Ordinary membership of this council was confined to retired Spartans aged over 60 who, once elected, held office for life; a king might succeed to his position in his 20s and over the years build up a body of political experience that no Elder could match. In relation to the fully qualified citizens (Spartiatai) who were *homoioi* or 'peers', there was a democratic element in the persons of the five annual ephors, who were by Herodotus' own day the most powerful men in Sparta, competent to bring kings to trial[135] and secure their conviction. These magistrates were elected by the whole Spartiate assembly. The oligarchic element lay in the Gerousia, to which the ephors in office had right of access; there policy was framed; and when these decisions were put to the vote there were no speeches from the floor, but only from the platform. In the famous debate recorded or at least depicted by Thucydides,[136] the assembly is addressed in turn by an ambassador from Corinth, one from Athens, King Archidamus and Sthenelaïdas, senior (eponymous) Ephor of the year. His is the winding-up speech – no question of throwing the motion open to the house – and he promptly puts the question to the vote. This seems to conform with accepted oligarchical practice.

Herodotus greatly admires Sparta in general, regarding her leadership in the Persian War as natural and inevitable. This will be dealt with in Chapter 6. Of her politics and constitution he has little to say. There is the remark on the 'good government' (*eunomia*) which flowed from the reforms of Lycurgus.[137] We should resist the temptation to hammer Herodotus for accepting without question what was no doubt accepted by everyone in Sparta, namely that their constitution and social system was a coherent package produced by one man; in no sense could an antiquarian survey of the origins of Spartan magistracies have fallen within his criteria of

---

[134] The '400' in Athens, who declined to create an Assembly at all, are the classic example of this.

[135] As they did to Cleomenes in c. 494 (vi.82), who was however acquitted. Full discussion of the ephors' powers lies outside the scope of this work, as does the question of Sparta's population. Suffice it here to say that the full citizens formed quite a small and highly privileged minority in the Spartan body politic. For a rather dramatised but fundamentally true picture of this, cf. Cinadon's conspiracy, 399 BC, in X. *Hell*, iii.3.4 ff., when the imbalance of population was more marked than ever. For an accessible and readable treatment of Spartan history, W.G. Forrest, *History of Sparta 950–192 B.C.* (Hutchinson, London, 1968) is recommended.

[136] Th.i.67–87.

[137] i.65.

relevance in Book I. When he narrates the quarrel of kings Cleomenes and Damaratus in Book VI he turns aside to a consideration of the origin of the dual kingship (passing on an indubitably unhistorical explanation for it) and the kings' privileges.[138] This section does have a strongly antiquarian flavour: the dual monarchy was a real curiosity. It is a pity that Herodotus fluffs two points, one the matter of the kings' proxies in the Gerousia, already discussed, the other the right 'to lead military campaigns against whatsoever country they choose'. The latter clause seemingly implies a power of initiative, hence many modern translators simply render the phrase 'to declare war upon . . . '. This may have been the case in archaic times if both kings acted in unison, but it was certainly not the case in Herodotus' own day, which is what he implies.[139]

As late as c. 506 Cleomenes, by then well-established and a dominant personality, seems to be raising an army on his private initiative, but with the support of his fellow king Damaratus, to crush the rising Athenian democracy. This enterprise collapsed when Damaratus withdrew, thereby perhaps destroying the legitimacy of the campaign.[140] As a result, that power was forced to lapse. It is rather as though Herodotus, who is very well aware that the Spartan state had undergone no revolutions or changes of régime for centuries (unlike everywhere else), has overlooked some subtle but important changes that became established by custom and practice.

Just one comment does Herodotus make on Spartan politics. With Athens evacuated for the second time, Athenian ambassadors were sent to Sparta to beg for an army to drive Mardonius' force out of Attica and Boeotia. The ephors put them off from day to day, ten days in all, during which time the work of fortifying the Isthmus was pressed ahead with all possible zeal;[141] eventually they were convinced that the Isthmus wall would be of no value if Athens Medised, as she was then tempted to do. The sequel came in the final phase of moves before the battle of Plataea was joined. The obstinacy of Amompharetus caused a hitch in the Greek retreat, for the Spartans did not move off at the agreed time. The Athenians thereupon stood their ground too, 'knowing full well the Spartan tendency to say one thing and mean something else'.[142] A pardonable comment, or attribution of motive, after what had gone before: perhaps Herodotus meant only to suggest that the decision-making behind closed doors that the ephors had gone in for would not have been possible in the open democratic society of Athens.

---

[138] vi.56 ff.

[139] Th.i.67–87 again; but not even in 479 either, to judge from ix.10.

[140] v.74 f.

[141] ix.8.

[142] ix.54.

Herodotus gives us a little more on democracy. There is the finely dramatised set of speeches delivered, obviously to the Council of 500, by Alexander of Macedon and a Spartan delegation, with the Athenian replies, at the end of Book VIII: here the official Athenian line is put across in ringing tones.[143] A more sinister side of democracy when roused is the ugly episode of Lycidas, a member of the Council of 500, who was lynched (as were his family later) for proposing that a hearing at least be given to Mardonius' overtures for a settlement.[144]

There are, however, two celebrated comments. One is that already quoted:[145] Athens has successfully repulsed an early attempt to strangle the Cleisthenic constitution by squarely routing armies from both Boeotia and Chalcis. 'Isegoria [here, evidently, 'democracy'] proved, not only in one respect but in all, what a noble thing it is . . . Evidently, when they were held down, they refused to do their best, for they were working for a master; but when they were freed, each man was eager to make an effort for himself.' On the face of it this was unfair to the Peisistratid régime, which was both successful in itself and beneficial to Athens in the short and the long term. But Peisistratid policy had been based on friendship and diplomacy; there were no wars with any of Athens' neighbours. What Herodotus here commends is a newly free people, with its back seemingly to the wall, striking back devastatingly at an attempt to rob it of its hard-won gains. We may fairly doubt whether Herodotus would have extrapolated this eulogy to cover success in aggressive wars, however: to fight in defence of your own liberties is quite different from fighting to deprive others of theirs. The remark cannot, therefore, be taken as evidence that Herodotus necessarily approved of Athens' military policies in his own day. I suspect that he did not.

The other comment is made on the occasion of Aristagoras' visit to Athens in 499.[146] Rebuffed by Sparta, the Milesian windbag (as depicted by Herodotus) came to Athens soliciting aid. 'There was nothing he did not promise them, until he won them round. It is apparently easier to pull the wool over the eyes of many than of one, seeing that Aristagoras had failed with Cleomenes on his own, but succeeded with 30,000 Athenians.' A witticism, obviously, which could only have point if the decision made by the Athenian democracy were a bad one and Cleomenes proved right. In Herodotus' judgement that was precisely the case. He regarded, or seems to have regarded, the Ionian revolt as an ill-conceived enterprise which could only have been justified by success, and Aristagoras as an unadmirable

---

[143] viii.140–4.

[144] ix.4 f.

[145] v.78.

[146] v.97.

leader whose motives were less than purely patriotic. It follows that he regards Athenian participation in the revolt as a blunder. The sailing of their ships was 'the beginning [not the 'cause'] of great evils, both for Greeks and barbarians'. And so they were, incontrovertibly: Ionia had been under barbarian supremacy for many decades before Darius, before the coming of the Persians in fact, without the mainland states getting involved. Although Herodotus handles some of Greece's most glorious martial exploits, he does not glorify war for its own sake; and although he plainly recognises that Persia and mainland Greece would have collided sooner or later once Persia was in Europe – the Thracian campaign saw to that – he equally plainly regrets that the collision came about in such a way. His treatment of the Ionian revolt will be considered in some detail in Chapter 4; here all we need say is that he is not such an uncritical admirer of democracy as to give blanket approval to any decision a democratic assembly may take.

That seems fairly to epitomise Herodotus' views on politics and politicians. He gives or withholds admiration and approval according to the quality of the rule and the nature of the decisions taken. We have seen how this was so in his treatment of the tyrannies, to which he generally gives credit when it is due. His admiration for Sparta and her *eunomia* did not blind him to the rather discreditable nature of her political manoeuvres in 479; and the same goes for Athenian democracy. Balance and fair-mindedness characterise Herodotus in his handling of political themes. It is fairly clear that he broadly sympathised with democracy as practised in his day, but was no fanatic or doctrinaire. If he has strongly held views, he does not allow them to colour the narrative or distort its interpretation. The thing that he, like most Greeks, valued most highly was 'freedom' in any or all of the senses discussed earlier; and he had the vision to see that that commodity was more likely to be secured under a democratic constitution than any other.

APPROXIMATE CHRONOLOGY ASSUMED IN THIS CHAPTER[147]

656/5	Beginning of the Sicyonian tyranny.
c. 655	Cypselus becomes tyrant of Corinth.
c. 630	Cylon's attempted coup in Athens.
c. 625	Periander succeeds Cypselus.
615	Alyattes becomes King of Lydia (i.25). Thrasybulus is tyrant of Miletus (no terminal dates ascertainable).
by c. 600	Cleisthenes is tyrant at Sicyon.
c. 585	Periander dies; succeeded by his nephew.
c. 582	End of the Corinthian tyranny.

---

[147] See preliminary note to chronological appendix to Ch. 1, p. 45.

101

c. 575	'Trial of the Suitors' at Sicyon.
569	Amasis becomes Pharaoh of Egypt (iii.10).
561	Peisistratus' first (short-lived) tyranny.
558	Croesus succeeds Alyattes.
556	Peisistratus' second (short-lived) tyranny. End of Sicyonian tyranny.
546	Peisistratus' final return: his tyranny established.
544	Fall of Croesus. Harpagus begins his campaign in Ionia.
c. 538	Polycrates becomes sole tyrant of Samos.
530	Cambyses succeeds Cyrus as King of Persia.
528/7	Hippias succeeds Peisistratus at Athens.
52	Polycrates allies with Cambyses. Death of Amasis. Cambyses' Egyptian expedition; end of Egyptian independence. Unsuccessful Spartan expedition against Polycrates.
522	Cambyses dies in Syria; usurpation of the Magus. Polycrates murdered by Oroetes; Maeandrius in power in Samos.
522(late)	Darius and his fellow conspirators overthrow the Magus; Darius becomes king.
518	Maeandrius flees Samos; Syloson installed by Persia. Maeandrius fails to win Spartan support.
514	Aeaces, son of Syloson, by now tyrant in Samos. Murder of Hipparchus in Athens. Darius' European campaign; Histiaeus of Miletus is the leading Greek commander. Histiaeus is given Myrcinus in Thrace, then recalled to Persia as Darius' adviser. Aristagoras deputises in Miletus. Coës installed as tyrant in Mytilene.
510	Hippias forced out of Athens by Spartan intervention.
508	Democratic reform of Cleisthenes in Athens.
507/6	Spartan invasion of Attica foiled by defection of Corinth and quarrel of Damaratus and Cleomenes. Athens defeats Boeotia and Chalcis.
c. 503	Sosicles of Corinth talks Sparta out of restoring Hippias.
499	Aristagoras' abortive attack on Naxos; he launches Ionian revolt. Coës killed, other Persian appointees deposed.
498	Athens sends 20 ships to Ionia.
494	Battle of Lade and fall of Miletus.
493	Death of Histiaeus.
492	Mardonius installs town-council democracies in Ionia.
491	Gelon usurps power at Gela.
490	Last appearance of Hippias, at Marathon.
485	Gelon takes over Syracuse.

4. ON WAR, CAUSES OF WAR AND MEN IN WAR

CROESUS AND HIS MOTIVES; THE POWER OF PERSIA; PERSIAN MOTIVATION; GREEK IDEAS OF WAR; THE IONIAN REVOLT; MARATHON; TACTICS AND STRATEGY IN BOOKS VII–IX; CONCLUSION

Herodotus proclaims his purpose in his opening paragraphs: '... so that the marvellous achievements, both of Greek and barbarian, should not go uncelebrated, in particular the causes for which they went to war with one another'. He follows this with a light-hearted dismissal of all the mythological reasons traditionally cited for the hostility of Europe and Asia:[1] 'Concerning all this, I am not proposing to say anything as to its truth or falsity. What *I* know is this,' and then he begins the story of Croesus the Lydian.

On the face of it, Herodotus' qualifications for writing on war were not all that impressive. Thucydides and Polybius were generals, Xenophon an officer of varied experience. Herodotus resembles more closely Livy and Tacitus, in that what knowledge he has of military campaigns comes from the eyes of others, and his evaluation of that knowledge is fallible. But of individual battles and campaigns we shall speak later. Here we shall concern ourselves with the more general theme of war.

The idea that war bulked large in the minds of the Greeks of the classical age is certainly one that seems to emerge from the historians. Thucydides narrowed his scope most intensely, so that the content of Books II to VII is almost entirely a narrative of military campaigns, or of politics and international diplomacy which have a direct bearing on the course of the Peloponnesian War;[2] Book I deals, or attempts to deal, with the causes and antecedents of that war, themselves very heavily biased towards the military side; there is no picture of the many years of peaceful splendour from 445 onwards; Book VIII has the immensely interesting account of the domestic political upheaval that produced the oligarchy of the Four Hundred, but otherwise is heavily taken up with complex naval and military manoeuvres. The impression of almost continual warfare involving

---

[1] The 'abduction of women' theme is stylishly parodied by Aristophanes, *Acharnians*, 524 ff. (425 BC) – in effect a parody of a parody.

[2] Pericles' Funeral Speech is arguably an exception; but the accounts of, for example, the plague and the civil war in Corcyra are not, in my opinion.

almost every state at one time or another emerges even more forcibly from the (often arid) pages of Xenophon's *Hellenica*, Books III to VII.

'The Greeks came to accept war as a natural fact like birth and death about which nothing can be done,'[3] and did not generally speculate on the causes of war itself, but they, or their historians, were extremely interested in the causes of particular wars. Thucydides, in his preface, announces his intention of explaining the causes of the Peloponnesian War 'so that no one may be in doubt about what led to this great war falling upon Greece'.[4] Scholarly controversy on the point has raged ever since. A recent 400-page book deserves to lay the arguments to rest, but probably will not.[5] Will such a book ever be written on Herodotus and his treatment of the causes of the Persian Wars? I think not, for although making less fuss about it than Thucydides, he has actually given us the answers in a form that does not require such portentous exegesis.

CROESUS' IMPERIALISM

Herodotus' historical sense in beginning with Croesus is sure and sound. As we have seen,[6] there is a tiny inconsistency in his making Croesus the first barbarian to injure the Greeks, when Gyges, Ardys and Alyattes had all made war on individual cities of Ionia; but there is no reason to think that their wars formed part of an imperialist pattern. With Croesus it was otherwise. He definitely aimed at extending his empire to the Asiatic seaboard, and to that end 'attacked all the Ionians and Aeolians in turn, beginning with Ephesus, on various pretexts, substantial where possible, otherwise trivial'.[7] This, therefore, is a systematic attempt at conquest, an attack on 'the Greeks' rather than on any particular state. The chain of causation runs from there: Croesus, having incorporated Ionia and Aeolis into his empire, then becomes embroiled with Persia, and his defeat effectively presents to Cyrus an Ionia already habituated to the loss of independence and unable to mount any really effective resistance to Cyrus' generals. Croesus, in other words, created the conditions for Persian rule in Ionia and ultimately precipitated it.

The difference, from the Ionians' point of view, was that while Croesus was indeed their master, he was of a broadly philhellene outlook; of the

---

[3] A. Momigliano, 'On Causes of War in Ancient Historiography' in his own *Studies in Historiography* (Weidenfeld & Nicolson, London, 1966), p. 120.

[4] Th.i.23.

[5] G.E.M. de Ste Croix, *The Origins of the Peloponnesian War* (Duckworth, London, 1972), highly recommended. A similar fate has overtaken Th.'s account of the plague of 430 (Th.ii.48): he describes the symptoms fully 'so that it may be recognised for what it is if it breaks out again'; but agreement among medical historians has proved elusive.

[6] Ch. 2, p. 50.

[7] i.26.

attitude of the Persians, at first, little or nothing can have been known, but there was no evidence for supposing that Greeks would enjoy any special privilege or position under them.[8] Cyrus' grimly humorous parable of the piper and the fishes, a genuinely oriental touch[9] – 'We piped unto you, and ye did not dance' – probably reflected all too accurately what the new conquerors felt.

We considered in Chapter 2 the way Herodotus cites Croesus as an example of cyclical justice; the oracle told Croesus that he was expiating the sin of his ancestor Gyges. We must frankly admit that there is present in Herodotus a mild case of schizophrenia: his faith in Delphi leads him to believe in the explanation of 'retribution deferred for four generations'. On the other hand, the plain facts of Croesus' life were a marvellous lesson in the folly of human presumption. Herodotus knows full well that Croesus alone was responsible for his decisions: he may have been encouraged by the oracle but he was certainly neither compelled nor even manipulated by it.[10] Croesus wanted empire, and he made a strong bid for it.

There is no real discrepancy between the two passages where Herodotus discusses Croesus' motives.[11] In the first, Croesus is made to cease mourning for his son Atys, tragically killed, by the news that Cyrus the Persian has overthrown Astyages, King of the Medes. Only later are we told that Astyages was Croesus' brother-in-law, and by thus deferring the information Herodotus is playing down the personal motive on Croesus' part – surely rightly.[12] The power of Persia under Cyrus was increasing and Croesus is represented as planning a pre-emptive operation to curb this growth. Again this is surely right, for Croesus' best hope of eastward expansion into Cappadocia must have lain in the timing of his invasion, when the new dynasty was still establishing itself at home and was vulnerable to pressure from without. In the second passage we are told that Croesus, having received the oracle (and missed its meaning), began preparing his campaign 'in the hope of bringing down Cyrus and the power of Persia'. As Cappadocia was then the westernmost province of the empire, formerly Median, now Persian, Croesus could hardly have expected to wrest it from Cyrus without at the very least inflicting some signal defeat on him. Imperialist expansion has always been a wholly adequate motive for aggression; the Athenians did not launch the Sicilian expedition of 415 in

---

[8] The evidently genuine liking that Darius felt for various individual Greeks in the next generation does not of course come into this.

[9] i.141; cf. St Matthew, xi.17.

[10] For a somewhat similar example of historian's schizophrenia cf. Tacitus, *Agricola*, which in part reads like a eulogy of *libertas* yet glorifies Agricola himself for depriving British tribesmen of their liberty.

[11] i.46 and 71; for a contrary view, cf. A.E. Wardman, 'Herodotus on the Cause of the Greco-Persian Wars', *AJP*, 1961.

[12] i.74.

quest of better trade facilities, nor did Alexander overthrow Persia in order to spread the blessings of Greek civilisation.

THE POWER OF THE PERSIANS IN WAR

At this point we begin to learn the power of Persia. As the story unfolds, book by book, we realise what an awe-inspiring power it was. The Persian approach to war was professional and comprehensive. Probably only the Romans among ancient peoples could match them for versatile efficiency. To defeat Croesus' celebrated cavalry, Cyrus improvised a camel corps from his baggage train.[13] In his advance on Babylon Cyrus had to get his army across the river Gyndes (Diyala), a tributary of the Tigris. Rather than risk a crossing of this formidable obstacle by boat, Cyrus embarked on one of those colossal engineering operations that we become accustomed to reading of in the wars of the Persians. The river was tamed by being made to flow in 360 channels. It flows into the Tigris at a point roughly north of Babylon, below the city of Opis, and it seems that Cyrus' objective was to get behind Babylon's main defence, namely the 'Median Wall'[14] about 80 miles north of the city. This line ran between the Tigris and the Euphrates, on which Babylon stood. As to the next phase of the campaign, Herodotus' narrative is impossible – the Euphrates could not have been drained in the manner described – and so he must have been misinformed, or may have misunderstood information to the effect that Cyrus captured Babylon by means of river diversions, not unnaturally concluding that the Euphrates was meant. It has been suggested, however, that the Tigris was the river so treated – this being just possible geographically – and that the combined lowering of the Gyndes and the Tigris enabled the Persians to cross to a point inside the great outer fortification.[15] The disloyalty of the Babylonian priests to their king did the rest and the city fell easily. Babylon was the most strongly fortified city in the ancient world and its capture was a tremendous coup.

An engineering work on an even greater scale, though apparently not this time for a military purpose, was the canal that Darius had cut from the Nile to the Red Sea.[16] Discussion of these stupendous projects prepares us for the most famous one of all, the cutting of the canal at the base of the Athos promontory in preparation for the invasion of 480. This was to prevent a repetition of the heavy losses sustained by Mardonius a decade

---

[13] i.80.

[14] For this name, X. *Anab.* i.7.15.

[15] So G.H. Maspero *Histoire Ancienne de l'Orient* (Paris, 1895), iii, p. 635; accepted by A.R. Burn, *Persia and the Greeks* (Edward Arnold, London, 1962), p. 55, among others. H's story, i.188–91.

[16] ii.158.

earlier when rounding Athos in bad weather.[17]

Cambyses' successful invasion of Egypt required massive preparation. Perhaps the most interesting detail is the excellent plan for crossing the Sinai desert: with the aid of the local Arab ruler a host of camels was assembled, all laden with water-filled camel skins; the desert was safely negotiated.[18] We need not take too seriously Herodotus' comment on Cambyses' further progress into Ethiopia: that he began the march without ordering the provision of supplies, and the men soon found themselves eating their pack-animals, and ultimately resorted to cannibalism – every tenth man drawn by lot.[19] This is not by any means the only nor even the grossest fiction in one of Herodotus' less impressive passages. Tradition hostile to Cambyses has somehow taken over. The camel-skins, however, prepare us for the immense care taken over the invasion of 480. We read of five places selected as depots for food supplies, established before Xerxes' army arrived.[20] They were strategically spaced out: Leuce Acte (White Cape) on the Sea of Marmara; Tyrodiza, near Perinthus in eastern Thrace; Doriscus; Eion on the Strymon; and the fifth somewhere in Macedonia, presumably at Therma (present-day Thessaloniki) where the army halted for a while. All these places were in territory controlled by Persia; round the corner from Therma Xerxes could count on sustenance from his friends in the rich agricultural lands of Thessaly. Herodotus also tells us of the arrangements to supplement these dumps – requisitions of meals from towns on the routes in between, such as Abdera, a heavy burden which was, however, borne; the orders had been given long in advance.[21]

By the time of Xerxes' invasion, Persian engineering techniques had reached new heights, often with the aid of Greek experts. The first example of a major bridging project is the Bosporus crossing. Darius shared Cyrus' unwillingness to hazard large bodies of soldiers in water-borne crossings, and for his great European campaign of 514 he commissioned a bridge over the Bosporus from the Samian engineer Mandrocles. He was delighted with the result, and Herodotus saw in the Heraion at Samos – a notable art gallery – the picture of Darius enthroned beside the bridge that Mandrocles dedicated there out of his rewards. Next, for the Scythian phase of the expedition, the Danube was spanned by a pontoon bridge built by the naval contingent. As we saw in Chapter 3, this consisted mainly of Ionian Greeks under the leadership, actual if not titular, of Darius' friend Histiaeus of Miletus. Consequently we are not taken aback by the bridging of the

---

[17] vii.22 f., cf. vi.44; for a post-Herodotean example of similar work, cf. Th.i.109: a channel in the Nile Delta is drained, stranding the Athenian fleet (454 BC).

[18] iii.9.

[19] iii.25.

[20] vii.25.

[21] vii.118–20.

Hellespont in 480, an operation of which Herodotus gives a good semi-technical description.[22]

When beginning his invasion of Scythia Darius also ordered the construction of eight fortified block-houses spaced between 7 and 8 miles apart. They were left unfinished when it became apparent that they would be of little use against a nomadic enemy;[23] but the record is interesting as it suggests what may have been a regular Persian method of controlling newly-won ground in city-less areas. Yet another facet of Persian versatility is shown by Aryandes' use of sapping and mining techniques in his siege of Barca (c. 514); these were, however, ingeniously countered by the defenders. Neither of these methods was actually employed in Xerxes' invasion; one novelty which does appear is the stone pillar erected, as a kind of miniature lighthouse, on a reef off the coast of Magnesia. A small reconnaissance squadron, sent ahead no doubt for just such purposes, had run foul of it.[24]

Much of this does indeed resemble mature Roman methods of making war, as practised under such generals as Caesar and Trajan, who fought their campaigns scientifically and with a constant eye on minimising their casualties. For nearly all the examples we have considered show a calculated and systematic approach to war. Unnecessary risks are cut out, potential dangers from natural hazards are minimised. Everything possible is done to ensure the most economical and efficient use of manpower; the men who followed Cyrus and his successors to war must have had the feeling that their lives were not going to be frittered away. It is this which makes so improbable such tales as the repeated frontal assaults on Thermopylae, executed at tremendous cost; or Darius' deliberate sacrifice of thousands of men in order to retake Babylon.[25]

Then there is the question of the size of Persia's armed forces. The figures quoted by Herodotus are not worth discussing in themselves;[26] he is merely the first of a long line of Greek historians who attribute impossibly large forces to Persian sovereigns. 'Xerxes' millions' were not, however, his invention: the figure of three million comes in the first of the three epigrams quoted by him on the dead at Thermopylae, set up presumably in 479. The number thus became at once part of the sacred tradition. Xenophon gives Artaxerxes II, at Cunaxa (401), 900,000 infantry, 6,000 cavalry and 150 scythed chariots; to Cyrus, 100,000 barbarian infantry, 20 scythed chariots, 2,500 Greek light infantry and 10,400 Greek hoplites. As Cyrus was pinning

---

[22] Mandrocles: iv.87 f.; Danube: iv.89; Hellespont: vii.36.

[23] iv.124. The connection between these forts and the Scythian expedition of Darius is, however, doubtful; they seem to be placed too far to the east.

[24] Barca: iv.201; Magnesia: vii.183.

[25] Respectively vii. 210-2, iii. 155-8.

[26] How & Wells, Appx XIX, use H's figures as the basis for a mathematical computation of Xerxes' host, which still leaves him with numbers that are *a priori far* too high, 180,000 men, 800 ships.

his hopes of victory upon the last-named (and, from the purely tactical point of view, they did in fact win the battle) we can draw our own conclusions about the rest. Arrian gives Darius III, at Gaugamela (331), one million foot, 40,000 horse and 200 scythed chariots, a host that was of course comprehensively and decisively beaten by Alexander's modest and manageable force. An honourable exception, as might be expected, is Thucydides, who refers to a Phoenician fleet of only 147 ships at Aspendos in 411.[27] 'The Greeks and Macedonians . . . seem to have regarded it as more glorious to picture themselves defeating a countless horde of worthless Asiatics than an efficient army of realistic proportions.'[28] I would settle for Xerxes leading an army of five-figure strength that was comparable with or not sensationally larger than other major expeditionary forces of antiquity: Alexander's, around 40,000; Hannibal's, just under 60,000, fewer than half of whom actually made it to Italy. It should still be realised that an army of even this size would have been colossal by any Greek city-state standards, more than a match for any four or five put together, full-time, professional and under unified command. The full 'paper strength' of front-line troops under Pausanias at Plataea was 38,700, in 21 separate contingents; the Persians ought to have won the Persian Wars.

What gave the Persians such a driving motivation for war? Herodotus again supplies the answer. He does so twice, the same answer in different contexts. Each context is unhistorical, but contains substantial truth. This is the idea that war is the proper business of a Persian king.

The first scene is set in Darius' bedroom. To this 'Homeric' setting we are skilfully led by the tale of Democedes the physician and his adventures. All this illustrates quite well one of Herodotus' techniques of composition. There are folk-tale elements in Democedes' story, but a solid substratum of truth (Herodotus will have got the story from Democedes' home city of Croton during his own period of residence in southern Italy); precisely how much need not bother us, because it soon becomes clear that the doctor's appearance in the narrative is historically motivated. He would probably have earned no more than two paragraphs, as a distinguished captive from Samos who made good in Persia, had not Herodotus made him the link with Queen Atossa's curtain lecture. Herodotus has chosen this format because it was the sort of thing that was familiar from Homeric epic, his only serious antecedent in the narrative art.[29] The choice of Atossa was cunning too, for

---

[27] vii.228, X. *Anab.* i.7.10 f.; Arr. *Anab.* iii.8.6; Th.viii.87.

[28] George Cawkwell intro. to Xenophon: *The Persian Expedition* (Penguin, Harmondsworth, 1972) (*Anabasis*), p. 36. He argues, from an analysis of the tactics adopted at Cunaxa, that the king, on home ground and in defence of his throne, led an army of '120,000 men at the most, possibly a very great deal less'. *A fortiori* Xerxes' forces in Greece are likely to have been smaller, bearing in mind the need to garrison some of the potential trouble spots like Egypt. I accept these conclusions.

[29] Cf. (e.g.) *Iliad*, xiv.292 ff. (Hera and Zeus). On all this cf. K.H. Waters, 'The Purpose of Dramatization

she had occupied the leading role in Aeschylus' successful play, the *Persae* of 472 (and probably revived from time to time). What Herodotus has done, in other words, is to convey serious historical arguments (as opposed to narrative) through the mouth of a familiar character, and in a manner that an audience as yet unversed in historical narrative techniques could appreciate.

The arguments advanced by Atossa are two: that the King of Persia, lord of great resources, ought to be active in adding to his dominions and performing some great feat to impress his subjects; and that in war the Persians will have their energies sapped and have no leisure to conspire against the king. (In the *logos* of course Atossa, prompted by Democedes, urges an invasion of Greece; but that is immaterial, for the motivation is identical for that which Darius actually has in mind, namely the campaign in Thrace and Scythia.) The second of these motives is fitting and probable in its historical context, for Darius, having achieved the throne by means of a conspiracy, has only just succeeded in putting down widespread revolts in the empire following the murder of the Magus.[30] The first, the programme of straightforward imperial aggrandisement, we have already considered in relation to Croesus – a perfectly adequate motive for aggression. (The same argument is developed at rather greater length in the speech which Thucydides puts into the mouth of Alcibiades in support of the Sicilian expedition.[31])

This motivation is emphasised by Herodotus in the course of the Scythian episode itself, again by use of direct speech; envoys from Scythia visit a conference of neighbouring chiefs, and in appealing for aid against Darius, they attribute to Persia an aim of universal conquest – us today, you tomorrow. Every good invasion, however, needs a pretext: no power will (as a rule) simply attack another without some public justification of its conduct. Herodotus reports as a fact Darius' desire to be revenged upon the Scythians for their invasion of Media a century and more earlier, and it is

---

in Herodotos', *Historia*, 1966, who argues, rightly in my view, that many of the speeches in the mouths of Herodotus' characters are not mere literary décor but serve to convey vital historical information. One of the numerous arguments in support of this is the fact that some speeches are delivered by nonentities (e.g. Mnesiphilus, viii.57), groups like 'the Ionians' (vi.12) or even anonymous individuals (e.g. the Athenian envoy to Gelon, vii.161). In none of these cases can the speeches be motivated by 'characterisation'. Many of H's speeches actually serve the same purpose as those in Thucydides, but the fact has been overlooked because, unlike Th., H does not announce his aim. 'From a literary point of view [Th.'s] use of this technique is . . . less successful; the speeches are far more obviously composed and inserted at selected points, and they are not the sort of speeches most people make, whereas Herodotus' characters talk like human beings' (Waters, ibid. p. 171). Waters does not add that H spares us pre-battle harangues by generals, one of the curses of later historiography.

[30] Most of this H omits, except for Babylon (iii.150 ff.) and Oroetes the disloyal satrap (iii.126 ff.). For an accessible narrative based on eastern sources, see Burn, *Persia and the Greeks*, Ch. VI.

[31] Th.vi.16–18.

extremely probable that some such reason was publicly aired.[32] Herodotus knows, however, that kings do not usually undertake major wars on such remote or sentimental grounds (we have already seen how he played down Croesus' motive of avenging his brother-in-law). Although he did not formulate it as clearly as Thucydides did, he understood the difference between what an aggressor might say to justify himself, and what really motivated his aggression.[33]

This contention is most clearly supported by his handling of an interesting minor episode, the Persian invasion of Libya and the capture of Barca.[34] Arcesilas III of Cyrene, while living as an exile in Barca, had been murdered by some Cyrenians who had earlier suffered under his oppressive rule. The queen mother Pheretime (one of Herodotus' most memorable viragos) went to Aryandes, satrap of Egypt, and appealed to him to avenge her son's death. This she justified by alleging (falsely, as Herodotus shows) that Arcesilas had been murdered on account of his Medism: it was he who had put Cyrene under the power of Cambyses. Aryandes 'took pity on her, and placed at her disposal the entire land and naval forces of Egypt . . . but before launching the campaign he sent a herald to Barca inquiring who the murderer of Arcesilas was; to which the Barcaeans replied that they were all responsible, for they had suffered much at his hands'. This answer was the signal for the expedition to begin. Herodotus then comments 'Now this was the cause that was used as a pretext; in fact (in my opinion) the expedition was sent in order to subjugate Libya; for Libya contains many peoples, few of whom were subject to Darius; most cared nothing for him at all.' Most of us would probably go along with Herodotus' 'opinion'.

The second major passage on this theme is that close to the start of Book VII, Xerxes' cabinet meeting. Mardonius has been sedulously preparing the ground, urging an attack on Athens after polishing off the Egyptian revolt. He begins with the argument for revenge, then continues 'so your name may be great in the world, and men will in future take care not to invade your dominions'. Europe, he added, was a lovely land, full of good things, too good for any other man than the king. In due course, then, Xerxes summons his advisers and announces his programme. 'No need to tell you of the achievements of Cyrus, Cambyses, and my father Darius, and the nations they added to their empire. Since I became king, I have been thinking about how not to fall short of my predecessors, and how to add no

---

[32] Chiefs: iv.102, 118; Darius: iv.1, cf. vii.20.

[33] H sometimes fails, e.g. at i.201, 204 Cyrus attacks the Massagetae because he wants to; and at iii.1 he gives as reason for Cambyses' Egyptian campaign what could only have been the 'pretext'. C.W. Fornara (*Herodotus* p. 29 f.) goes too far, however, in denying that the theme of Persian imperialism is present in Books I–VI; the Scythian and Libyan passages I discuss suggest otherwise.

[34] iv.164–7, 200–5; cf.iii.13. H calls the king Arcesileōs in the Ionic dialect.

less to the power of Persia than they' – the familiar message, war is the king's business. He then continues, like Mardonius, with a reference to the fertility of Europe, and dwells upon the motive of revenge for the Athenians' role in the Ionian revolt and at Marathon. (Here we see the 'real causes' coming first, with the 'pretext' following.) He concludes, though, with a ringing restatement of his original aim, 'that the sun shall not look down upon any land that lies outside our own . . . for I hear that, once we have got the Greeks out of the way, there will be no city nor nation that will be able to stand up to us in battle'.

Mardonius takes up the theme, echoing Xerxes' sentiments and adding a neat *a fortiori* argument: 'We have subdued and enslaved the Sacae, Indians, Ethiopians, Assyrians, and many other powerful peoples, not for any wrong they did us, but to enlarge our empire: it would be very strange if we fail to punish the Greeks who *have* injured us without provocation!' – again, the motive of revenge is made subordinate to the real thing. And even Uncle Artabanus, in arguing against the project, tacitly acknowledges that aggrandisement is the motive.[35]

This must be the belief that underlies the separate anecdotes of Oeobazus and Pythius. The former had asked for one of his three sons to be released from service on the Scythian expedition. To Oeobazus' surprise and delight, Darius smilingly agreed that all three should be left behind: so they were, with their throats cut. Pythius the Lydian millionaire, probably grandson of Croesus, had entertained Xerxes' army and placed his fortune at the king's disposal, an offer that Xerxes graciously declined. Presuming upon this, Pythius made a similar request in respect of the eldest of his five sons; this time it was only the cherished eldest who was sought out and killed.[36] It is perhaps characteristic that Herodotus should make Darius act in a calculating way, suggesting a ghastly practical joke – *pour encourager les autres*, possibly – whereas Xerxes acts in a fit of furious temper. Whether or not the stories are true in every detail (and there seems no reason to doubt their central substance) they show how Persian kings were thought to be capable of behaving; and the rigorous enforcement of personal military service is consistent with the picture we have now formed of the place of war in Persia's priorities.

THE GREEKS IN WAR

So, Xerxes invaded on the pretext of the defeat at Marathon; the Marathon campaign was launched on the pretext of revenge for Athens' aid to Ionia.

---

[35] This entire passage is discussed from the theological point of view in Ch. 2.

[36] Respectively iv.84, vii.27–9, 38 f. There are no comparable acts of cruelty that H records of Darius, but (as Burn, *Persia and the Greeks*, pp. 102 f., 119 points out) Darius' own Behistan inscription tells of the brutal punishments he inflicted upon rebels: DB II in Kent, *OP*.

But then it was the Greeks who were the 'aggressors', and it is time to consider in turn the Greeks in war. A most celebrated, indeed notorious, criticism of Greek methods of warfare occurs in the speech of Mardonius at Xerxes' cabinet meeting, already discussed. What the Persian general is made to say is not necessarily Herodotus' own view, but, if we accept the principle that his speeches are sometimes used to convey historical information, we may conclude that Mardonius' strictures are such as might plausibly be uttered.[37] 'The Greeks go to war without any planning: they find the most fair and flat piece of ground they can, and come down and fight on it. The winners do not come off without heavy loss, and I needn't speak of the losers – they are wiped out. As peoples of a common tongue, surely they should use diplomacy . . . or anything rather than war; but if there was no alternative to fighting, they should seek out a position where they would be hardest to conquer, and there make their stand.'

Herodotus, through Mardonius, has put his finger upon one of the apparent curiosities of Greek warfare: Greece is a land dominated by mountains and ranges of hills, with relatively little cultivable plain in between. But the armies maintained by the city-states (in so far as they were 'maintained' at all) were equipped and trained with a view to those plains. 'Whichever side could dominate the plain could wreck the other's crops; and the narrow margin on which Greece subsisted meant that few states could survive such devastation two years running, even if the first did not bring it to capitulate.'[38] The hoplite, a heavily armoured infantryman, and the tactics that hoplite formations employed, had been evolved in the seventh century when wars were a matter of one city-state fighting its neighbour for possession of some precious strip of disputed territory. The cavalry arms of the states were negligible, useful perhaps to pursue and cut down beaten enemies, but with no capacity to decide a battle. The hoplite could still give a good account of himself on gently sloping ground, as the Spartans did on the little foothills of Cithaeron in 479; in genuinely rugged terrain they were terribly vulnerable to harassment by more mobile light-armed troops, as Demosthenes the Athenian learned to his cost in Aetolia in 426.

It is a fair enough generalisation to say that the Greeks disliked war, important part of their lives though it was. It is very difficult indeed to find anything in classical Greek literature, including most emphatically Herodotus, that could be construed as a glorification of war *per se*, though

---

[37] I think that in fact this *does* represent H's views, and the speech would have had impact at the time of its composition, namely the early phases of the Peloponnesian War. H's hatred of war in general will be discussed later in this chapter.

[38] A. Andrewes, *The Greeks*, (Hutchinson, London, 1967), p. 147.

the military virtues might be admired because they were so necessary. What turned them to frequent war with one another was the desperate quest for a bit more land to support the population, or a desire to prevent any one state from achieving a dangerous eminence among its neighbours. Wars of genuine aggrandisement were extremely rare; it is difficult to say whether this was the cause or the effect of the remarkable lack of tactical and other development over nearly three centuries. (Genuine tactical innovations came in the fourth century, most spectacularly under Epaminondas the Theban, but it was the introduction of entirely new formations, and a dramatic change in the strength and role of the cavalry arm, that enabled Macedonia to conquer half the world.)

Herodotus gives us some useful illustrations of Mardonius' points. When Croesus is examining the Greek states in the search for a powerful ally, his choice falls upon Sparta. By that time, the 540s, Sparta was by some way the strongest state in the Peloponnese; but barely a generation earlier she had been soundly defeated by Tegea, the nearest city of Arcadia to Sparta's own borders. In the eighth and seventh centuries the Spartans had subdued their neighbours the Messenians, and made them into helots, working on the land to sustain the ultra-privileged minority who were the enfranchised Spartan citizens. That long-drawn-out and tragic episode lies well outside Herodotus' frame of relevance and chronology; the melancholy and ultimately disastrous effects it wrought on Spartan social life and policy-making are too well known to need discussion here. What concerns us is that by the 570s the Spartan policy-makers evidently felt secure enough to extend the system to Arcadia.[39] The cunningly phrased Delphic oracle, discussed in Chapter 2, clearly points to the land of Tegea being surveyed and divided into allotments for the benefit of Sparta. Sparta lost that encounter, and that was the last war of aggrandisement she ever embarked on. That defeat was probably, almost certainly, a blessing. The effect of a great accession of new helots upon Spartan life can only be imagined. In future engagements Sparta evidently bested the Tegeans sufficiently to be able to press them into her alliance, and this was the policy she followed steadily from then on.

The existence of the state of Argos was an aid to Sparta in extending her alliance. Argos had been the most powerful state in the Peloponnese when Sparta was relatively unimportant, and that supremacy had endured until well into the seventh century. Those who look only at the classical age see Argos as a power constantly on the defensive, forever at a disadvantage in her dealings with Sparta. A visit to Argos, however, will show why the city was for centuries a great power in Greece. The huge plain of Argos remains to this day a wonderfully fair and fertile area. Ringed by hills,

---

[39] i.66.

commanded by fortresses under Argive control, it guaranteed the city's continuing prosperity and provided a base for the extension of her power over her neighbours. In the age before the Spartan supremacy, not only the cities of the Argolid, such as Epidaurus, and the island of Aigina, but even Corinth herself, had been within Argos' sphere of influence. As we saw in Chapter 3, Cleisthenes of Sicyon waged war, both militarily and culturally, with Argos; with what result we do not know. There is little doubt that the continued existence of Argos as a *potentially* great power secured, from at least the middle sixth century onwards, the loyal support of the north-east Peloponnesian cities for Sparta. For a century and a half or more, Corinth was one of Sparta's firmest allies, despite the immense difference between the ethos of the two states which Herodotus stresses:[40] the Spartans (like most Greeks) despised those who 'worked with their hands'; the Corinthians had no such snobbish prejudice. Sparta and Corinth were never competitors.

A splendid example of what Mardonius had in mind also occurs in Book I. At the time of Croesus' appeal to Sparta under the terms of their recent alliance, that city was unable to respond at once. She was at war with Argos over the possession of the border country of Thyrea, a bone of contention for a century and more, which Herodotus is careful to point out was properly part of the Argive patrimony.[41] The two sides agreed to settle the matter by a contest of 300 picked champions, the remainder of their forces retiring from the scene lest they be tempted to intervene. The object of this was presumably twofold, to minimise casualties and to make it a genuine test of quality. Unfortunately, the rules were not absolutely clarified before the 'match' and when the two sides had slaughtered one another, leaving only two Argives and one Spartan alive, both sides claimed victory as the Spartan had despoiled the enemy dead. Consequently the full forces of both were engaged after all, and this time (needless to say, after heavy casualties) the Spartans won decisively. Thyrea was the last piece of real estate acquired by Sparta in her entire history.

Argos had just about recovered from this disaster when her next war with Sparta supervened. More than once Sparta had to turn down appeals for overseas aid because of her Peloponnesian commitments, and she was limbering up for a new bout with Argos when Aristagoras of Miletus visited King Cleomenes in 499 – not that he would have sent aid in any event, we can be sure. The battle was fought at Sepeia in Argive territory, c. 494. Herodotus does not enlighten us as to the motive for Cleomenes' invasion nor even the pretext for it; he merely states that an oracle of Delphi had predicted the capture of Argos.

In the 'Battle of the Three Hundred' almost everything (though not, as

---

[40] ii.167.
[41] i.82, cf. Th.v.41 (420 BC).

it turned out, *quite* everything) had been done to ensure fair play. This time it was the exact opposite. Cleomenes overreached the Argives by a stratagem that anticipated Lysander's at Aigospotami in 405; and followed up the victory with a massacre of some Argive survivors in a grove sacred to (the hero) Argos. But here is the significant point: Cleomenes did not go on to capture Argos itself, which many thought he could and should have done. He was put on trial before the ephors on his return and he may indeed have defended himself on the grounds given by Herodotus, namely that by taking the sacred grove of Argos he had fulfilled the oracle. The Spartans in general had a reputation for piety, whereas Cleomenes himself took a light-hearted view of such things: at different times he is recorded as bribing the Pythia at Delphi, and committing sacrilege upon the Athenian Acropolis, at the sanctuary of Demeter and Persephone at Eleusis, and at the Heraion near Argos (where he had a priestly attendant dragged out and flogged).[42] We may guess, however, that his real motive was to cripple Argos for yet another generation, but to leave the city in existence as a potential threat, thereby ensuring the continued loyalty of Sparta's northern allies. Be that as it may, the king's calculated ruthlessness rendered a service to Greece, for by the time of Xerxes' invasion Argos had not recovered enough to be of more than trivial nuisance value; she afforded no effective aid to the Persians at all.

The disunity of Greece was a commonplace. Time and again the prickly independence of the city-states threatened to undermine their capacity for effective military action. We saw in Chapter 3 how Gelon's offer of military aid was rejected because he claimed the supreme command over Sparta and Athens. (Events would have prevented him from sending aid in any case, but that is not here the point.) Evidence for this comes in the first book. The Ionians and Aeolians of the Asian coast were subject to Lydia, and when Croesus invaded Cappadocia, Cyrus called upon them to revolt in his rear. Perhaps understandably, they did not. Even more understandably, the victorious Cyrus declined to accept their belated submission and treated them as enemies; all except Miletus, whose relationship with Lydia had been governed by treaty. Cyrus thus neatly detached the most powerful state from the ranks of the opposition. It soon became apparent that the Ionians had no contingency plan of any kind. They began to build walls, and delegates from the cities met at the Panionion, their communal cult centre. It was decided to appeal to Sparta for aid; none was forthcoming, and the cities were picked off one by one by Harpagus the Mede, Cyrus' able general. The Ionians either abandoned their cities *en masse*, like the Teians and Phocaeans, or defended their walls against Harpagus' siege-works until the

---

[42] Respectively vi.66, v.72, vi.75 and 81; battle of Sepeia, vi.76 ff. More fully discussed in Ch. 5, pp. 171-7.

inevitable end came. No plan for common action was adopted, though Herodotus records a tradition that Bias of Priene proposed one.[43]

THE IONIAN REVOLT

As far as Herodotus is concerned, hostilities involving the Greek states pass outside his frame of relevance for many years. We are given some details of the unsuccessful Spartan attack on Polycrates of Samos; we hear of the attempts by Sparta and Athens' neighbours to crush the new-born democracy, but are told nothing of military interest. These enterprises have been discussed in Chapter 3, in connection with Sparta's policy of opposition to tyrants. But the theme of war makes an emphatic return with the narrative of the Ionian revolt, and from then on is never far removed from our minds. Herodotus' handling of the revolt is one of the most controversial of the major passages in his work. He has been criticised for an inadequate account of its causation, hostility towards its protagonists, and a general prejudice which leads him to play down what successes it achieved. It must be frankly admitted that he cannot be wholly acquitted of these charges; without embarking on a full narrative of the revolt we shall examine his treatment of it.[44]

As we have seen, Herodotus has a clear idea of the real causes of the expansionist wars of Croesus and the Persian kings, even though he does not always state them explicitly. His account of the causes of the Ionian revolt, however, has come under heavy critical fire. The usual grounds are that he concentrates on personal motivation and makes no attempt to grapple with any 'deeper causes', even through the medium of direct speech put into the mouths of protagonists. A second objection is the improbability of the Histiaeus story – the coincidence of the 'tattooed head' with Aristagoras' resolve; the alleged supposition that Histiaeus was more likely to be sent back to Ionia in time of revolt than in time of peace, and so on. This latter group may well be disposed of rapidly: they probably all form part of a tradition deriving from no less an authority than Histiaeus himself! Until we come to the crop of tales linking him with the revolt, we find in Herodotus no reason to suspect that Histiaeus was anything other than a loyal supporter and servant of Darius (other than the unsubstantiated suspicion of Megabazus). Histiaeus was never formally relieved of his tyranny in Miletus (Aristagoras only ruled as his deputy) and probably was quite sincere in his belief that he could put the situation in Ionia to rights. On reaching the coast, however, he fell foul of Darius'

---

[43] i.76, 141, 152, 164, 168 ff.

[44] The most useful modern narrative of the battles and campaigns in H v–ix is that of Burn, *Persia and the Greeks*. I do not aim to re-cover that ground.

brother Artaphernes the satrap, who openly accused him of instigating the revolt: 'This is how it is, Histiaeus: you stitched the shoe; Aristagoras put it on' – a *bon mot* with an authentic ring to it. He left Sardis in a hurry and tried to get himself accepted by Chios and later by Miletus itself, without success; the Milesians had had enough of tyranny.[45] It is probably to this phase of his career that the tale belongs: in establishing his *bona fides* he tried to convince these Ionian communities that he had been the brains behind the revolt.[46]

The other criticism is more serious and deserves examination. Discontent in Ionia there must have been. We can hardly blame Herodotus for not adducing 'economic pressure' when the very concept of economics did not exist; on the other hand, having already listed the tribute payable to Darius from Ionia and its neighbouring sub-satrapy he could have pointed out that this was oppressive (if, indeed, it was). The sum provided annually by the 'Ionians, Asian Magnesians, Aeolians, Carians' with the coastal communities as far round as Pamphylia totalled 400 talents;[47] this was roughly the same as the annual tribute paid by the *entire* Delian League to Athens in the 440s. To make matters worse, the cash would have been largely taken out of circulation, whereas a fair proportion of Athens' income found its way back into the Aegean world.

Again, Herodotus knows that tyrannies were by now unpopular. We have already seen his remark about Miletus' attitude to Histiaeus and his comeback; having tasted freedom, she wanted no more of tyranny. This of course comes late in the story. Later still, in the aftermath of the revolt, Mardonius suppressed the Ionian tyrannies (though not all, as we later discover) and installed town-council democracies instead, thereby removing at a stroke a clearly perceived source of discontent. In the very first phase of the revolt, the most exciting development was the deposing of many of the Asian Greek tyrants, while Aristagoras resigned his title at Miletus (continuing, however, to exercise effective command). This coup was carried out swiftly, easily and almost bloodlessly, Coës of Mytilene being the only recorded casualty.[48] The system the Persians had steadily supported collapsed overnight. This could not or at any rate would not have occurred had the tyrannies been at all popular. The institution was outmoded in mainland Greece. We can be sure that the Ionians and Aeolians were well aware of the sensational progress of democratic Athens in the short time

---

[45] v.106, vi.1–5. For the jealousy of Persian nobles for Greek advisers, cf. Ch. 3, pp. 94 f. and note 121.

[46] Well argued by J.A.S. Evans, 'Histiaeus and Aristagoras', *AJP*, 84, 1963, pp. 123–8. He explains Histiaeus' subsequent curious and ambiguous moves as aimed at restoring Persian-backed tyrannies in Ionia under his own leadership, 'salvaging something from the wreck of the revolt', whereas Artaphernes aimed at clear military victory.

[47] iii.90.

[48] Mardonius: vi.43; Coës etc: v.37 f., cf. Ch. 3, p. 93.

since Hippias' expulsion; the other mainland states had shed their tyrannies decades earlier. Herodotus could have laid stress on this political factor as an original cause of the revolt.

But even when all this is admitted, men seldom undertake hazardous military enterprises in defence of abstractions like 'liberty' or *isonomia* or the like. It is specific acts of injustice or oppression, and the reports of such things gaining circulation, that motivate individuals, and ultimately communities, to revolt.[49] We may draw our own conclusions as to the nature of Coës' regime, but we know too little of the other Ionian tyrannies to be able to say whether, and if so how far, their regimes were oppressive. What we can confidently say is that Aristagoras rapidly built up a large following, and the spread of the revolt to the Hellespont and Cyprus suggests more popular discontent against Persia than Herodotus manages to convey. A further point is that the only sources Herodotus could possibly have drawn upon for his narrative were accounts passed orally through at least one generation, and these are more than likely to have stressed the personal motivation; he could hardly be expected to have ignored these.

Much doubt has also been expressed over Herodotus' account of the events that sparked off the revolt; but here there seems far less reason. Not absolutely every detail is above suspicion. It is improbable that Megabates the Persian commander tipped off the Naxians about the impending attack – improbable but not utterly incredible, given the frequent jealousy of prominent Persians for influential Greeks. If there was a breach of security, it is quite easy to imagine how it may have occurred, despite Megabates' clever feint to the north; his fleet was conveying the Naxian oligarchic exiles who started the whole business, and it may be that one or more had been in communication with relatives at home. The allegation of treachery on Megabates' part may have stemmed from recriminations between different units of the fleet when the siege of Naxos failed to prosper.[50]

Again, while Aristagoras certainly had a prominent role in the Naxian expedition, it cannot have been in any greater capacity than political and diplomatic adviser to Megabates – the Persians did not as a rule allow the tail to wag the dog – and though we may well believe in the quarrel between these protagonists, we cannot believe Aristagoras' alleged claim that Artaphernes put Megabates under his orders. Perhaps this is an early indication of the sort of person Aristagoras is – a figure with an inflated

---

[49] W.G. Forrest, *The Emergence of Greek Democracy* (Weidenfeld & Nicolson, London, 1966), p. 119 (on the issues that precipitated the coming of tyranny to Corinth): 'Even among the active politicians [they] may have been far more immediate, far more practical, far more accidental than we who generalise about Greek history are inclined to think they were. Little men probably followed Cypselus because a Bacchiad had pushed them off the pavement . . . or fined them a sheep for an offence which had only brought their neighbour a caution.'

[50] v.33 f.

notion of his own importance. In any case, in the quarrel Aristagoras vigorously champions the rights of a Greek officer against the Persian admiral, and for this he must have earned himself great popularity among the Greek units of the fleet. Was it this that gave him the idea to seize a moment to revolt?[51] There are reasons for thinking that this was so.

First, it is quite believable that Aristagoras, having personally vouched for the feasibility of the Naxian expedition, should consider his position untenable after the fiasco. Secondly, the rest of Herodotus' narrative (and we have no other) bears out the supposition that everything was arranged in a hurry after the return from Naxos. Aristagoras called a meeting of his partisans to discuss what to do next. The fact that support for a revolt was not unanimous suggests that there was no pre-existing conspiracy. Hecataeus the geographer, whose role in all this Herodotus will have learnt from his own writings, first argued against revolt at all, doubtless drawing on his 'professional' knowledge of Persian resources; then proposed the seizure of the temple treasures of Branchidae near Miletus to pay for a fleet. (Later, when things were going badly, he suggested that Aristagoras should fortify the island of Leros and lie low there.[52]) Anyway, the decision to go ahead was taken. There followed the deposing of the tyrants, the appointment of generals in the cities and the mission of Aristagoras to Sparta: as in the 540s, the quest for a powerful ally began when the die had already been cast. The whole story speaks of haste and improvisation.

Aristagoras got no joy at Sparta. The entertaining story of the bronze map and the timely intervention of Cleomenes' daughter is not, perhaps, in accordance with the strict rules of the Spartan constitution, but is realistic enough in so far as Cleomenes in 499 was by far the leading voice in Spartan policy-making. He had been on the throne 20 years already and easily outgunned his colleague Damaratus. (Note that Cleomenes is represented as personally ordering Aristagoras out of Sparta, whereas less than two decades before he had had to request the ephors to expel Maeandrius of Samos.[53]) Again Herodotus rather personalises the motivation – of course the *logos* was far too good to pass up lightly! – saying nothing about the Spartan policy of 'no overseas adventuring' after their fiasco at Samos in 525, nor about the war with Argos, already discussed, which was probably starting to loom. On the other hand the passages of direct speech, like others we have considered, do contain some reference to real issues. Aristagoras' implicit comparison between the Persian

---

[51] See Evans, 'Histiaeus and Aristagoras', p. 119.

[52] v.36, 125. The fact that neither of these pieces of advice was very good may tell in favour of their authenticity. An act of gross sacrilege would have antagonised too many Ionians to make the results worthwhile; and Leros, a little island about 30 miles south-west of Miletus, would have been a base of very doubtful utility unless supported by a powerful fleet.

[53] v.49–51, cf. iii.148. Spartan isolationism did not long outlive the fall of Ionia, however.

infantryman and the hoplite is valid: the Greeks were far more heavily armoured than their opponents (a fact which helps to explain authentic disparities of casualty figures like those at Marathon)[54] and, man for man, Asiatic infantry could never stand up to a hoplite charge unless well supported by cavalry. Probably the real 'truth' of Aristagoras' address is the fact that he was a persuasive talker whose tongue, however, outran his brains, and for that matter his military virtues. Equally Cleomenes' reply embodies a cardinal point of Spartan policy, not only of that age.

And so to Athens. As we saw in Chapter 3, Herodotus thought that to decide to support Aristagoras was the worst thing the Athenians could have done. Judging from after the event, they embroiled themselves with Persia without gaining anything themselves, they provided Persia with a pretext for imperial expansion into Greece, and their initial involvement and swift withdrawal was undignified, to put it no more harshly. But even without the benefit of hindsight, they were taken in by the plausible Aristagoras and his promises. Herodotus does here give us some clues to their motivation. He skilfully ends his great digression on recent Athenian history with an account of Hippias' intrigues with Artaphernes and the Athenian rejection of the satrap's order to take Hippias back. This they did with their eyes open to the consequences – hostility with Persia.[55]

But why did they provoke open war? When dealing with any kind of sovereign assembly like Athens' Ecclesia, where a majority of votes carries the day, this question is almost impossible to answer. Few individuals take any major decision from absolutely unmixed motives, and when these are multiplied hundreds or thousands of times over one really cannot distinguish what was 'the' cause. A reason that may seem to us ill-informed, misconceived or just plain bad, if it secures a majority of votes becomes *ipso facto* an adequate one. Thucydides felt the same about the decision to send the great expedition to Sicily – the people had no idea of what they were letting themselves in for.[56] At any rate the modest scale of the help sent to Ionia – 20 shiploads of soldiers – suggests that there was no overpowering majority in favour of aiding the rebels.

Aristagoras had energy and at least some of the qualities of a leader. His 'nominal'[57] abdication of the tyranny (for he continued to be in effective control at Miletus) was a shrewd political move designed to win popular support. He evidently had no great confidence in his own generalship, however, for he delegated the command of the revolt's opening campaign to his brother and another Milesian. But Herodotus judges him harshly.

---

[54] vi.117. Probably a higher proportion of Greeks sustained non-fatal wounds from Persian arrows etc.

[55] v.96.

[56] Th.vi.1—but still it should have succeeded (Th.ii.65)!

[57] *logōi* is H's word, v.37.

Aristagoras approached the refugee tribe of the Paeonians of western Thrace (whom Darius had forcibly resettled in Phrygia) offering them the chance to return to their home on the river Strymon; and this was successfully accomplished. Instead of rating this a useful blow at Persia, by causing a diversion, possibly even opening a 'second front' in Thrace,[58] Herodotus says that 'no good could come of this to the Ionians; it was only done to annoy Darius'. And after a narrative of the ups and downs of the war (the downs predominating in Cyprus, the Hellespontine and Carian areas) Herodotus makes Aristagoras, 'a poor-spirited creature, as it became apparent', cut out and run for it, dismayed at his own handiwork in throwing Ionia into chaos. Possibly true; possibly not. He went to Histiaeus' old settlement of Myrcinus in Thrace; Herodotus does not discuss the reasons for this choice, but he hardly needed to because Aristagoras was soon killed in a skirmish with some natives.[59]

The revolt proper lasted five years,[60] with mopping-up operations extending well into the sixth. Herodotus' information on much of the story is rather low-grade, and no clear chronological picture emerges for the middle years 497–5; and it is not in any case the intention of the present work to reproduce a narrative of events. Matters came to a head at Miletus in 494, both by land and by sea; almost all else had fallen away by then, Cyprus, the Hellespontine Greeks and Caria (the last only after terrific fighting with heavy losses on both sides); and the enthusiasm of some at least of the Ionians themselves was wavering. A council meeting at the Panionion took the decision, strategically right, to throw everything into naval operations and let Miletus defend her walls as best she could. The stakes were unequal. A naval victory by Persia must necessarily lead quite quickly to the complete investment and fall of Miletus, and the collapse of the revolt; even if the Greeks won a complete victory, it could not have been decisive; a long and hard struggle lay ahead.

The battle of Lade was the first of the heroic contests between Greek and Persian. The Ionians, true to the decision taken, had assembled at Lade (an islet off Miletus) a colossal fleet, 353 ships dominated by contingents from Chios (100), Lesbos (70), Samos (60) and Miletus herself (80). Inevitably the Persians are awarded 600 ships; for a realistic assessment of their numbers, we may attach more weight to the statement that the Persian high command was alarmed by the great number facing them, and were not confident of their ability to defeat them.[61]

The command of this armada was a tricky question. It went to

---

[58] So Mabel Lang, 'Herodotos and the Ionian Revolt', *Historia*, 1968, Paeonians: v.98; cf. v.15.

[59] v.124–6.

[60] vi.18.

[61] vi.8 f. For '600', cf. iv.87 (Scythia); vi.95 (Marathon).

Dionysius of Phocaea, by then a sadly attenuated city that furnished only three ships to the fleet. Some have seen in this (possibly rightly) an intention to obviate jealousy between the Big Four.[62] It is attractive, however, to think of this appointment as recognition of Dionysius' personal qualities. Herodotus introduces him with a magnificent speech – brief, forceful and presenting the real issues with stark clarity.[63] Leading by example, he put his men through a vigorous programme of training in tactics and physical fitness. But conditions at Lade cannot have been good; the island must have been badly overcrowded, for the crews were not allowed ashore, and in the summer heat sickness broke out. 'We must have been mad to take orders from this swollen-headed Phocaean who has provided only three ships! The way he treats us is outrageous, many of us are ill, others will be soon . . . any suffering would be better than this!' – such are the grumbles that Herodotus puts into the mouths of the Ionians. They effectively mutinied, refusing to undergo any further training.[64]

Meanwhile the Persians had opened a discreet propaganda campaign through some of the deposed ex-tyrants, hoping to reduce the formidable Ionian fleet by some defections. At first the overtures were rejected, but the Samian officers reconsidered their attitude in the light of the mutiny (the approach to them had been made by Aeaces, son of Syloson), and when the great battle commenced, 49 of the Samian ships left the western end of the line and sailed for home. The large contingent from Lesbos, next in line, finding themselves exposed and vulnerable, did the same, as did some of the small units. The Chians got a terribly rough handling but fought spectacularly well, inflicting as well as suffering heavy losses; finally their survivors broke through the enemy line to escape home. Some badly crippled ships were beached at Mycale (on the mainland opposite Samos) and the crews began a northward march; but when they reached the vicinity of Ephesus, they were massacred by a force of Ephesians who claimed to believe that they were marauders. The Milesians also fought on; they had nowhere else to fly to. Miletus later fell to a tremendous assault and the revolt was effectively over.

Herodotus gives us an interesting footnote on Dionysius, who had shown his quality in the battle, capturing three ships; when he saw that all was lost he cleverly made a run for the Phoenician coast, ransacked and sank some merchant vessels, then sailed to Sicily, where he pursued the

---

[62] E.g. Burn, *Persia and the Greeks*, p. 211: cf. choice of unimportant capital cities for federal states, like Ottawa, Canberra.

[63] I am not meaning to imply that the speech put into his mouth is anything other than H's own composition, handling issues in the manner discussed in note 29 above. The arresting opening phrase 'On the razor's edge' *might* be an authentic recollection (vi.11).

[64] For Ionian dislike of discipline, cf. the story of Pausanias and the transfer of hegemony in 478: Th.i.95, Plut. *Arist.* 23 (with colourful details).

congenial career of a pirate preying upon Etruscan and Carthaginian trade – never Greek. We may suspect that he was returning to an earlier occupation, and that his known prowess in that field may have helped to secure his appointment to high command.

As we have seen, Herodotus' treatment of the revolt is less than generous – the unflattering picture of Aristagoras, the aura of ambiguity that surrounds Histiaeus (but he *was* an ambiguous figure in his latter days, if any historical personage ever was), the tenderness of the Ionians before Lade. Why this attitude on the part of one who is usually so fair-minded? Why did he not represent the revolt as a brave – at times heroic – but ultimately unavailing blow struck on behalf of freedom? It will not do to say that Herodotus' judgement is formed by the fact that the revolt failed. Failure is not *per se* a crime in Herodotus' eyes. He accepts the Spartan myth that represented the most miserable failure of the entire Persian War, the fall of Thermopylae, as a triumph of heroism in defeat; and that although it was brought about by criminal negligence on the part of the Spartan king, and led to the collapse of central Greece and the destruction of Athens.

The explanation must be sought in the reason for the failure of the revolt, and an impartial reading of the facts of Herodotus' account (discounting any 'colouring') shows that it failed through infirmity of purpose: disunity and at times outright treachery were what killed it. In Cyprus, resistance to Persia had got off to a promising start and a strong fleet was sent from Ionia in support. But in the middle of what proved to be the decisive land battle, the contingent from Curion quit the line; they were followed by the chariot force from Salamis. (They probably favoured the pro-Persian ruler Gorgus, who had been thrown out of Salamis by his brother Onesilus, leader of the Cypriot revolt.) After this mass desertion, there could only be one result; the heroic Onesilus and many others were killed; the Ionian fleet withdrew, and from then on it was only a matter of time before this phase of the revolt ended – less than five months, in the event. Meanwhile, in the Hellespontine area, Daurises (a son-in-law of Darius) conducted a lightning campaign among the Greek rebels there. When we are told that he took one day each to reduce five cities, not all insignificant ones, we may conclude that the mere threat of his presence was sufficient to induce surrender.[65] And then came the tragedy of Lade; as he begins his narrative of it, Herodotus wearily records the mutual recriminations that bedevilled the accounts of the battle – still continuing in his day, if we lay stress on his use of the present tense.[66] In the sequel, the slaughter of the Chian survivors by the men of Ephesus suggests that the latter city had

---

[65] Cyprus: v.102, 108–15; Daurises: v.116–18.
[66] vi.14.

already made its peace with Artaphernes and in this dishonourable way was seeking to rehabilitate itself with the victors; their plea, reported by Herodotus, that they had not heard about the battle, is not seriously credible. Finally, no Greek reader of Herodotus could miss what he does not need to stress, for the facts speak for themselves: the fiercest resistance was put up by the non-Hellenic Carians. There was, in short, much to be ashamed of in the course of the Ionian revolt.

MARATHON AND ITS ANTECEDENTS

Herodotus prepares us for the Marathon campaign with the immortal scene of Darius hearing the news that Sardis has been burned by the Athenians and Ionians. 'He paid no regard to the Ionians – *they* would not escape punishment! But he asked who the Athenians were; and on being told . . . shot an arrow towards heaven, and prayed: " O Zeus, grant that I be revenged upon the Athenians".' Those who comb Herodotus' text for slights upon the Ionians duly find one here.[67] But the historian is being realistic. The Ionians were a known quantity. Persia had taken their measure back in the 540s. But the introduction of a potent new ally, whether Darius had heard of them or not (and surely Artaphernes had reported to him their acrimonious diplomatic exchanges?), could have completely altered the balance. It is natural that the king's interest should have been specially aroused. In these wonderful few lines Herodotus tells us that Athens is now definitely on Darius' agenda, with a 'pretext' ready supplied.

But first there was the question of Thrace. This European province of Persia, acquired by Megabazus early in Darius' reign, needed attention after the revolt, and in 492 Mardonius marched right through it with an army and up to the further borders of Macedonia, which submitted to the king. Mardonius' accompanying fleet suffered a disaster from the weather off Mount Athos, his army suffered some casualties from tribesmen in the Strymon area and he himself was wounded. But despite this, and Herodotus' description of it as 'inglorious', the expedition achieved some solid and valuable results. Herodotus says that it was aimed at the punishment of Athens and Eretria (which had also sent help to Ionia), but this looks like an inference from its resemblance in scale and method to Xerxes' invasion of 480. More probably it was intended to bring Persian power right up to the borders of Greece proper, whence diplomatic pressure could be exercised upon potential Medisers – look what happened to Thessaly in 480. It is after this campaign but before Marathon that demands are made of the cities and islands of Greece for 'earth and water';

---

[67] E.g. Lang, 'Herodotus and the Ionian Revolt' (on v.105). I am not arguing that all such alleged 'slights' are imaginary. See Appendix One, pp. 230 ff.

many, including Athens' enemy Aigina, complied.[68] Persia, no squanderer of manpower, preferred to win subjects by diplomacy than by force of arms.

The Marathon campaign is full of interest from the strategical point of view, for it shows clear evidence of an ability to learn from the mistakes of others. Here as usual we shall be examining Herodotus' treatment of military themes rather than reconstructing a narrative of the engagement. Herodotus' account is far from being above criticism, yet he does have some grasp of the strategical principles involved, and believable accounts of 'what happened at Marathon' can be fashioned from his narrative.

A short stretch of archaic polygonal masonry on the acropolis of Eretria, which survived the Persian sack in 490 (vi.101). (Deutsches Archäologisches Institut, Athens)

Eretria, the first selected target, applied to Athens for aid. Athens did not adopt the potentially suicidal[69] course of sending her army across to the island, but 4,000 Athenian settlers living next door at Chalcis would have been a splendid reinforcement. But 'in Eretria, after all, there was no sound policy' – the familiar Ionian symptoms of disunity and treason. The 4,000 Athenians were tipped off about this and crossed to Attica. The Eretrian strategy, if that is the word, was to sit tight behind the walls. Apart from

---

[68] Mardonius: vi.43 f.; Aigina: vi.49.

[69] Not realised by How & Wells on vi.99–101: 'Herodotus is anxious to justify the Athenians for not sending succour from Attica.' What would have appened if the Persian fleet had then sailed round to Athens?

the opening remark just quoted, Herodotus refrains from overt criticism, but the facts speak for themselves. The Eretrians had learnt nothing from the fate of Miletus, which was not starved out but taken by storm; and they utterly underestimated the damage traitors could do. The Persians launched one of their powerful assaults on the walls, and after nearly a week two of the Medising party within got their chance to open the gates – and 'all Greece was weakened by the loss of a fine city'.[70]

Expecting to give Athens a taste of the same medicine, the Persians, guided by Hippias, put in to Marathon, 'for that was the most suitable ground in Attica for cavalry manoeuvres'. A genuine comment on a strategical issue – but is it valid? Even though today the plain of Marathon is thickly planted with olive groves and other trees, the visitor is struck by the breadth and evenness of it – surely excellent cavalry country in antiquity. But it is not clear that that is the reason why the Persians landed there. First, when the battle took place, the Persian cavalry played no recorded part in it; it was an infantry set-piece. Secondly, Hippias himself, with his Thessalian allies, had won a fine cavalry action back in 512 at Phaleron, routing Anchimolius' Spartans; why not try the same ground again? The 'same ground' theory might, however, explain Marathon in a different sense: more than 50 years earlier Hippias and his father had landed there to rally support (successfully) among their partisans of the 'Hill', thereby launching Peisistratus upon his third and durable tyranny. Hippias, now an old man, may well have been living in the past.[71]

The Athenians marched out to Marathon to meet them. This decision must have been influenced by what happened at Eretria. Everyone knew that there were traitors or (less emotively) supporters of the Peisistratidae in Athens. The most valiant efforts of the army might be frustrated by them. Nor were Athens' allies likely to come to her aid unless they saw that she was wholeheartedly committing herself to a fight – compare Eretria again. In the event faithful Plataea and, belatedly, Sparta sent contingents to Marathon. Later tradition records[72] what Herodotus does not, namely that the proposal to march out to Marathon was Miltiades'; likely enough, as he also argued for the bold course on the battlefield.

What is certain is that both the overall strategy of the Athenians and

---

[70] vi.106.

[71] For completeness' sake I should record my opinion that the Persian plan was to leave a containing force at Marathon strong enough to hold or at least fight a drawn battle with the Athenians, while running troops (including cavalry) round by sea to catch Athens undefended, and to rely on the 'collaborators' to open the gates. What went wrong was that the containing force failed to contain. This is not the place to argue the points.

[72] E.g. Nepos, *Milt.* 5.

their tactics on the day involved a truly heroic degree of risk; it was going to be a case of 'winner take all'. The Athenians were waiting for their Spartan allies to arrive, and to seize the opportune moment to attack when they had not yet come was the sort of decision that no commander would choose to face. When Herodotus records that five generals were in favour of the orthodox 'safe' course, even though the best hope of safety lay in boldness, this is entirely credible. So much of history, not only ancient, shows that it is the really great commanders who estimate the risks and take the plunge on an accurate calculation. Themistocles' plan of battle at Salamis was of a similar order: only by fighting in the narrows did the Greeks have any real prospect of winning a decisive victory; and yet, if things went wrong, there was no escape, they would lose all. Small wonder, as Herodotus realistically records, that the nerve of some of the officers broke. From elsewhere we think of Hannibal thinning out his line against superior numbers at Cannae, Africanus' capture of New Carthage and Caesar's retention of his reserve at Pharsalus, among others. A negative example comes from Thucydides:[73] Lamachus' proposal to capture Syracuse by a *coup de main* stood no chance of acceptance by his colleagues, and we may legitimately doubt whether he himself was doing anything more than putting it up as a discussion point. An Africanus or a Nelson (in Copenhagen style) would have certainly carried it off.

Miltiades knew all about Persian tactics and did not want his splendid hoplites softened up by long exposure to Persian arrows. The Athenians advanced upon the Persians at a brisk light-infantry pace[74] – the Persians thought they were mad – which meant that they were fighting hand-to-hand before any really serious casualties were suffered. His detailed tactics, as set out by Herodotus, were original but simple: knowing that a victory in the centre would leave his wings terribly exposed to the more mobile and lightly armoured Persians, he threw everything into winning on the wings, with only a token depth in the centre. This succeeded brilliantly, for even the Persians who broke through the weak centre found themselves cut off from their ships by the victorious wings that had now joined hands. It was a strategical and tactical coup of the highest class, and the casualty figures given by Herodotus bear this out; having been counted on the field of battle, they are likely to be authentic. Later writers like Justin are plainly disappointed by Herodotus' moderation – he quotes the number of 200,000 Persian dead![75]

---

[73] Th.vi.49.

[74] *Not* 'at a run', which so many translations perpetuate. Herodotus' word (*dromôi*) is used by Th. (iv.78) to describe Brasidas' march through the length of Thessaly! For a discussion of Miltiades' role as effective commander, see Ch. 1, pp. 43 f.

[75] Justin, ii.9.20; cf. Plut. *MH*, 862B.

TACTICS IN XERXES' WAR

Books VII to IX show Herodotus in his fullest splendour, and yet they illustrate some of his weaknesses too. Here, beginning with the Thermopylae campaign, we shall discuss some details of his handling of the great battles, leaving to the end the question of his overall strategical grasp.

Some weaknesses are apparent in his account of Thermopylae. He has fallen completely under the spell of the Spartan myth that turned a catastrophe into a triumph of sorts. In a sense this was fair, because Leonidas and his band *were* heroes at the finish, and by their self-sacrifice they did enable a large body of Peloponnesian hoplites to retreat in safety and fight another day. But Herodotus does not emphasise (what was surely true) that Thermopylae was a far more 'winnable' battle than Plataea, and by losing it the Greeks gave themselves a far greater and more difficult task to accomplish in the next round; nor that the loss came about through the commander's blunder: in full knowledge of the Anopaia path, and having posted a guard there, he failed to ensure that they knew their orders or were in a proper state of readiness. Hydarnes' Immortals could and should have been stopped. Again, 'epic' elements have found their way into his account and probably figured in the oral tradition from a very early stage – the Medes being ordered to 'capture those men alive and bring them before the king!'; Xerxes thrice springing up from his throne in terror for his army; the masses of expendable Persians being whipped into battle – as we have seen, utterly foreign to Persia's economical military practices.

There is also a bit of racial prejudice. The Theban contingent at Thermopylae is blackened, and Boeotian Plutarch for once is on to something when he hammers Herodotus at considerable length for this.[76] While 400 was a pathetic total for a great city to send (especially when little Thespiae managed 700), they cannot have been 'held there as hostages' by Leonidas, for they would have helped to tie his hands when he needed every man in the fighting line. One blunder by Leonidas is credible, a piece of stupidity like that is not. Herodotus could have discussed other reasons for the Thebans' presence: were they political opponents of the ruling oligarchy?[77] Polycrates of Samos sent *his* political enemies to what he hoped was death in Egypt under Cambyses. Did Leonidas, by keeping the Thebans to the end, hope to embroil their city in the war on the loyalist side? Or did he regard them as expendable, knowing that their city was certain to fall soon? The Theban general, Leontiadas, had a son named Eurymachus, who was killed in 431 in the Theban attack on Plataea,[78] and the usual explanation of Herodotus' 'malice', that he has listened too carefully to anti-

---

[76] vii.222, 233; cf. Plut. *MH*, 864D–867B.

[77] Diodorus, xi.4.7 actually says this; a guess of Ephorus? For Polycrates, cf. Ch. 3, p. 87.

[78] Cf. Th.ii.2.

Theban gossip in Athens, is probably right. (This is exactly paralleled in the case of Corinth, as we shall later see.)

But a great deal of gold remains. There is some fine dramatisation: the conversation of Xerxes and Damaratus, in the now familiar manner, conveys to us some real historical truths: the way the Spartans smarten themselves up before battle symbolises their superb discipline: if Xerxes can defeat *them*, he has won the war.[79] Prophetic words! There is some vivid descriptive narrative: the rustling of the oak leaves underfoot, the Phocians caught off watch, Hydarnes' anxiety – these cannot be Spartans, surely? – and the Persians' rapid passage past; the bold attacks of the Greeks when they knew their last hour had come. There are some charming vignettes: the self-sacrifice of Megistias the seer, the *bon mot* of Dienekes the Spartan, the precious epigrams.[80] More seriously, there are useful remarks on Spartan tactics: their trick of pretending flight, then rounding upon their disordered pursuers, is one that only a highly trained and disciplined force could have successfully brought off.[81] Finally Herodotus gives us as full a picture of the ground as could be imagined, short of an actual map. The topography of Thermopylae does raise some problems, but all solutions are squarely founded on the numerous details he gives in his text.[82]

In parallel with the fighting at Thermopylae the Greek fleet was actively engaged off Artemisium, northern Euboea. Here Herodotus gives us realism, for no mythology sprang up around these encounters, valuable though they were to the allied cause. After a roll call and a brief discussion of Athens and her cession of supreme command, he begins his narrative with an all too credible picture of the first sight of the Persian armada by the Greeks. The Persians had suffered less from the violent storm of the preceding days than the Greeks had expected, and there was an air of nervous alarm, even some talk of withdrawal. We may doubt whether this was ever contemplated by the high command, for to do so would have exposed Eurybiadas' fellow Spartans to certain death at Thermopylae; the role of Themistocles we shall discuss in a later chapter (p. 189). But most of the Greek sailors would have had far less idea of Persian power than, say, the Ionians had had at Lade. At once we see the efficient Persian war machine swing into action. As their fleet came up to Aphetae and the tactical situation was summed up, a strong squadron was immediately detached to sail round Euboea, come up through the Euripos from the south and take the Greeks in the rear, while the main body reorganised itself and

---

[79] vii.209.

[80] vii.218, 228.

[81] vii.211.

[82] W.K. Pritchett, 'New Light on Thermopylae', *AJA*, 62, 1958, p. 211, the best modern study (based on a long personal survey of the possible routes of Hydarnes, including a jeep ride along the favoured candidate) regards H's topographical description as 'unquestionably faithful'.

remained inactive, as usual not wishing to risk unnecessary casualties.[83] The speed with which the tactical appreciation is turned into operational reality is impressive; and a route was chosen to escape the notice of the Greeks at Artemisium. This aim was, however, frustrated by the deserter Scyllias of Scione, who brought some valuable intelligence to Artemisium.

At this point Herodotus seems to skip a couple of days in his account, for he definitely states[84] that the three days of engagements were synchronised with the three days of fighting (as opposed to waiting) at Thermopylae. However, assuming a two-day lapse, it was the Greeks who took the initiative. Knowing now that the Persians at Aphetae were not at full strength (since the detachment of the encircling force) they waited till late afternoon and rowed across to the Persian station, 'wishing to gain experience of battle against them, in particular "breaking the line" '. So, initial nervousness has given way to rational confidence. 'These men are mad' thought the Persians – familiar reaction – for not only were they more numerous but they had better sailing ships. This was the result of centuries of high-level seamanship, contrasted with the hastily built Athenian vessels whose crews, in many cases, had probably only just completed their basic training. Some of the Ionian contingent in the Persian fleet could not withhold some patronising sympathy for the gallant Greeks, sailing into battle against hopeless odds; others were less tender in their feelings. But in the fighting the Greeks did well, carrying off 30 ships including that of the brother of Gorgus, King of Salamis in Cyprus (and therefore of the valiant rebel Onesilus). The Persians 'fared far less well than they had expected'; one disappointment for the allies, however, was that only a single vessel from Xerxes' Greek contingent deserted to the loyalist side, that of Antidorus of Lemnos, probably an Athenian by origin.

The Persians had already suffered terribly from the weather and had lost 15 vessels to a Greek patrol before the commencement of battle proper;[85] now their encircling squadron was destroyed off the 'Hollows of Euboea', news of which disaster reached Artemisium at the same time as an Athenian reinforcement of 53 ships.[86] The second day saw another late-afternoon skirmish in which the Greeks pounced upon the Cilician squadron and sank several, returning under cover of night. On the third and last day the Persians, realising they were in danger of losing the initiative, 'and afraid of what Xerxes might do to them', got their fleet to sea by midday and a general action ensued. Herodotus describes the Persian tactics: they

---

[83] viii.7.

[84] viii.15. On H's own showing a slip of two days must be assumed in the 'parallel diaries' of land and sea operations. Burn (*Persia and the Greeks*, p. 396), How & Wells (ii, p. 372 ff.) and others offer reconstructions differing in minor details. For consistency's sake I follow Burn.

[85] vii.194.

[86] viii.14.

formed a great crescent, that is, advancing with recessed centre and wings leading, in order to surround the Greeks. In the first day's fighting the Greeks had adopted an inverted crescent formation, with centre leading and wings turned somewhat outward,[87] and if they did so on this occasion too they would have met the barbarians head on – which is probably what they would have wished.

The great numbers of the Persians caused some measure of mutual interference as they pressed in from a broad front towards a smaller target; but the battle was long and hotly contested, being finally broken off when both sides had evidently had enough. Quite heavy casualties were suffered on both sides (in particular half the Athenian ships were in need of repair), so much so that the allies 'began to consider fleeing[88] further into Greece' and were plainly in no condition to renew the contest next day. But the final decision to withdraw was effectively made for them by the news brought by boat from Thermopylae, that it was all up with Leonidas' force. After a good meal of roast mutton (commandeered from the Euboeans) the fleet headed south in the darkness. No attempt was made to pursue them. Next morning, when the Persians learned that they now commanded the seas off Euboea, Xerxes proclaimed a day's rest and 'Cook's Tours' of the battlefield of Thermopylae were laid on for the sailors.

Herodotus has given us an account, very good as far as it goes, of an indecisive battle. Both sides learnt a lot about each other. The Phoenicians and the rest would have developed a healthy respect for Greek courage and proficiency; no 'Lade' attitude was in evidence here. The Greeks, by skilful exploitation of surprise, inflicted minor but useful losses on the enemy for two days and proved that the Persians were not invincible. But the hard-fought general action on the third day banished any complacency that might have started to take the place of nervousness.

Herodotus' account of Salamis must be considered a bit of a disappointment. Elements of epic and the miraculous figure in his story, but there is a good dash of realism and solid narrative as well; less, however, than he might have given us, and leaving several questions unanswered; whereas on Artemisium he tells us quite efficiently most of what we need to know.

The evacuation of Athens was not complete; a garrison of sorts was left on the Acropolis behind a wooden palisade, partly no doubt, as Herodotus says, as an insurance policy against the oracle;[89] but conservative opinion in Athens would probably have been opposed to total abandonment anyway. The Persians tackled this obstacle in their usual resourceful way, shooting

---

[87] viii.11.

[88] A strong word, but *drēsmos* means just that.

[89] viii.51.

fire-arrows from the Areopagus Hill opposite, setting fire to the woodwork and reducing the defenders to dire straits. True to form the Persians did not bother with a direct assault; improbable as it sounds, a climbing party found a way up the eastern end of the Acropolis and the citadel was taken in a manner recalling the fall of Sardis. The temples were duly destroyed by fire. Herodotus tells us that the loss of the Acropolis had a demoralising effect on the Greek fleet, now drawn up at Salamis, and some commanders were actually preparing to leave station without awaiting a decision; and the decision to withdraw to the Isthmus was in fact made.[90]

It may seem surprising that such demoralisation followed the fall of the Acropolis, which had virtually been abandoned in the first place as indefensible. But the picture of alarm is surely realistic. The conventional military thinkers among the naval commanders would have had grave doubts, or worse, about defending a country which was no more.[91] The move to the Isthmus would lose Megara, Aigina and the refugee-packed island of Salamis itself to Persia,[92] but a majority of 'voting' commanders evidently thought this was bearable. The task facing Themistocles was to get the decision reversed by bringing to bear the genuine arguments of higher strategy that applied to the case. A nonentity[93] named Mnesiphilus makes an historically motivated intervention here to pull the trigger, as it were, that would launch Themistocles into action. Mnesiphilus' political and psychological arguments, and Themistocles' tactical arguments in the reconvened meeting, are an excellent summary of the realities. The heavier Greek ships would suffer terribly in the open water of the Isthmus; the Phoenicians would run rings round them. In the narrows they had a chance, especially as the Persians could not bring their superior numbers to bear efficiently. Themistocles reinforced this with a threat to withdraw if his policy was not adopted; and Eurybiadas the Spartan supremo was convinced.[94]

Realistic, too, is the picture of renewed dismay in the Peloponnesian ranks when the Persians arrived at Salamis, and the criticism of Eurybiadas' foolish policy.[95] The generals again met, but it is hard to believe that the question of withdrawal to the Isthmus was ventilated yet again, as Herodotus implies. The main danger to the allies now was of the

---

[90] viii.56.

[91] viii.49.

[92] Burn, *Persia and the Greeks*, p. 436 f., rightly emphasises the importance of Salamis island as a military objective, containing as it did not only refugees but also Athenian troops and the organs of government. Its fall might have knocked Athens out of the war.

[93] But not completely: his name occurs on ostraka, possibly of the post-479 period (*Arch. Deltion*, no. 23, p. 28 f.).

[94] viii.57–63.

[95] viii.70, 74.

progressive deterioration of their forces, morally and physically, unless a battle were brought on soon. It is not likely that food supplies on Salamis, even after the well-planned and executed evacuation, were comfortably adequate for both the refugees and the 60,000-odd sailors; and pressure from the rank and file to withdraw to their homes might have grown to the point of being irresistible.[96]

This, then, is the context of Themistocles' message. Doubts have been cast on the historicity of this; on the contrary, if there had been no evidence for it, it would almost have been necessary to invent it.[97] It is generally agreed that in waters like those of the Salamis narrows the Greeks were at their most formidable as compared with the Persians. Why, then, should Xerxes have committed his fleet to battle in a situation of his opponents' choosing? Even allowing for the fact that Xerxes evidently wanted a sea battle,[98] some explanation is called for. The answer must lie in recent history. The last great clash of fleets before Artemisium had been Lade, and the memory of that encounter must have been familiar to Xerxes' senior commanders. Secret diplomacy and political warfare had saved the Persians literally thousands of casualties on that day. It was one thing for the Greeks to fight bravely at Artemisium, when there was everything still to play for, but now central Greece had collapsed, Athens was destroyed, Megara and Aigina were threatened. When a secret message came intimating defections among the allied fleet, the reaction of the senior Persian commanders was surely 'we have been here before', and the decision to fight was settled.

To make sure, the Persians spent the night in preparations, bringing their ships up towards the narrows to prevent any Greek escape and landing a small force on the islet of Psyttaleia (Lipsokoutali)[99] to deal with any Greek wrecks or swimming survivors. Herodotus does not mention the despatch of the Egyptian squadron round the western end of Salamis island,[100] but it would have been very un-Persian if some such manoeuvre had not been attempted when we remember what had happened off Euboea.

Naval battles are confused and confusing affairs. Literary attempts to re-fight the battle of Jutland are apt to leave the reader befogged. All the more is this likely when far greater numbers of vessels are involved, and in a confined space, as at Salamis. To arrive at a general picture of what was happening at any one moment, or to try to distinguish tactical manoeuvres from movements forced by the pressure of circumstances, is almost

---

[96] These arguments appear in Artemisia's speech (viii.68), yet another vehicle for 'issues'.

[97] We should not exclude the possibility that to send the message was a joint decision of the allied high command; nor should we assume that we have Themistocles' *ipsissima verba*!

[98] viii.69.

[99] W.K. Pritchett, 'Toward a Restudy of the Battle of Salamis', *AJA*, 63, 1959.

[100] Diodorus xi.17 records this. H does however twice bring reports to the Greeks that they are surrounded, one from Aristeides, one from a Tenian ship deserting Xerxes (viii.79 ff.).

impossible without the aid of aerial cinephotography! Thucydides gives us an unforgettable picture of the watchers on shore at the last battle in Syracuse harbour. Unable to perceive the overall trend of the titanic struggle, each man identified the fortune of his side as a whole with the particular clash that was before his eyes.[101]

Herodotus' account of Salamis is a bit like this. Some sound tactical detail is given: the broadest outlines of the order of battle – Spartans on the right (eastern) wing facing the Ionians, the Athenians on the left facing the Phoenicians (the Greeks were drawn up on the shore of Salamis island and not strung out across the narrows); and the opening manoeuvre of the Athenians (Herodotus actually says 'the Greeks', but the context seems to imply the Athenians) backing water – presumably to encourage the Phoenician wing deeper into the narrows – before beginning the combat. Other tactical details that go to make modern reconstructions have to be drawn from other sources – above all, *The Persae* of Aeschylus, Athens' only surviving historical verse drama; he makes the messenger to Persia report such details as the Greek right (the Spartans) leading, therefore presumably rowing down-channel past the advancing Phoenicians until they came opposite to the Ionians; and that the Greeks managed to keep outside the Persians and struck in at them.[102] This latter fact helps to explain Herodotus' picture of the Persian battleline degenerating into a shambles. Ship fouled ship as the defeated front endeavoured to escape and those behind pressed forward in their eagerness to impress Xerxes.[103]

Otherwise Herodotus gives us a number of disconnected incidents, and for good measure, a couple of miraculous apparitions: the self-preservation of Artemisia – 'Amazon Queen',[104] or rather perhaps a female Themistocles! – an anecdote well worth its two paragraphs; the Homeric struggle of the Samothracians and Aiginetans, illustrating in a nutshell the furious mêlée that much of the battle must have been; the gallant Polycritus of Aigina showing Themistocles what poor Medisers the Aiginetans were; Aristeides' hoplites landing on Psyttaleia and slaughtering the Persian detachment there. That force had been utterly irrelevant to the battle since the Persians fell into the Greek trap and committed their fleet to the narrows.

Two points remain to discuss – the Corinthians and the mole. Herodotus reports an Athenian allegation that Adeimantus of Corinth hoisted sail in a panic at the start of the battle and sailed off westwards. At the end of the story he repeats his emphasis that it is an Athenian tale and says that the rest of Greece supports the Corinthian version of events. The

---

[101] Th.vii.71.

[102] A. *Pers.* 399, 417 f.

[103] viii.86, 89.

[104] So Burn, *Persia and the Greeks*, p. 448, apparitions, viii.84, 94.

sailing off can hardly have been invented, it was seen by too many. Its tactical purpose may have been to engage the Egyptians in the western channel or, more probably, to put some flesh upon Themistocles' message by giving a genuine impression of flight to the enemy.

Adeimantus had already lost two verbal bouts with Themistocles and was represented as having to be bribed to stay at Artemisium.[105] As in the case of the Thebans at Thermopylae, Athenian prejudice has left some mark in Herodotus' story, for Adeimantus' son Aristeas was a thorn in Athens' side from 432 to 430; he led a Corinthian contingent in support of the Poteidaean revolt. For his treatment of Corinth Herodotus has his knuckles rapped by Plutarch,[106] again with some justification, and the latter skilfully quotes four inscriptions which support the Corinthians' contention that they played a distinguished part in the battle.

Finally, the mole. Herodotus says that Xerxes began work on a mole from the mainland of Attica, to reach Salamis[107] – presumably with the help of a pontoon bridge. Herodotus puts this immediately after the defeat and represents it as a futile attempt by Xerxes to cover up his intention to retreat. Though not impossible, this is doubtful, for his workmen would have been operating under the noses of a victorious enemy fleet. More likely work was begun earlier; it would have been a tremendous operation, no more so however than some of the military engineering feats described earlier; but would have needed local superiority at sea to carry off successfully. How Herodotus came to misplace the episode (if indeed he did) can only be guessed at.

The victory of Salamis, and the retreat of the Persian fleet, took the military pressure off the Peloponnese. But the decision to leave Mardonius with the hard core of the Persian army to winter in Thessaly meant that at best only a breathing space could be hoped for. The clear implication of Herodotus' narrative that spans Books VIII and IX is that Greece was in just as much danger in 479 as in 480, and that diplomatic and political warfare was Persia's substitute for the fleet. But this will be fully discussed later as part of grand strategy; here we shall merely consider Herodotus' handling of the battle of Plataea, the most controversial engagement of the Persian Wars. Did the Greeks win because of Pausanias' tactical brilliance? Was it the supremely good fighting qualities of the Spartan hoplites that ensured victory, despite muddled and indecisive leadership? Or was it that for Pausanias, a sound and competent commander, everything went right on the day, including a fatal blunder by the enemy?

A case can be made out for each view: not much of one for the first, on

---

[105] Respectively viii.94, 59, 61, 5.

[106] Plut. *MH*, 870B–871A.

[107] For the military importance of taking Salamis, cf. note 92 above.

the evidence of Herodotus' text, but the brief résumé Thucydides gives of Pausanias' operations in 478 (when he headed the allied league making aggressive war on Persia) suggests high military capacity.[108] For the second, an unusually large number of things seemed to go wrong at Plataea – wrangles about positions in the line, alleged disobedience of orders, the interception of a supply train, difficulties over water supplies, and an ill-conducted retreat that left some contingents out of touch with the battle when it occurred. As for Spartan hoplites snatching victory from tactical failure, one only need examine Thucydides' account of the battle of Mantinea (418):[109] King Agis, in a classic demonstration of the military axiom 'order, counter-order, disorder', left his line terribly vulnerable to the enemy, who were however prevented from fully exploiting the blunder by the steadiness and quality of the Spartan rank and file. There is most to be said for the third view, in so far as it is difficult to point to any real mistakes made by Pausanias, whose manoeuvres do seem to have been designed to bring on the battle upon ground that favoured him; but he was lucky in that Persian impetuosity played, undeservingly perhaps, into his hands. As for the things that went wrong, they may form a realistic and authentic picture of what happens in an allied army of 21 separate contingents, each with its own civic pride and traditions. The barrel had been scraped to put this huge Greek host into the field, and a fair verdict might be that Pausanias did as good a job as could have been expected in turning it into something like a united force.

The topography of Plataea need not detain us; the problems, and the colossal bibliography thereon, have largely arisen because many of Herodotus' reference points (scrupulously given and suggesting careful inspection of the ground) have disappeared. 'Herodotus' contemporary with his text in hand would have had little difficulty in forming a clear picture of the whole battle.'[110]

The campaign proper opened with the advance of the Peloponnesian forces to the Isthmus and the retirement of Mardonius from Attica. He reasoned (correctly) that Attica was poor cavalry country and he stood a better chance of bringing on battle on his own terms in Boeotia, on the edge of the great plain south of Thebes, his effective base for supplies.[111] The forces were probably well-matched. Herodotus gives the Greeks 38,700

---

[108] Th.i.94.

[109] Th.v.70–3.

[110] W.K. Pritchett, 'New Light on Plataea', *AJA*, 61, 1957, p. 28, whose indefatigable survey of the topography has as usual laid many of the problems to rest. He works on the (inherently probable) assumption that when H describes the Greek army as being at a point (map reference style) he refers to Pausanias' command post on the right. The Greek line would of course have extended for about three miles.

[111] ix.13.

hoplites, a total which is both quoted by itself and as the sum of the 21 individual contingents; it is an entirely credible figure bearing in mind the 'last throw' atmosphere that must have prevailed.[112] It was easily the largest Greek army so far put into the field and remained so until well into the fourth century. A large number of light troops – Spartan helots and others – were in attendance, according to Herodotus 69,500, a number which may or may not be true, but it hardly matters as their value as combat troops was probably negligible. At this period the tactical possibilities of light infantry had barely been explored, let alone exploited, and these personnel would have been employed on such duties as guarding the baggage and escorting supply trains. The battle would be won or lost on less than 40,000 men.

Mardonius' forces were broadly similar (as with the campaign of 480, Herodotus' figures for the Persians are not worth discussion); his strategy suggests that he had no overwhelming superiority of numbers and relied on choice of ground to decide the issue. What he did have was a unified command and an infinitely superior cavalry arm. The anecdote of Thersander the Orchomenian and his Persian friend, apart from its theological interest, suggests that some of the Persian officers regarded themselves as being on to a hiding; perhaps Mardonius had underrated the power of the Greeks to unite and put a massive army into the field when their backs really were to the wall. A similar note is struck on the field of Plataea itself, before the main engagement: Artabazus, not in favour of risking a battle, urges that they disengage, withdraw to Thebes and from there step up their programme of aggressive diplomacy, purchasing with gold the support of the leading men in the cities[113] – a ploy that Philip of Macedon made full use of in the next century. This advice was not of course taken.

Waiting, waiting, waiting – again and again this is the preliminary to the great battles between Greek and Persian. Several days at Marathon; four days at Thermopylae; but with twelve, Plataea beat them all. When the stakes were so high, the commanders wanted to make quite, quite sure. Pausanias' force was being augmented all the time by men streaming over the Cithaeron passes from the south,[114] so on the face of it delay was profitable to him. But for Mardonius there was perhaps even less incentive to join battle. He was securely supplied from Thebes, with shorter lines of communication (though Alexander of Macedon allegedly reported to the Athenians that Mardonius was running short). By cutting the allies off from

---

[112] ix.28 f.

[113] ix.41. This argument is actually in indirect speech, a variation on the technique discussed in note 29. The same advice had been tendered by 'The Thebans', ix.2.

[114] ix.38.

their supply trains and access to water[115] he could make the position of the Greeks untenable and perhaps even cause the break-up of the great army. Mardonius enjoyed that most powerful combination of military advantage, a strategic offensive with a tactical defensive – like the German forces on French and Belgian soil from 1914 onwards. There was a greater onus upon Pausanias to begin battle, bearing in mind the fact that Greek citizen hoplite armies could not be held together for more than about six weeks, what with the pressing needs of domestic agriculture and so on.[116] Equally, Mardonius' forces were better suited to waging a contest of attrition – as in fact they did during the waiting period, the cavalry earning its keep well with some effective harassment. Pausanias' hoplites, on the other hand, could only really justify themselves in a decisive battle – provided that one could be brought on.

Herodotus represents the early phases of Plataea as a battle for position. If his account seems confusing, we can be fairly sure that the event itself must have seemed utterly confusing, baffling and frequently pointless to the rank-and-file soldiery who merely marched where and when they were told but may not have known why (not having been privy to the secrets of the generals' council). And it was only such men whom Herodotus could have spoken to – young in 479, middle-aged or elderly when they gave him their recollections; Pausanias, unlike so many modern generals, left no memoirs.

There is, then, a good deal of valuable realism and enough detail to make reconstruction of the manoeuvres possible. For such a great and successful encounter, the amount of 'epic', miraculous or generally fictitious material is less than might have been expected, no more than on Salamis and Marathon, considerably less than on Thermopylae. There are inevitably some misunderstandings, and there is also a bit of the racial prejudice that shows in the accounts of the earlier battles. To consider the weaknesses first: there is a touch of glamorisation about the 'five hundred picked Athenians' going as volunteers, 'when no others would', to the aid of the hard-pressed Megarians. In the final order of battle the Athenian contingent was separated from the Megarians only by 600 Plataeans; probably it was the same in the opening phase when this episode occurred. The Athenian force also included archers, who proved to be the decisive factor in driving off Masistius' cavalry and killing that officer himself. Surely, they were the obvious troops to send.

Again, it may very well be that the Athenians and Tegeans wrangled for precedence in the battleline, and quite possible that mythological arguments were adduced to tip the scale. But no one need believe that the

---

[115] ix.39, 49 f.; Alexander, ix.45.

[116] Cf. the Spartan invasions of Attica from 431.

dispute occurred on the very battlefield itself during the period of waiting; there were some questions that could be settled beforehand. Herodotus is taking the opportunity to put something into the otherwise empty space of the wait.[117]

Much doubt has been cast on the story of the right and left wings changing places to bring the Athenians to face the Persians, and the Spartans to face the Boeotians and other Medising Greeks.[118] We may question whether any such move took place on the very morning that battle was confidently expected – after the alleged tip-off from Alexander of Macedon – for it could have hardly taken less than an hour to execute. Nor need we believe that the move was a frightened reaction by Pausanias to the news reported from Alexander; a ridiculous suggestion. But it could have been a tactical ploy of Pausanias to keep the enemy guessing during the days of inaction, or even to try for a winning formula; it was much more likely that the Spartans would win a quick victory over the Medisers than that the Athenians would, and if that occurred it would release the full might of the Greeks to concentrate on Mardonius' Persians. But Mardonius was too wily to be caught by this. He carefully followed the Greek move so as to keep his best troops opposite the Spartans, in whose sector of the line he knew the battle and the war would be lost and won.

It is at this point that Alexander of Macedon takes his final bow. The ins and outs of this Histiaeus-like figure, and his intrigues with Persians and Athenians, make diverting if not entirely convincing reading. Obviously a survivor *par excellence*, he probably managed, as Artemisia and Damaratus may have done, to get accepted after the war a version of events that put him in a favourable light.[119]

Then there is the story of Amompharetus the Spartan *lochos* (battalion) commander. As it is narrated it is difficult to believe. Even the *bon mot* – 'with this pebble, I vote against running from the strangers', as he drops a boulder at Pausanias' feet – even this sounds wrong: it was Athenians not Spartans who voted with pebbles. There is nothing incredible about Spartan officers disobeying ridiculous orders; at Mantinea again, two *lochos* commanders disobeyed King Agis' foolishly belated order to change position in the line when they were actually closing with the enemy; for which insubordination they were subsequently tried and exiled from Sparta.[120] But in our case Pausanias' order was utterly sensible, designed to

---

[117] Megarians: ix.20 ff.; Tegeans: ix.26 f. 'Filling-in' was suggested by Munro, CAH, iv, p. 332.

[118] E.g. Munro in *CAH* makes this a part of the Greek move to their second positions, with the two wings in turn marching behind a screen of troops. The exchange of wings however seems to be a 'public fact' known to thousands (Burn's concept), and it seems best to regard it as a thwarted tactical move, especially as Munro's explanation disregards the Persian counter-moves.

[119] ix.44–7.

[120] Th.v.71.

get the allies out of a position that had ceased to be tenable. Amompharetus was also wrong in his interpretation of Spartan traditions: if sound tactics required it, retreat – or even flight – was a perfectly valid option, otherwise presumably Pausanias would not have entertained the idea either. The Spartans' pretended flights at Thermopylae had proved most effective. Had this been a case of real insubordination we can be sure that Pausanias would have called Amompharetus' bluff and set off much sooner. The whole story of the violent row between Pausanias and Amompharetus rests on the sole testimony of an Athenian messenger – or what those who heard him said that he said – and cannot be regarded as 'public fact';[121] there may have been an urgent last-minute transmission of orders. The trend of Herodotus' story does in fact support the generally held modern view that Amompharetus' force was a rearguard, perhaps with the additional purpose of acting as a bait to draw the Persians forward. Herodotus gives us a good piece of military detail when he makes Amompharetus give Pausanias' men a start of over a mile,[122] and then begin to move at a measured pace; he rejoined the main body just before the leading Persian cavalry began their harassment – marvellously well-disciplined timing.

Racial prejudice – Athenian, that is, for the story of Plataea seems to betray a heavier dependence upon Athenian information than might have been expected – is less virulent than the anti-Theban and anti-Corinthian passages of the Thermopylae and Salamis accounts. Such as it is, it is largely at the expense of the minor contingents of the allied centre, including Megara and Corinth, states that were bitterly hostile to Athens at the time that Herodotus was preparing his work for publication. He tells us that at the time of the imminent retreat to the third position, the Greek high command decided 'to send half the army to Cithaeron, to rescue those who were escorting the food supplies' who were cut off by Persian harassing attacks. The force detached on this errand was the centre (because the subsequent narrative concentrates on the right and left, Sparta and Athens) and Herodotus does not tell us if it accomplished its mission; but there is no reason to think it did not, before retiring to Plataea. Again, Herodotus makes their withdrawal to Plataea a 'flight', but they seem to have halted and grounded arms in good order outside the city.[123] Furthermore, in the battle itself, they are not made to come into action until the battle is as good as decided; but then 'they set off in no sort of order, the Corinthians and their neighbours . . . to the temple of Demeter; the Megarians . . . across the plain'; but the latter forces ran into the Boeotian cavalry and 600 of them

---

[121] Burn again, *Persia and the Greeks*, p. 532, a good point.

[122] '10 stades' (MSS), wrongly emended to 4 stades in Hude's OCT, on a preconceived idea of topography (ix.57); Amompharetus' pace—*badēn* (as opposed to *dromōi*). For the traditional Spartan slow march into battle, cf. Mantinea again (Th.v.70).

[123] ix.51 f.

were killed; 'they died without honour'. An unjust comment, for (as Herodotus' own narrative shows) this force must have taken pressure off the Athenian left, who had been having a tough battle with the Medisers. For when the battle really was settled, the Boeotian cavalry was employed not in cutting up Megarians but in screening, quite effectively, the flight of their defeated infantry.[124]

But when all criticisms are made, how much of worth remains! The valuable picture of the role of cavalry – one of Persia's crack forces, but not hitherto seriously engaged in the war – harassment, cutting-out of supplies and rapid pursuit; the first picture we have of Greek, as opposed to barbarian, archers in action, their brilliant feat in slaying Masistius, and the effect this had on Persian morale; the canny approaches of the two generals, each determined to choose the ground: no death-or-glory rushes here (when Mardonius advanced, he did so because he thought he had the Greeks on the run; and so he had, almost); the insights into the problem of keeping a great army fed and watered, and the effect this has on tactics and strategy; the wonderful discipline and steadiness of the Spartans; the final storming of the Persian camp. The whole narrative forms a fitting climax to Book IX and to the history as a whole.

The battle of Mycale, though immense with respect to its consequences, and of much political-strategical interest, was a relatively small-scale affair in itself.[125] Herodotus' account is good, brisk and straightforward. Corinth this time gets a good press; so, of the minor states, does Sicyon, whose general Perilaus fell.

There is a touch of realism in the Athenians urging each other on to make it *their* victory this time (they were probably fed up with Sparta taking so much credit, whether or not the news of Plataea had arrived). Herodotus also singles out from the enemy the native Persians for commendation. When the Greeks rushed their camp wall, the enemy broke – except for the Persians. Forming themselves into small groups they kept resistance going until the entire Greek force could be brought to bear on them.

HERODOTUS ON STRATEGY

On military tactics, then, Herodotus is fallible though far from hopeless. On questions of strategy he is really rather impressive. His description of Xerxes' great preparations (discussed earlier in this chapter) shows that he

---

[124] Megarians etc: ix.69 f.; Boeotian cavalry: 67 f.

[125] ix.102.1 seems to imply a very constricted battleground, barely enough even for the small Greek force to deploy. A minor point of interest at Mycale is that the Athenian and Spartan commanders evidently got on well. Thucydides (ii.13) records the hereditary friendship of Pericles, son of Xanthippus, and King Archidamus, grandson of Leotychidas.

understood the physical and logistical problems of moving a huge army over long distances – even through territory already controlled, like Thrace and Macedonia. He puts remarks into Artabanus' mouth warning Xerxes of the 'enmity' of the land and the sea to a force like his: how vulnerable will his fleet be to storms at all points of the route, when there cannot be harbours big enough to accommodate all the ships together; and the further his army advances, the more danger will there be of its supplies running out. Xerxes soundly rebuts the latter contention of his pessimistic uncle, but says nothing of the former: prophetic stuff, for the Persian fleet did in fact suffer heavy losses from the weather, but there is no record of any breakdown of the commissariat.[126]

It is more or less generally agreed that the Persian strategy was the simple and effective one of keeping the fleet and army moving in some sort of harmony, and using the fleet to support the army if ever the latter was held up by some hostile force. Herodotus does not stress this; it is really too obvious to require that. His narrative does clearly imply it, both in such things as the Persian detachment sent round Euboea to turn the Greek position; and in his masterly sketch of the topography of Thermopylae and Artemisium.[127] It is explicitly stated in Achaemenes' speech: he is rebutting Damaratus' suggestion that a large part of the fleet be detached to capture the island of Cythera (off Sparta). 'If the army advances in conjunction with the fleet, each will help the other; if you split them up, you will be of no use to the fleet, nor they to you.'[128] The Greek allies had evidently penetrated the Persian strategy (not, perhaps, an excessively difficult task), and the interdependence of Thermopylae and Artemisium is clearly apparent. Whatever happens, and whatever grumbles or fits of nervousness there may be among officers or men, the naval high command will not pull out of Artemisium because it knows that by doing so it will be abandoning Leonidas' men to certain death. Once Persian ships could land men behind Greek positions, all fortifications (and courage) were set at nothing.

In passing, we may as well examine Damaratus' proposal to take Cythera. It is quite possible that later both Damaratus and Artemisia put about versions of events on the lines that 'Xerxes could have won the war if only he'd listened to me'. Whether that is so or not, Herodotus is true to form in attributing such a plan to Xerxes' adviser on Spartan affairs. If it succeeded, it would ensure Damaratus' speedy restoration to the Spartan throne, probably with minimum casualties (and therefore bitterness) among

---

[126] vii.49. For a similar example of historian's prophecy-by-hindsight, cf. Th.vi.10, where Nicias is made to anticipate accurately all sorts of things that actually did help to ruin the Sicilian expedition. I suspect that Th. (who did not always interpret his own words at i.22.1 in the same way) meant Nicias to say the sort of things he ought to have said if he had had his wits about him.

[127] vii.175–7.

[128] vii.236.

his subjects. Any such move would be necessarily a gamble to some extent, and Achaemenes' reply (along with the familiar Persian antipathy towards influential Greeks) embodies the orthodox strategical principle of *tout le monde à la bataille*. Sideshows, however well-conceived, may detract from one's ability to win a decisive victory.[129] But it would be surprising if the Cythera question had not been at least discussed in Xerxes' council. The prophetic remark attributed to Chilon may be authentic; in Herodotus' own lifetime, Tolmides of Athens had taken Cythera during his successful naval expedition round the Peloponnese (456/5); and when Herodotus' work was before the public, the exploit was repeated by Nicias (424).[130]

As the invader, Xerxes held the initiative, and the Greeks' counter-measures would necessarily be dictated by their reading of the Persian strategy. Herodotus is good on this too. The opening move, to put a stop to existing disputes among the patriotic states, is neatly described.[131] What poignant reading this paragraph must have made in the Peloponnesian War, when Herodotus' work appeared! The reasoning behind the abortive expedition to the vale of Tempe is put, in the now familiar manner, in a speech addressed to the council of the patriotic delegates. The Thessalian appeal embodied the strategical principle that the defence of the common soil of Greece required a common effort; the further north the Greeks could mount their defensive effort, the more states would remain firm in their loyalty. The vale of Tempe, the famous beauty spot, is a pass on the line of the river Peneius, and the Greeks expected Xerxes to advance towards central Thessaly along the line of the present *route nationale* between Athens and Thessaloniki. The force sent north was entirely adequate to defend that position, and the inhospitable coast of Magnesia was sufficient security against naval landings in their rear: the Artemisium position would have served Tempe just as well as Thermopylae. But Herodotus has already prepared us for failure. Xerxes' forces had begun to clear a route by tree-felling round behind Mount Olympus; and Herodotus (implicitly dismissing the rather silly story of, inevitably, Alexander of Macedon) records his opinion that it was on learning of this route that the Greeks fell back. We may guess that they discovered not only the existence of the route but also the fact that the local Thessalians were going to make no effort to defend it.[132] (Herodotus does seem to let the Thessalians down rather

---

[129] How & Wells call Achaemenes' strategical maxims 'puerile', but it is extremely easy to find examples ancient and modern to vindicate him. Athens in the 450s lost badly in Egypt and achieved no decisive success in the First Peloponnesian War; in 1915 the allies' simultaneous heavy commitment to the Western Front and Gallipoli prevented success in either theatre.

[130] Paus.i.27.5; Th.iv.53. Chilon: Damaratus had married into his family (vi.65), and see genealogical table, p. 201. For the possible publication date of H's work, cf. note 1 to this chapter.

[131] vii.145.

[132] Tempe: vii.172–4; Olympus: vii.131.

lightly in this episode, as compared with his later treatment of the Thebans.)

It is notable that the Greeks had no prepared fall-back position, but returned to the Isthmus, and it was a force that was not only smaller but different in the details of its composition that was sent to the next defensible point, Thermopylae. Thessaly was, therefore, sacrificed; but she was probably beyond saving anyway, with the most prominent ruling family (the Aleuadae) heavily committed to Persia.[133] Thermopylae was in all other respects a better bet than Tempe, as Herodotus points out. The Greek policy-makers did not know of the encircling path, but Leonidas was told of it on his arrival. The most striking thing to emerge from Herodotus' account is the small size of Leonidas' force, considerably smaller than the 10,000 quoted for Tempe. And yet this puny force was nearly adequate. Leonidas only detached the 1,000 Phocians to guard the back path; he could have done with more, though if the Phocians had known their orders properly all might still have been well.

It has been argued that the small army and large fleet in the parallel campaigns of Thermopylae and Artemisium suggest that the Greeks wished to decide the issue at sea. The facts suggest otherwise. Not only does Herodotus' account clearly make the naval manoeuvres subordinate to the campaign on land,[134] but the large fleet might just as well suggest lack of confidence in what was, after all, a relatively untried arm; the hoplite force was small but abundantly proven. Leonidas' force put it about that they were only an advance guard for a much larger force, but, as Herodotus points out, this was mainly to induce the central Greek states to send contingents – successfully, in two cases. We need not believe in the literal truth of this propaganda, but some further forces would have had to be sent north if only to make good any losses suffered by attrition. The sad fact, recorded by Herodotus, was that the allies, with their minds on the Spartan Carneia and the Olympic Games, did not expect the Thermopylae campaign to be decided so rapidly.[135] Once the decision to defend the pass had been taken, it should have been implemented in full, without delay.

Herodotus' model account of Artemisium does not stress one strategical point of consequence. The fact that the Greeks were in defence of the narrows of northern Euboea served to delay for several days the entrance of the Persian fleet into safe waters: and that must have been a crucial factor in the terrible losses suffered by the Persians from the weather.

The strategical question over Salamis was simply, for both sides, 'to

---

[133] vii.175, 177. Aleuadae: vii.6, 172 etc.
[134] viii.21.
[135] vii.206.

fight or not to fight?' The Greeks had no real option; they must either prepare to fight in the narrows of Salamis, or to make a stand at the Isthmus adjacent to the fortified position on land. This issue we have already discussed; there was no third option of avoiding battle altogether. A failure to inflict a decisive defeat on Xerxes' fleet would open up the Peloponnese to seaborne landings. Xerxes, however, did have such an option, and its expression is put, characteristically, into the mouth of Artemisia. 'Do not rush in to attack the Greeks, but bide your time. In time the Greek forces will break up and return to their homes.' It is the familiar idea that citizen forces could not be held together indefinitely, which we earlier discussed in the case of Plataea – 'Salamis is running short of supplies; and if you threaten the Peloponnese by land, you may detach Peloponnesian units from the fleet.'[136] Possibly another example of 'how Xerxes could have won the war by listening to the right advice'; but his rejection of Artemisia's counsel could have been soundly based. Herodotus represents Xerxes as being eager for battle to enable his forces to redeem themselves after their relative failure off Euboea. But this will not quite do. We have already seen that the Persians did well on the third day at Artemisium, and the Greeks could not afford another 'Persian failure' like that; the view of the Persian high command may well have been that to pursue a waiting strategy, though sound in itself, might impair the morale of their sailors. One option that was not open to Xerxes, and Herodotus makes no mention of it, was simply to sail past the Greeks to the Peloponnese. The Persians would never have dared risk a landing on enemy soil with an unbeaten fleet in their rear.

Strategy and politics are always difficult to disentangle. As we have seen, the original decision to defend Tempe was politically motivated, a bid to keep Thessaly loyal. If the Greek fleet had stuck to the original majority decision and abandoned Salamis, the political consequences could have been incalculably disastrous. But few campaigns in ancient history measure up to those of 479 as illustrations of the interdependence of strategy and politics. Herodotus grasps this fully, and the account he gives of the manoeuvres behind the scenes, not always creditable, is convincing and realistic. Reduced to the barest essentials, the political-strategical questions were these: for Mardonius, whether he could detach Athens from the allied cause and, with her fleet, neutralise the Isthmus wall; for Athens, whether she could induce Sparta to send something like her full force into central Greece to drive Mardonius off Athenian soil for good and all; for Sparta, how low a price could she get away with paying in order to retain the loyalty of Athens.

To convey his overtures Mardonius employed first, the ubiquitous

---

[136] viii.68.

Alexander of Macedon, second, a Hellespontine named Murychides. The Athenians heard Alexander, and before they replied, a Spartan delegation pleaded with them, offering sympathy for the loss of their homes, and support for their families for the duration of the war. Not a word about invading central Greece! The Athenians then rejected Alexander with lofty disdain, and then turned, in rather pained tones, to the Spartans. They thanked them for their kind offer of support, but insisted that the only 'support' they were interested in was an army north of the Isthmus.[137]

This reply of the Athenians caused Mardonius to reoccupy their city, and Murychides his second emissary actually went to Salamis, but got no further than Alexander had done. But behind the scenes furious diplomacy, often acrimonious, was going on: Athens began to put real pressure upon Sparta. As the summary above shows, Athens held the trump cards: Persia wanted her, Sparta needed her. With Athens, Persia would win the war; without her, Sparta would very certainly lose it. So, in reproaching the Spartans for their inaction, the Athenians could not only remind their allies of the concessions promised by Persia if they changed sides, but also hint that, if Sparta continued reluctant, Athens would look to her own safety.[138]

Herodotus stresses, by mentioning the fact three times, that the fortification across the Isthmus was by now as good as complete,[139] and this, he maintains, conditioned Spartan strategical thinking. This is likely enough and certainly consistent with Spartan policy both before and afterwards; but it could not last. The Athenian fleet and the threat of its falling into Persian hands ensured that the correct decision was made. As usual the issue is spelled out in direct speech, here put into the mouth of an influential Tegean named Chileos. He makes a historically motivated intervention to state what most thinking Spartans will have known in their hearts, namely that there was no alternative to mobilising a massive allied force and committing it to central Greece, 'traditional Spartan policy' notwithstanding.[140] The Spartans had, however, to reckon with possible interference from Argos, whose neutrality was *de facto* in Persia's interests. In the event strict Spartan security and speed ensured the safe passage of her forces out of the Peloponnese, and Argos proved a broken reed. That momentous strategical decision having been taken, it was thereafter up to the generals to get to grips with the foe on ground of their own choosing; and we have already examined the tactics of Plataea.

After Salamis, the naval war languished. Themistocles' proposal to sail

---

[137] viii.140–4.

[138] ix.4–6.

[139] ix.7.1, 7b.1, 8.2.

[140] ix.12; Chileos: ix.9. If it is a genuine tradition that has preserved his name, we may guess that his visit to Sparta had something to do with the prominence of Tegea in the subsequent campaign.

to the Hellespont and cut off Xerxes' retreat was rejected. The surviving Persian vessels returned to Asia and regrouped at Samos, guarding against a possible revolt in Ionia.[141] No attempt was made by the allies to pursue them, and a large proportion of the Greek fleet was stood down. A mere 110 ships assembled at Aigina, waiting for something to happen or for some decision to be made. Leotychidas the Spartan king was in command; Herodotus gives no figures for individual contingents; a pity, for knowledge of them might clarify the strategical picture. Athens sent a contingent (Herodotus records its commander, Xanthippus the father of Pericles) but it would be interesting to know if it was of more than token size. The most likely interpretation of the events of 479 is that Athens withheld the bulk of her fleet from the allied war effort until it was clear that Sparta was really going to take the initiative on land. This could certainly explain the apparent timorousness of the Greek fleet at first – when appealed to by a group of Ionian exiles to sail over and liberate their homeland, 'they were with difficulty prevailed upon to advance to Delos; anything beyond that was full of terrors to the Greeks, who had no knowledge of the area, and supposed it was all full of the enemy's forces; Samos, they imagined, was as far away as the straits of Gibraltar'. The Persians for their part were too scared to sail westward from Samos, so Herodotus satirically concludes: 'Their mutual fear guarded the area between.'[142]

As regards the Greeks, this would be poppycock if the Athenians had been on hand, or at least on call, in reasonable force. As it stands it may be a valid comment, possibly a remark made by one of Herodotus' informants, an impatient Samian friend who could not understand the allies' dilatoriness. When Herodotus resumes the story,[143] however, he does for once fail to grapple with a strategical issue (though he does make Hegesistratus and his fellow Samians argue that the appearance of the Greek fleet off Ionia would cause a general Ionian revolt). It is not clear from Herodotus why it was all right for Leotychidas to sail for Ionia in the summer of 479 when it had not been after Salamis, and his explanation of the 'omen' contained in Hegesistratus' name ('leader of the army') is pleasant but hardly adequate.

The truth probably lies in the tradition, recorded by Herodotus, that Plataea and Mycale were fought on the same day. If it is indeed true that Athens did not release her naval forces for an Ionian campaign until Sparta was definitely committed to a campaign in Boeotia, it is quite possible – bearing in mind the many days of waiting at Plataea – that the brisk

---

[141] viii.130.

[142] viii.132.

[143] ix.90. Xanthippus may of course have been a more cautious leader than Themistocles, who after Salamis had advocated the bold ploy of sailing to the Hellespont.

amphibious operation at Mycale did more or less coincide with the decisive phase of the land battle. It seems that Herodotus, as we have seen, faithfully recorded the early stages of the Athenian diplomatic pressure on Sparta, but did not spell out what this meant in practice, namely refusing to put her fleet under Spartan command until the last moment. That, however, is a minor blemish on what is for the most part a clear and convincing picture of a war that was fought out on a high strategical level.

CONCLUSION

As we observed earlier in this chapter, Greek writers in general did not glory in war, but rather viewed it as an inevitable evil, a distaste that Herodotus shares in full measure. On the face of it that might seem surprising, when he chronicles the most glorious exploits in the history of Greece, but his humanity never lets him forget that war means suffering, making wives widows and children orphans. It is certain that he was finishing his work during the Archidamian war, and published it, probably, in 425 BC. The outbreak of that war between the two states that had done most to defeat Xerxes, and which he admired beyond all others, must have been a source of great sadness to Herodotus, and lent poignancy to many of his passages. Here there is no need to do more than cite a handful of passages that shed light upon his attitude.

It was this hatred of war that made him condemn Athens' decision to help Aristagoras and the Ionians, already discussed. The ships that Athens voted to send were 'the beginning of evils, for Greeks and barbarians alike' – war, purely and simply. While leading up to the account of the Marathon campaign, Herodotus tells of the portentous earthquake at Delos, a divine warning of evils to come, 'for in the reigns of Darius, Xerxes and Artaxerxes – a bare three generations – more evils fell upon Greece than in the twenty generations before Darius: some, indeed, stemmed from Persia, but others from their own leaders struggling for supremacy': in respect of casualties, the 'First Peloponnesian War' (459–446) and the Archidamian War down to 425 were far more costly to the states than all the campaigns of the Ionian revolt, Marathon and 480–479. An especially significant passage occurs before his narrative of the naval war of 480, when Athens, in the interests of Greek unity, waived her claim to command the allied fleet despite her preponderant contribution: 'They set great store by the survival of Greece, and they knew that if they fell out over the question of leadership, Greece would go under. They were quite right, for internal strife is a greater evil than united war by the same measure as war is worse than peace.' Chilling reading in the 420s! More sinisterly, Herodotus goes on 'but after driving off the Persians and carrying the war on to Persian soil, the Athenians – using the pretext of Pausanias' tyrannical conduct – deprived the Spartans of their command'. And so Athens was launched on her imperial career, which led tragically and inexorably to the wars with Sparta. It is almost as though Herodotus sees Athens, the principal beneficiary of the allied victory, caught up in the same vicious spiral as Persia had been, a successful power with a restless urge to expand.[144]

Not surprisingly, Herodotus sometimes uses direct speech to convey the same message. The likeable exile Damaratus of Sparta extols the virtues of his former countrymen to Xerxes: their courage, their hatred of slavery, their freedom under the law. Yet, when twitted by Xerxes for his supposed exaggeration of Spartan prowess, he does not reply by boasting. Instead he says 'I do not claim to be a match for ten men, nor two. I would not even fight with one if I had the choice. But if I had no choice – if there were some great issue to spur me on – with the greatest possible pleasure would I do battle with one of those champions of yours who claim to be as good as three Greeks.' The rest of Damaratus' speech is strongly prophetic, and we can be sure that this passage too is intended to be taken most seriously as an illustration of how even the Spartans, a military-oriented people, thought about war.

Finally, an example from one of Herodotus' favourite characters, Croesus of Lydia. Cyrus had just saved him from the pyre, and asks him why he became his enemy and invaded his land.[145] Croesus replies 'When I did what I did, luck was with you, and the misfortune was mine; the god of the Greeks is to blame for that, by urging me to go to war. For no one is such a fool as to choose war in preference to peace: in peace sons bury their fathers, in war fathers bury their sons. It was the gods' will that things should have turned out so.' Croesus has passed through his ordeals and learnt from them, and every word he utters to Cyrus in this passage is pregnant with wisdom. In this beautifully phrased epigram we will not be wrong in hearing the voice of the historian himself.

---

[144] Respectively v.97, vi.98, viii.3. A similar note to the last is struck at ix.117: the Athenians besieging Sestos (479/8) are wearying of the task and press to be taken home. The generals refuse, unless ordered by the Athenian government, 'so content were they with the way things were' (i.e. with the new Athenian policy of aggressive war against Persia). Correctly explained by Fornara, *Herodotus*, p. 81.
[145] Croesus: i.87; Damaratus: vii.104.

5: SOME HERODOTEAN PERSONALITIES

DARIUS AND HIS PREDECESSORS; CLEOMENES AND DAMARATUS; THEMISTOCLES AND PAUSANIAS

Herodotus is by no means enslaved to any sort of biographical treatment of history; but given that one of his aims is to record the marvellous achievements of men, it is inevitable that some dominant figures will emerge from his narrative; inevitable, too, for one of his cast of mind, that among the secondary characters some should exercise a particular fascination. Several such characters have been considered already in different connections and there is no need to re-cover the ground here. Among the dominant figures, Croesus and Xerxes have been treated in Chapter 2, and Miltiades in Chapter 1; Aristagoras, Histiaeus, Artemisia and many other of the secondary figures have also been discussed from the political or military viewpoint. The intention of this chapter is to consider Herodotus' treatment of a few outstanding personalities not separately covered.

The remaining Persian kings are obvious candidates for inclusion. We shall not, however, consider Cyrus and Cambyses at length. The whole of Cyrus' story is contained within Book I: there is not one piece of fresh material concerning him in any later book, until the moral anecdote with which Herodotus concludes his entire work. The story is heavily overlaid with elements of folk-tale, but some seemingly authentic touches of character do show through. Cyrus was evidently a man with a sense of humour, albeit a grim one at times: the parable of 'the piper and the fishes' is a good example, and so is his reply to the Spartan envoys who urged him to keep his hands off Ionia. More spontaneous perhaps was his unmalicious laughter when the defeated Croesus asked his permission to reproach the Delphic Apollo.[1]

Of Cambyses little more need be said. He has suffered the fate of rulers who follow a long, successful and popular reign, *comparatio deterrima*[2] – the invidious contrast that heightens the virtues of the first and magnifies the failings of the second. In fact Cambyses' reign was successful enough for its relatively short duration: every square mile of real estate acquired by Cyrus was retained, and to that already great empire

---

[1] Respectively i.141, 153, 90.

[2] Used by Tacitus, *Ann.* i.10, of the Augustus-Tiberius succession.

were added Phoenicia by treaty[3] and Egypt by conquest. But in the account of his reign truth and fiction have become inextricably intertwined. He emerges as a sort of cross between Caligula and Henry VIII (in his blacker moments) and membership of his court must have resembled living on the upper slopes of a volcano. He was unpredictably capable of insensate cruelty and the grossest sacrilege – his burning of Amasis' corpse offended both Persian and Egyptian custom; he was impossible to please – delighted that Croesus had survived his impulsive orders for him to be killed, he nevertheless punished with death those who had disobeyed the orders;[4] yet he was not devoid of that courtly generosity that marked the typical oriental monarch – witness his gracious treatment of the defeated Psammenitus, a clemency which the latter was unwise enough to abuse.[5]

We can be sure that, as the son of the almost superhumanly successful Cyrus, Cambyses felt a need to assert himself forcefully. How far this extended towards the point of personality disorder and ultimately madness can only be guessed at. The fact that he left no successor with an interest in rehabilitating his memory has given the hostile portrait an unchallenged field.

DARIUS AND HIS REIGN

In Darius we meet the first great personality in Herodotus who is the subject of full-length treatment that is unambiguously historical, with minimal adulteration by elements of folk-tale, unbalanced hostility or (as in the case of Croesus) theology. Darius is mentioned more often than any other individual in the *Histories*, and is arguably the greatest figure of the entire work. He casts his shadow before him by being quite frequently mentioned before he enters the story proper as one of the seven conspirators against the two Magi. The revolt of Media early in his reign is briefly noticed in Book I; so is the act of sacrilege he contemplated (but did not carry into effect) in the temple of Babylonian Bel, and his desecration of Nitocris' tomb in the same city – one of his less felicitous enterprises. In addition we get a rich example of the type of *post eventum* prophecy with which potentates tended to be invested, in this instance a dream allegedly sent to Cyrus, then about to embark on his last and fatal campaign. In Book II we find the anecdote of Sesostris' statue at Memphis to which Darius yielded pride of place – Sesostris having succeeded in subduing the Scythians! – and a colourless reference to the canal that Darius had cut between the Nile and the Red Sea; and in Book III the delightful story of the

---

[3] iii.19.

[4] iii.16, and 29–37 for various examples of his cruelty.

[5] iii.15.

test by which Darius proved the truth of Pindar's aphorism that 'Custom is king of all.'[6]

There are two noteworthy points about this little list: one is that all of them date from Darius' period as king (apart from the 'prophecy' vouchsafed to Cyrus, the story of which includes the interesting incidental piece of information that Darius was about 20 and too young for military service at the time of Cyrus' campaign against the Massagetae; he was, therefore, born in about 550 BC). The only thing we ever learn about him before the episode of the Seven Conspirators is told out of sequence as part of the second digression on Samian history: Darius first met Syloson, brother of Polycrates and future tyrant of Samos, while serving in Egypt as a junior officer 'of no special importance' in Cambyses' guard. Darius was not marked out for greatness early, and no body of legend clustered round his cradle. His father Hystaspes, a man of distinction, was actually holding a satrapy in Cambyses' reign;[7] but although Herodotus mentions Darius' membership of the Achaemenid house, his actual relationship with the kings was not all that close: to be precise, he was Cyrus' second cousin, once removed.[8] There must have been many closer kin at the time when Darius gained the throne, a fact which may help to explain the tremendous wave of disaffection in the empire which followed the fall of the Magian régime.

The second point to note is that the anecdotes are not especially well harmonised: they are fitted in out of sequence as footnotes (as it were) to the main topic under discussion, and they betray their sources: Darius, the hammer of the Babylonians, is represented as being restrained from an act of sacrilege only by a failure of nerve, and in the 'Nitocris' episode he is made to appear both avaricious and foolish. In these tales we can detect a kind of anecdotal revenge taken by a defeated people; similarly, Egyptian sources are probably assuaging their own injured pride in the tale of Sesostris' statue – Egypt had once been ruled by a better man than Darius! Certainly as regards the Babylonian tales, the idea of Darius the sacrilegious is not readily compatible with the picture of the respecter of ethnic religious tradition, as seen in the anecdote of 'the power of custom'.

When Darius enters the story proper, however, a more consistent picture does seem to emerge. He did not originate the conspiracy of the 'Seven' – that was Otanes, who had discovered the truth about the Magian usurpation by romantically devious means, and compared notes with two friends. Darius arrived hurriedly at Susa[9] apparently knowing that the

---

[6] Respectively i.130, 183, 187, 209; ii.110 (cf. 99), 158; iii.38.

[7] iii.70, 139.

[8] There are some problems in Darius' family tree but this much is certain—derived from i.111, vii.11 and Persian sources. See How & Wells, Appx IV for fuller discussion.

[9] Not in fact where the murder of the Magi occurred according to Darius' own inscription (DBI in Kent, OP); an unimportant point.

throne was occupied by an impostor (how, Herodotus does not explain) and was promptly added to the existing group of six conspirators – the original three, who included his father-in-law Gobryas, having each co-opted an accomplice. All were members of the Persian nobility, the ruling class of Cyrus' empire; Herodotus goes out of his way to tell us that outside Persia itself the regime of 'Smerdis' the Magus and his brother was popular and their demise lamented.[10] Having joined, Darius effectively took over the leadership by his vigorous advocacy of swift and decisive action. When Herodotus makes him justify deliberate lying to achieve entry to the usurper's quarters, he has not forgotten what he has earlier told us about the Persians' abhorrence of lying,[11] nor is he merely indulging in a bit of petty sophistry for the enjoyment of contemporary Athenians (though they would certainly have enjoyed it). Rather he is preparing us for the kind of person Darius is – calculating, ruthless when necessary, fixing his gaze upon ends and not being over-nice about means. Darius has already threatened to expose the conspiracy to the Magus unless his plan is adopted.

The 'debate' that followed the success of the conspiracy has already been examined in Chapter 3. Here we need do no more than notice two things: first, that Darius concludes his theoretical debating-club arguments for monarchy with something slightly more concrete: 'This, then, is my view, that having been given our liberty by one man, we should preserve that system, and, apart from that, we should not do away with ancestral customs that are perfectly sound.' An appeal to Persian conservatism ('custom' again!) bolstered by the example of the great Cyrus, was irresistible. Secondly, in his attack on monarchy, Otanes cites all sorts of traditional vices of despots, but it is notable that during his long reign Darius did not in fact (or at any rate in Herodotus) display these unpleasant qualities.

The tale of how Darius actually gained the throne is amusing, and, whatever the source from which it stems, derogatory to the king in so far as it gives the credit for his elevation to the stratagem of his groom Oebares. Whatever the true facts may have been (and remember that Darius was the only Achaemenid among the Seven) it is obvious that Darius became king with the full agreement of at least five of the rest; for the families of these men continue to hold prominent places under Darius and Xerxes – in particular, all five had sons or grandsons holding senior commands in the invasion of 480. The sixth, Intaphrenes, was put to death early in Darius' reign, together with most of his immediate family, as punishment for breaking the rules agreed among the Seven concerning access to the king. Intaphrenes was no doubt presuming upon his intimate friendship with

[10] iii.67.

[11] iii.72, cf. i.138.

Darius; the latter for his part was asserting the Persian king's claim to absolute obedience from his subjects. This is the sort of characteristic that one tends to associate with Xerxes rather than Darius, but the Oeobazus affair is a further example. It is perhaps natural that Darius, as a successful conspirator, should suppose that Intaphrenes' insubordination portended a conspiracy against himself; he shrewdly summoned the other five, separately, and by cross-questioning established that as far as they were concerned there was no conspiracy, and that they disapproved of what Intaphrenes had done. Upon that, Darius struck. His somewhat sweeping reprisal upon Intaphrenes' family did enable him to display the familiar regal 'generosity' by sparing his wife, brother-in-law and eldest son.[12]

Directly after narrating Darius' accession, and even before the Intaphrenes affair, Herodotus gives us the famous picture of the Persian empire under Darius, the satrapies, their constituent peoples and the tribute they furnished annually. Herodotus explicitly states that it was Darius who put the tribute on a fixed and regular basis. (He does not actually state, but we may confidently assume, that he also cancelled the 3-year tax holiday proclaimed by the Magus.) The derogatory name *kapēlos* ('shopkeeper') was applied to Darius no doubt by those who had suffered from his financial and administrative skills in practice.[13] At any rate Darius resembled Augustus in that he gave to his empire a shape and a system that were the foundation of all its subsequent history, destined to be altered in details but not in substance.

Darius' accession was followed by widespread uprisings across the Persian empire, and it must have seemed as if it was on the verge of breaking up. Our knowledge of all this comes largely from Darius' own inscriptions in Persian; Herodotus gives it much less attention than might have been expected; one might have supposed that the terrible difficulties of Darius at the beginning of his reign were most relevant to Herodotus' overall story, but we know extremely little about Herodotus' criteria of relevance. The fact that very little of all this directly involved the Greek world may be the answer. The cause of the revolts may have been regret for the Magus' benevolent regime, with its generosity to the provinces; possibly the existence of Persian nobles in governorships who thought they had a better claim to represent the Achaemenid house than Darius; more probably, it was simply a case of numerous conquered peoples regaining their breath after an interval and striking a blow for freedom; most had been acquired during the whirlwind career of Cyrus, and the lapse of time is roughly comparable with that between the Roman conquest of south-east Britain and Boudicca's rebellion. Other Roman parallels are possible.

---

[12] iii.118 f.

[13] iii.89.

What we do get in Herodotus is the fleeting glance, in Book I, at the revolt of Media, already referred to; more substantially, the punishment of the disloyal satrap Oroetes, discussed in Chapter 3; and a yet fuller account of Darius' suppression of the revolt of Babylon.[14] As I suggested in Chapter 4, Herodotus' account of the last can hardly be historical; in the story Darius, falling in with Zopyrus' plan, deliberately sacrifices no less than 7,000 soldiers in order to delude the Babylonian high command, a policy that ill conforms with Persia's traditionally economical and efficient ways of making war. Herodotus does not need to underline what every Greek reader would have found deeply shocking, namely the use of huge masses of men as mere cannon-fodder – something unthinkable for the city-states with their small armies of citizens. However, the point of the story is that Herodotus believes this is the kind of decision that Persian kings could make, the sort of power that they could wield. Darius' reprisals, too, after the capture are on an heroic scale – 3,000 leading Babylonians are impaled. But Darius is also given an opportunity to show his more human and generous side – his horrified indignation at the self-mutilation of Zopyrus and his remark that he would have preferred Zopyrus unmutilated to 20 more Babylons. He showed his appreciation to that faithful servant in many ways, including giving him his sister in marriage. Somewhat similar is Darius' reported comment on his marshal Megabazus, conqueror of Thrace – that he would like to have as many of him as there are seeds in a pomegranate, in preference to becoming master of Greece.[15]

The episode of the punishment of Oroetes offered Herodotus another opening for the motif of regal generosity: again, the story of Syloson and the flame-coloured cloak may be considered inadequate motivation for a major advance of Persian policy, but Darius was certainly most generous to Syloson. He made a point of ordering that Samos be handed over to him undamaged, which was both politic and fair – after all, the Samians had done nothing to offend Darius – but this desirable outcome Maeandrius and his brother contrived to prevent.

Some consistency does, in fact, become apparent in Herodotus' portrayal of Darius and his treatment of conquered peoples and captured territories. Babylon, which had offered him the gravest provocation and stood a particularly lengthy siege, was punished, as we saw, with the execution of 3,000 prominent citizens and the partial destruction of her fortifications. But then Darius' anger evaporated. He had the place resettled, drafting in womenfolk from all around. Somewhat similar were

---

[14] Respectively i.130, iii.126–8, iii.150–fin. Babylon actually revolted twice under Darius; H's narrative does not agree entirely with *either* of the revolts that figure on Darius' inscription, DBI and III in Kent, OP.

[15] iv.143; Zopyrus and D's sister: iv.43.

the cases of Miletus and Eretria. The city that had led the Ionian revolt did not, at the final collapse, suffer a wholesale massacre; the survivors were resettled by Darius near the mouth of the Tigris. The surviving Eretrians, 'who had injured Darius without provocation', were deported from their homes but subjected to no further ill-treatment; the king settled them on land near Susa. The remarkable story of the Paeonian tribespeople bears some resemblance to this. Darius had them transplanted from their homes (by the Strymon in western Thrace) into Phrygia; then Aristagoras of Miletus enabled them to return, under the cover of the Ionian revolt. Darius' motive here can only be guessed at; perhaps it was a carefully calculated demonstration of Persian power, designed to impress the yet unconquered tribes on the western edges of the empire. Whatever the truth be, there is no doubt that wholesale uprooting of peoples was a recurrent and recognisable feature of Darius' policy. Histiaeus of Miletus convinced the islanders of Chios when he (quite falsely) claimed that Darius was planning to interchange the populations of Ionia and Phoenicia.[16]

The Scythian expedition is the most controversial passage in Darius' entire reign, both in itself and as regards Herodotus' account of it. Here we shall concern ourselves only with the historian's treatment of Darius as he occurs in the story. By way of preface, it should be said that the whole story appears to be narrated from a hostile point of view, a fact that sets it apart from the other leading episodes involving Darius. Herodotus understood well enough why Darius launched the expedition – it was a straightforward case of imperialist expansion. Gossip, stemming presumably from Democedes the physician whose descendants Herodotus could have met in southern Italy, suggested that he was pushed into it by Queen Atossa, daughter of Cyrus. Herodotus is certainly aware that, while Artystone (Cyrus' younger daughter) may have been Darius' favourite wife, Atossa, mother of Xerxes, was the most powerful; nor is he blind to the realities of harem intrigues in Persia: the gruesomely tragic story of Xerxes and his womenfolk near the close of Book IX proves that. But as we have seen in Chapter 4, Atossa's intervention is historically motivated; she is employed to present the real arguments for military aggression. The idea that the expedition was a reprisal for an almost-forgotten raid into Media by the Scythians was no doubt aired as justification, and duly finds its way into Herodotus' text; the Scythians themselves were not deceived.[17]

---

[16] Respectively iii.159 (Babylon); vi.20, 119 (Miletus, Eretria); v.12, 98 (Paeonians); vi.3 (Histiaeus). Cf. also the Barcaeans, iv.204.

[17] iv.1 and vii.20, but cf. iv.118. For a full discussion of Persian motivation, see Ch. 4, pp. 109-112, and especially note 29. Artystone: vii.69. Atossa: previously married to her own brother Cambyses and then to the Magus, she was the first woman to be taken to wife by Darius after his accession; he was already married to a daughter of Gobryas the conspirator and was to take four more wives, two from the house of Cyrus, one a daughter of the conspirator Otanes and one his own niece. Xerxes and eleven other sons are recorded from these unions, all but one of whom served on the invasion of 480. See iii.88 and vii.2–3.

As Darius limbered up for the expedition, his brother Artabanus attempted to dissuade him – what inaccessible folk the Scythians were! Darius persevered with his preparations, however, no more deterred than Xerxes was to be when the same Artabanus offered the same advice to him before the great invasion of 480. Oeobazus, a Persian gentleman, attempted to get one of his three sons excused military service: Darius, pretending to agree, had all three put to death – a forcible reminder of the Persian king's claim to absolute obedience from his subjects, especially where war was concerned, and the king and members of his house were risking their own persons in combat. This too has its parallel in 480, with the case of Pythius the Lydian.[18] The two narratives differ in point of characterisation however – Xerxes is represented as acting in a fit of rage, while Darius deceives Oeobazus with a show of friendship, a calculated act designed to deter other possible applicants.

Darius duly gets under way, gets his army safely across the Bosporus by pontoon bridge and marches into Thrace; pausing for a while by the headwaters of the river Tearos, he erects a grandiloquent inscription, then proceeds to the Danube. The hostile picture continues, for here he has to be dissuaded (by Coës of Mytilene) from the potentially disastrous course of dismantling the pontoon bridge and leaving no rearguard. Evidently Darius agreed with Herodotus that 'neither the Ionians nor the rest of the Greeks know how to count'[19] for he does not trust the Ionian commanders to compute the 60 days that he expects to be the maximum length of his absence, but orders them to undo one knot per day on a leather thong with 60 knots in it. Then after making contact with the Scythian advance guard some three days' march away from the Danube he allows them to dictate his strategy for him as he pursues them through the trackless wastes. Frustrated by his inability to bring the enemy to battle, he challenges the Scythian king, by herald, to stand and fight or to surrender. Naturally Idanthyrsus does no such thing, except to the extent of stepping up cavalry harassment of Persian foraging parties, and making overtures to the Ionians and other Greeks at the Danube bridge.

Darius is represented as being at his wits' end when the puzzling gift of a mouse, a frog, a bird and five arrows arrives from the enemy.[20] For what is evidently the correct interpretation of this (a pessimistic one, naturally) he is indebted to his one-time fellow-conspirator Gobryas. His discomfiture is completed by the apparent contempt of the Scythians for him: when seemingly about to give battle at last, they suddenly disperse in

---

[18] iv.83 f. cf. vii.38 f.

[19] ii.16; Coës: iv.97 f.; Tearos: iv.91. Joking aside, date computation could pose problems: cf. Th.iv.89: Demosthenes' elaborate plan for a 3-pronged attack on Boeotia depended on strict synchronisation, but one of the forces (his own) arrived on the wrong day.

[20] Gift: iv.131; herald: iv.126.

pursuit of a hare that has darted across their front. This decides him – the Persians must pull out of Scythia without delay. Again prompted by Gobryas, he masks his flight by the ruthless and deceitful abandonment of his sick and wounded.[21] It was a diminished and demoralised force that reached the Danube crossing point and found the bridge apparently gone; the safety of the king and his army depended upon the loyalty of one man – Histiaeus of Miletus!

We need not feel obliged to accept the literal truth of all of Herodotus' account, but neither should we dismiss it as outright fiction.[22] In particular the picture of a highly organised army of a civilised power, ill-equipped to wage a campaign with nomad peoples, and being led a fearful dance in the wilderness, is highly convincing. Nor is there any question that Persia suffered a definite reverse; her power was never extended across the Danube. But what of Darius himself? For once he appears bankrupt of policy and generally cuts a poor figure. How is this to be accounted for? The answer probably lies in the similarities between the Scythian campaign and the great invasion of 480. Though superficial, they have led Herodotus to treat Darius in a manner that anticipates his picture of Xerxes. Artabanus' advice both to Darius and to Xerxes is overruled; Oeobazus has his parallel in Pythius. Both kings cross into Europe by way of a tremendous bridge; Darius sets up a boastful inscription, Xerxes utters impious and presumptuous words at the Hellespont. Both kings lean heavily on their advisers, with the difference, however, that Darius takes the advice of Coës and Gobryas to his profit, Xerxes rejects that of Artemisia and Damaratus to his cost. Both are forced to retreat in an undignified fashion.

Scythia was the one major failure of Darius' reign in which the king was personally involved – the Marathon campaign of course was conducted by his lieutenants – and to that extent at least it is credible that Herodotus was tempted to equate the role of Darius in it to that of Xerxes in 480. There, however, the resemblances end. Although Darius is not impressive in Herodotus' narrative, he is not pilloried in the way that Xerxes is. His enterprise is not made the vehicle for theological reflections upon hubris, the jealousy and anger of the gods and so on.[23] Even his boastful inscription escapes without comment. These differences in fact considerably outweigh the similarities, and a glance at the general historical context will explain why. Xerxes' defeat in 480/479 was a real turning-point in Persian history. Herodotus' early years were passed in an age when Persia was constantly in retreat, forced ever on to the defensive by the restless energy of Athens and

---

[21] Such abandonment was not however unknown even in Greek citizen forces if circumstances were dire enough; Th.(vii.75) gives a harrowing example in the Athenian attempt to retreat from Syracuse.

[22] As is done for instance by Bury (HG^3, p. 241).

[23] See Ch. 2, pp. 53 f., for a full discussion of this.

her alliance. Darius' setback, on the other hand, made no difference either to the fortunes of the Persian empire or to the pattern of his reign. The conquest of Thrace under Megabazus proceeded without intermission. Of the European Greek communities, Byzantium and Miltiades' Chersonese already acknowledged Darius, as their rulers served with the fleet at the Danube. Along with barbarian Thrace Megabazus took in more Greek towns, from Perinthus on the Sea of Marmara possibly as far as Acanthus in Chalcidice.[24] An invaluable foundation was laid for future expansion into Greece proper.

Darius was a keen expansionist in the tradition of Cyrus and Cambyses. In his reign not only was Thrace acquired, but also Samos and the other islands of the eastern Aegean; and Aryandes (apparently acting on his own initiative) conquered part of Libya. Mardonius' European campaign of 492 brought the Macedonian kingdom into subjection, and the wealthy island of Thasos too – if indeed that was not a reconquest of a community that had previously fallen to Megabazus, for the Thasians did not raise a finger against Mardonius. Following this success, Darius sent heralds all over the place demanding earth and water, tokens of submission, from the states of Greece. They got them, too, from many mainland states and all the islands visited, including, most spectacularly, Aigina. Darius gave his blessing to Aristagoras' scheme for taking Naxos, an ideal springboard for annexing the Cyclades as a whole; when Athens applied for a Persian alliance after Cleisthenes' democratic revolution, Artaphernes would only grant it in return for earth and water – he knew his royal brother would not be interested in any other terms. As regards the Marathon campaign, for all the frothy talk of destruction or enslavement, the presence of Hippias with the expedition strongly suggests that the aim was to make Athens an advanced base for expansion in Greece.[25]

The survey party that Darius sent from Sidon to Greece and western waters with Democedes of Croton would have had possible future military action in mind as well as the satisfaction of Darius' curiosity about the world – of which, more below; at any rate Aristophilides, king of Taras, was able to cover Democedes' flight by arresting his Persian escorts as 'spies'. Darius also despatched an exploring party to the east with orders to travel from the interior downstream to the mouth of the Indus. The party included Scylax of Caryanda, a town near Halicarnassus, and it may be that Herodotus got this information from members of his family. Anyway, having reached the Indian Ocean, the explorers then sailed westwards past the Persian Gulf into the Red Sea. This interesting journey was followed by a

---

[24] Acanthus: vi.44; Perinthus: v.1.

[25] Aryandes: iv.200 ff.; Mardonius: vi.44; heralds: vi.48 f.; Naxos: v.30 ff.: Artaphernes: v.73; Hippias: vi.109.

successful campaign against 'The Indians' (presumably those living around the Indus) and, Herodotus adds, 'Darius made use of this sea' – probably the 'shopkeeper-king' was exploiting the new conquests by way of trade, for we can detect a connection between Scylax's survey and the canal which Darius had dug between the Nile and the Red Sea.[26]

Although Darius very often acted out of calculation, he was not devoid of a more general curiosity; while his army was crossing the Bosporus bridge on the first phase of the Scythian campaign, he sailed to the northern mouth of the Bosporus and had a good look over the Black Sea – 'a sight well worth seeing'. It was also simple curiosity that made him enquire about the industrious Paeonians before he conceived any idea of transplanting the entire tribe to Phrygia[27]

Darius was a stern master but, so far as oriental monarchs ever were, a fair one. He had Aryandes, satrap of Egypt, put to death on a charge of insubordinate behaviour of some sort, and that despite Aryandes' successful Libyan campaign. (The story Herodotus tells, that the satrap minted his own particularly fine silver coins, is not incredible, but no such 'Aryandic' coins have been positively identified.) Before Lade, the first thought of the Persian admirals on seeing the size of the Ionian armada was fear that they would fail to defeat it and come to grief at the hands of Darius. But Darius did not normally act in a totally arbitrary fashion, nor is he reported to have lost his temper. The story of Sandoces is illuminating. One of the royal judges, he had been condemned by Darius for selling justice and crucified; while he was actually still hanging, Darius computed that his services to the royal house outweighed his offences and had him taken down. So he survived, ultimately to command a squadron in Xerxes' navy. Darius' second thoughts were in accordance with the Persian principle outlined by Herodotus in Book I: not even the king can have a man killed for one offence only, but an offender's faults must be weighed against his services, a nicety that Cambyses had failed to observe when punishing Sisamnes for a similar offence.[28]

Darius excelled (or, at the very least, was most fortunate) in his choice of subordinates and knew how to win the most loyal and devoted service from them – as was shown in an extreme degree by Zopyrus at Babylon. When Darius appealed for a volunteer to deal with the murderous satrap Oroetes, there was keen competition among 30 of the Persian gentlemen present to undertake this potentially most hazardous task; recourse was had to drawing lots; Bagaeus, whose name came out, accomplished the

[26] Western survey: iii.134–7; Taras was a colony of Sparta, hence its 'king'. Scylax: iv.44. H does *not* state that Scylax was in command.

[27] Respectively, iv.85, v.12.

[28] Aryandes: iv.165 f.; Lade: vi.9; Sandoces: vii.194; cf. i.137, v.25.

mission successfully.

It would be going too far to describe Darius as a 'philhellene', and it was probably sound statesmanship rather than šentiment that made him relieve his western generals of their posts after the Ionian revolt and give overall command to the youthful Mardonius, son of his old friend Gobryas and his own son-in-law. Mardonius, who no doubt had his instructions, removed at a stroke one of the grievances that helped to launch the revolt by suppressing the mainland Ionian tyrannies and installing town-council democracies in their stead. (The islands seem to have been unaffected by this.[29]) On the other hand, the list of individual Greeks who enjoyed the friendship or the favour of Darius is a long and impressive one. Mandrocles of Samos, the engineer who bridged the Bosporus, was laden with the most generous rewards. Syloson, as we have seen, was installed as tyrant of Samos, and Coës rewarded for services rendered in Scythia by being appointed tyrant of Mytilene. The opening of the Ionian revolt cost the latter his life – whether for the nature of his régime or for excessive loyalty to Darius Herodotus does not say.

Democedes of Croton, the physician who wrought successful cures upon both Darius and Queen Atossa, dined at the king's table and was given every privilege – 'save that of returning to Greece' – and had influence enough to save from execution the Egyptian doctors who had failed with Darius. When he went on the survey mission referred to earlier, Darius sent a shipload of gifts for his family in Croton. Democedes rather unscrupulously gave his escort the slip and never returned to Persia. The survey party were doubly in trouble, for on their return voyage they were shipwrecked on the heel of Italy and enslaved, presumably by the natives. They were found and ransomed by a wealthy exile from Taras named Gillus. Darius, pleased at their recovery, offered Gillus his choice of reward. He asked for restoration to his native town, adding patriotically that this should be effected by the men of Cnidos, rather than by a Persian force, 'so as not to throw Greece into uproar', Cnidos and Taras being on friendly terms. Both were Dorian towns; Cnidos had belonged to Persia ever since Harpagus' conquest of western Asia. This story did not end happily, for the Cnidians complied with Darius' instruction but failed to persuade the Tarentines to take Gillus back; and they were in no position to use force.[30]

---

[29] Bagaeus: iii.128; Mardonius: vi.43; for the persistence of island tyrannies, viii.85, 132 (Theomestor of Samos, Strattis of Chios).

[30] Mandrocles: iv.88; Syloson: iii.141; Coës: v.11, 38 and see Ch. 3, p. 93; Democedes: iii.132; Gillus: iii.138; Cnidos: i.174.

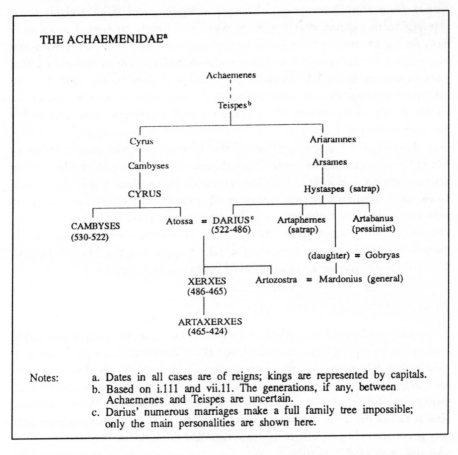

THE ACHAEMENIDAE[a]

Achaemenes
|
Teispes[b]

Cyrus — Ariaramnes

Cambyses — Arsames

CYRUS — Hystaspes (satrap)

CAMBYSES (530-522)

Atossa = DARIUS[c] (522-486) — Artaphernes (satrap) — Artabanus (pessimist)

(daughter) = Gobryas

XERXES (486-465) — Artozostra = Mardonius (general)

ARTAXERXES (465-424)

Notes:
a. Dates in all cases are of reigns; kings are represented by capitals.
b. Based on i.111 and vii.11. The generations, if any, between Achaemenes and Teispes are uncertain.
c. Darius' numerous marriages make a full family tree impossible; only the main personalities are shown here.

Darius was particularly generous to Greek exiles who sought refuge in Persia. To Damaratus, whom Cleomenes' intrigues had removed from the throne of Sparta, Darius granted a magnificent gift of land and cities – not, we may guess, for services rendered, but more in the expectation of services to come in a further invasion of Greece. The properties lay in southern Aeolis (on the Asian mainland opposite Lesbos) and still belonged to his family nearly a century later. We may, however, legitimately agree with Herodotus in doubting whether it was really Damaratus' advice that ensured the succession for Xerxes. Scythes, ruler of Zancle, who had been captured and enslaved by his supposed ally Hippocrates of Gela (in reality, evidently his overlord), contrived to escape and made his way from Sicily to Persia. Darius considered him 'the most upright man who ever came to him from Greece'; he obtained the king's permission to revisit Sicily, returning in due course to Persia, where he died, old and very prosperous. Slightly different was the case of the involuntary exile Metiochus, son of Miltiades, who had been captured by a Phoenician squadron while escaping with his father from the Chersonese. Although Miltiades had done Darius great damage in the Ionian revolt, his son was handsomely treated. Darius gave him an estate and a Persian wife, and he lived as a Persian gentleman thereafter. Of the greatest of Darius' Greek friends, Histiaeus of Miletus, enough has been said in Chapter 3.[31] Suffice it here to say that Darius' liking for him appears to have been genuine and sincere; he was indignant at his death at the hands of Artaphernes and Harpagus, and he had his head scrupulously buried.

The reign of Darius represented the apogee of Persian power, in terms both of area under direct control and of influence in the wider world. Darius was ambitious and acquisitive, but he achieved his aims much more often than not. His reign was long, he was well supported by his subordinates, he was methodical and efficient, and he enjoyed the good luck that the most successful rulers need from time to time. Herodotus' account as a whole suggests that he was an eminently worthy occupant of the Persian throne. He died in 486, having been king for 36 years.

CLEOMENES AND DAMARATUS

Cleomenes succeeded his father Anaxandridas as Sparta's king in the Agiad line not later than 519 BC and died, in rather mysterious circumstances, in 490 or 489. His reign was in many ways controversial, but he had a greater and more enduring influence upon Spartan history than almost any king before or after. Damaratus succeeded his father Ariston in the Eurypontid line perhaps not much later than Cleomenes – it is not ascertainable with any precision – but certainly at some time before 506,[32] and was deposed at the instance of Cleomenes in 491. The jarring reigns of these two men supplied Herodotus with a most interesting secondary theme, and enabled him to produce a pair of surprising and arresting portraits. For Cleomenes, who did more than anyone else to ensure that Sparta was firmly opposed to Persian expansion into Greece, is made the subject of treatment that is not always sympathetic; Damaratus, who after attempting to thwart Cleomenes' loyalist policies in 491 sought asylum with King Darius, and later returned to Greece as adviser to Xerxes, is shown as a likeable, even-tempered person, an undeserving victim of unscrupulous intrigue.

Obviously there is more in all this than meets the eye. The oddest remark that Herodotus makes is when, in speaking of the circumstances of Cleomenes' accession, he says that Cleomenes reigned 'for no long time'.[33]

---

[31] Damaratus: vi.70, vii.3, cf. X. *Hell*. III.i.6; Scythes: vi.24; Metiochus: vi.41; Histiaeus: see Ch. 3, pp. 93-5.

[32] v.75. H's words could be taken to imply that Damaratus was well established on the throne by then.

[33] v.48, Plataea: vi.108; cf. Th.iii.68.

Now, on Herodotus' own showing, his reign extended from c. 518 (when Maeandrius of Samos appealed to him for aid) to 491 (when he, with Leotychidas, coerced Aigina); and in fact his intervention in the affairs of Plataea is firmly dated by Thucydides to 519. Now it is true that kings of Sparta quite often came to the throne young and reigned for prodigious periods of time – Archidamus was *de facto* king in the Eurypontid line for a great part of Herodotus' lifetime, c. 476-427; and Pleistoanax son of Pausanias managed a similar stretch, 459-409, albeit with some coming and going. But even so it seems perverse to call a reign of 30 years 'short'. On the face of it this seems to resemble Herodotus' comment on Themistocles in 480, that he had 'recently come to the forefront', but as we shall see, that *suggestio falsi* is part of an elaborate dramatic entry for the hero. No such dramatic motive can be traced here, and it seems that Herodotus is either guilty of a chronological slip – not having done his sums, as it were, between Maeandrius and Leotychidas – or else he is no less carelessly reproducing part of a hostile package of information supplied to him by friends in Sparta.

Herodotus makes controversy surround Cleomenes from the moment of his accession, if not from his very birth. He is mentioned briefly in Book III in the Maeandrius episode, but the first substantial treatment of him comes in a long digression, triggered off, as so often, by a search for allies from outside – in this instance, by Aristagoras of Miletus. Herodotus is very naturally intrigued by the story of King Anaxandridas and his two wives. His second wife came from the family of the famous ephor Chilon, Sparta's representative among the Seven Sages. Curiously this linked Cleomenes with his future colleague and enemy Damaratus, for he – taking literally the Spartan custom of marriage by capture – carried off Percalos upon whom Leotychidas had had his eye; and Percalos may have been first cousin to Cleomenes' mother.[34] (Lest this be thought to throw the generations out of phase, Herodotus tells us that Archidamus married his aunt, or rather his father's half-sister, who was demonstrably younger than himself.)

Anaxandridas' second (bigamous) marriage, urged upon him by the ephors, had the desired result, a male heir in the person of Cleomenes. Herodotus implies what is probable enough in itself, that Anaxandridas promptly returned to his first love, taking no further interest in Cleomenes' mother or perhaps in the child himself; for when, shortly after, his original wife unexpectedly became pregnant, Cleomenes' mother's family made a great to-do – presumably because they feared a threat to Cleomenes' rights of succession – and the ephors were obliged to witness the birth of Dorieus.

---

[34] v.41, vi.65; cf. Plut. *Lycurgus*, 15. Archidamus: vi.71—Sparta was evidently not very strict about prohibited degrees: Anaxandridas' first wife was his sister's daughter; Leonidas' his half-brother's daughter (v.39, vii.239).

If that was so, their fears were not unfounded, because when the half-brothers reached manhood, Dorieus evidently thought he had a better claim to the succession on personal merit. Herodotus supports this view, saying that Cleomenes had gained the throne not through merit but strict primogeniture – the Spartans followed their usual custom in going for the first-born, ignoring Anaxandridas' marital pecularities; and that he was, if anything, 'slightly mad', while Dorieus was the finest young man of all his generation.

Cleomenes' Controversial Reign

When Cleomenes was confirmed as successor Dorieus was bitterly resentful, and, 'unable to bear the thought of having Cleomenes as king over him', asked the Spartan authorities for a body of men and left for a colonising venture in Libya. The area was one of some interest to Sparta: Cyrene, the leading Greek city of north Africa, was her granddaughter colony (through the island of Thera), and trade links between Sparta and Cyrene were quite strong.[35] But Dorieus' enterprise did not prosper. He cut short the formalities (failing to consult Delphi), provoked the Carthaginians and was back in the Peloponnese in less than three years. He took the precaution of consulting Delphi for his next scheme, a similar attempt in western Sicily (another area of Carthaginian influence). The encouraging reply he received was falsified by events. After intervening in the war between Sybaris and Croton, on behalf of the latter, he and his party duly reached Sicily; but they fell foul of the Punic colonies, and most of them, including Dorieus, were killed.

Dorieus' adventures are of no very profound interest except for the light they shed on the man himself: if he really was the *beau ideal*, a 'very model' of a Spartan prince, one cannot help feeling that he ought to have done better; though whether his double failure was the result of poor planning, mismanagement or his own evident impatience, we cannot say. Herodotus tells us rather more than we need to know about his activities in southern Italy and Sicily, probably for no better reason than that he possessed the information from his own residence there.[36]

Chronologically, the first event of Cleomenes' reign is his appearance in the vicinity of Plataea with an army in 519. The Plataeans, at war with

---

[35] H points out that men from Thera acted as Dorieus' guides (v.42).

[36] 'Dorieus' is obviously a significant name (=Dorian) and as such *may* represent a reaction by King Anaxandridas against the policy of 'peaceful co-existence' between the Spartans and the pre-Dorian or Achaean peoples of the Peloponnese—a policy usually associated with the great Chilon, Cleomenes' ancestor. Is the name then a protest against his enforced and unwanted second marriage? This is not strictly relevant to H, and cannot be gone into here (though cf. Cleomenes' remark on the Athenian acropolis). It is the subject of an interesting argument by George Forrest, *History of Sparta* pp. 74–7, 82 f. For H in Southern Italy, see Ch. 6, p. 212.

Thebes, were in difficulties and appealed to Cleomenes for aid. He advised them rather to put themselves into the hands of Athens – 'they are close at hand, and they are no mean protectors'.[37] Herodotus adds that this was not out of goodwill for Plataea, but rather to cause trouble between Athens and the Boeotians. He was of course writing at a time when bad relations between Athens and Thebes were one of the constants of Greek diplomatic life. It is not obvious that this was necessarily so in 519, but it certainly was in 506, when one of the early threats to the Cleisthenic democracy came from Boeotia. In any case, the whole business suggests the cunning and ingenuity that emerges from some other passages of Cleomenes' career. 'Divide and rule' was now established Spartan policy in relation to her Arcadian allies and the rest of the Peloponnese (as far as her influence extended); Cleomenes' action was carrying the process one stage further, north of the Isthmus. Sparta was on good terms with Hippias of Athens in 519 and had no reason to be on bad terms with Thebes so far as is known. But Athens was even more closely connected with Argos – Hippias' stepmother, Timonassa, was an Argive lady[38] – and Cleomenes can hardly have been blind to the possibilities of future awkwardness there. On the other hand no one could have construed his action as anything other than friendly to Athens at that moment; it was the Thebans who suffered by having their claim to the headship of Boeotia infringed. It was masterly diplomacy, and no one can read Thucydides' third book without being struck by the bitterness of the Thebans towards Plataea because of her friendship with Athens. On this occasion Athens and Thebes did indeed come to blows despite the mediation of Corinth, and Athens was victorious.

As to what Cleomenes was doing up north with an army, we can only guess. Perhaps he was securing the loyalty of the government in Megara, whose tyranny Sparta had abolished more than 40 years earlier.

Quite soon after this Maeandrius of Samos came to Sparta. As we saw in Chapter 3, he fled when Persian forces occupied the island in order to install Syloson as puppet tyrant. He must have had some hopes of winning support from Sparta, because in the reign of Cleomenes' predecessors Sparta had seen fit to send an expeditionary force over to Samos in the unfulfilled hope of evicting the tyrant Polycrates.[39] We do not know what was the motivation behind that expedition: was it one example, rather more ambitious than most, of Sparta expressing her dislike of tyranny (and hoping to gain the alliance of whatever docile régime succeeded it)? Or was it prompted by Polycrates' alliance with Cambyses for the purposes of the

---

[37] vi.108. Actually H says 'the Spartans' gave this advice, although he specifies Cleomenes as the leader of the army.

[38] *Ath. Pol.* 17.

[39] iii.54; this campaign is also discussed in Ch. 3, p. 87. Maeandrius: iii.148.

Egyptian expedition? Whatever the truth was, the considerations cut no ice with Cleomenes. Either he allowed Sparta to learn from her mistake of sending a seaborne expedition so far away or he was not unduly concerned by the thought of Persia taking over the offshore islands of Ionia, or (most probably as I suspect) he recognised that Maeandrius was not the man to put any money on – he seemed to have no support at home, let alone abroad.

Cleomenes emerges well from this episode: Maeandrius attempted to corrupt him with a technique reminiscent of that to which he himself had fallen victim at the court of the satrap Oroetes. But Cleomenes showed himself to be 'a man of the highest integrity', and recognising the danger that other Spartans might be corrupted, went to the ephors and secured his expulsion from the Peloponnese.[40] (It was too early in his reign for him to act entirely on his own initiative, as he did later with Aristagoras.)

Having hinted at Cleomenes' mental instability at the outset of his reign, Herodotus says that at the finish he went quite mad; but as to why, opinions differed. Argives said it was a punishment for an act of gross sacrilege at Argos, Spartans said that it was the result of intemperate drinking habits that he picked up from a Scythian embassy.[41] According to the story, the Scyths proposed an heroic scheme of invasion of the Asian continent (rather as Aristagoras was to do) by way of reprisal for Darius' unsuccessful invasion of their land; this would date the episode to about 512. Evidently the Scyths, like Croesus, were attracted by Sparta's reputation as the acknowledged leader of the Greeks; but they were not likely to succeed where Maeandrius' more modest and realistic proposals had failed.

The chequered history of Spartan intervention, actual or attempted, in Athenian affairs from 512 to 503 has been touched on in passing in earlier chapters.[42] Although it begins after Hippias started to look eastwards for friendship with Persia (or at any rate with Persia's vassal Hippoclus of Lampsacus), it would be a mistake to regard Spartan policy at this stage as opposed to 'Medism'. The dusty answer given to Aristagoras in 499 should dispose of that. Rather, since the murder of Hipparchus, Hippias' reign had grown more oppressive, and when that happened with a tyranny its days were usually numbered. The Delphic oracle, 'influenced' (corruptly or otherwise) by the Alcmeonidae, was urging all Spartans to liberate Athens. Cleomenes himself, as we know, had a somewhat cavalier attitude towards religious formalities and would not necessarily have paid any heed to this; but in such a public matter, Spartan public opinion, notoriously pious,

---

[40] H's phrase; not all of the Peloponnese was actually in Sparta's alliance but that would not deter Spartans from making the claim.

[41] vi.75, 84.

[42] v.62–93: see Ch. 1, pp. 28 f. and Ch. 3, p. 84.

might give a decisive push in the desired direction.

But it is easy to think of cogent reasons why it should have suited Cleomenes to intervene. If Hippias' regime really did seem to be moving towards an inevitable fall, was it not Sparta's plain duty to ensure that the successor regime was one congenial to herself? That was obviously Cleomenes' thinking, but subsequent events were to make him regret his desertion of his former friends the Peisistratidae. We are, incidentally, entitled to speak of 'Cleomenes' policy' here, for he was in personal charge of the second and third expeditions, and commanded the fourth jointly with Damaratus until the latter walked out; the first, under the admiral Anchimolius, was an unqualified failure.

From this series of events Cleomenes does not come out very gloriously. In 510 he was successful in expelling the Peisistratidae only through the lucky chance of capturing the children of Hippias and his party as they were being smuggled out of Attica. However, the deed was done, bloodlessly, and the regime that Cleomenes bequeathed to Athens was a conservative aristocracy led by Isagoras, son of Teisander. So far so good; but when in 508 Cleisthenes the Alcmeonid made his bid for popular support, and was well on the way to getting it, Isagoras called on Cleomenes to prop him up and prevent the democratic reforms. Cleomenes gladly complied – rumour hinted at an affair between him and Isagoras' wife in 510 – and Cleisthenes and his supporters withdrew from Athens: the blood-guilt of the Alcmeonidae, not for the first nor for the last time, was invoked against them.

On his arrival in Athens, Cleomenes attempted to abolish the constitution, including the Council of 400 (soon to be 500), and to replace it with an oligarchic clique of Isagoras' supporters. But the council resisted, the citizens rose *en masse*, and Cleomenes and Isagoras took refuge on the Acropolis. After a short seige they surrendered and left Athens. It was an undignified end to Cleomenes' intervention, for he had achieved none of his aims: he had replaced the basically friendly regime of Hippias and the Peisistratidae with an ungrateful and unreliable democracy. His clumsy handling made it hostile as well.

This was the occasion of his sacrilege on the Acropolis, when Athene's priestess attempted to bar his way: "'Go away, Spartan stranger. . . no Dorian is allowed in here." "Madam, I am no Dorian, but an Achaean"' – and he pushed his way in. Elaborate theories have been erected upon this slight remark, such as that Cleomenes was a supporter of the 'Chilonian' policy of breaking down barriers between Dorians and non-Dorians in the Peloponnese. Possibly he did favour his great ancestor's views. More probably it was a quick repartee – as a (supposed) descendant of Heracles he could claim to outrank any Dorian in pedigree, and the remark gains point when one sees the word used was *Dorieus* – the name of his hated half-brother!

Cleomenes' infelicitous handling of Athenian affairs continued when, with Damaratus (who now enters the story), he assembled an army of Spartans and allies to pay the Athenians back for their insulting treatment of his previous venture. He concealed from his force his other aim, which was to set up Isagoras as tyrant:[43] had such flagrantly inconsistent policy leaked out at the start, the expedition (the biggest so far) would not have got as far as it did, which was to Eleusis on Attic soil. Significantly the contingent from Corinth, a city that had shed its tyranny two generations earlier, was the first to back out of the enterprise, which then collapsed entirely when Damaratus also pulled out. With the two kings no longer unanimous the legitimacy of the expedition was perhaps undermined; in any event it returned home with nothing achieved, and Athens was left free to deal with the Boeotians and Chalcidians of Euboea, whose attacks were supposed to have been synchronised with the Peloponnesian invasion.

Sparta's prestige can scarcely ever have been much lower – almost every strand of her policy had gone wrong. This was, however, another mistake from which she was capable of learning. A rule was introduced prohibiting both kings from participating in the same expedition. Though Herodotus does not say so, we can imagine that a powerful dose of public displeasure fell upon Damaratus, who had let the side down badly: Cleomenes' policy, inconsistent and clumsily executed though it was, at least was seen to be serving Sparta's interests. More importantly, some sort of machinery was set up for consulting the allies before military expeditions and even letting them have some kind of informal vote on the project; there were to be no more blindfold adventures. When the Spartans opened the question of restoring Hippias in c.503 – this time Cleomenes is not named as being responsible – a preliminary meeting of the allies was held, and Sosicles of Corinth got the proposal quashed. This was the first beginning of the formal alliance known to historians today as the 'Peloponnesian League'. It was a major concession by Sparta, for it implied that she could now only lead her allies to war by persuasion and could not command them to follow wherever she might lead.

That particular proposal must have seemed every bit as amazing as Sosicles makes out in the opening words of his speech; the Spartans' justification, or at any rate pretext, for it was a group of oracles that Cleomenes claimed to have picked up on the Athenian Acropolis, and, more especially perhaps, the discovery that their original expulsion of Hippias had been corruptly procured. So much for their opposition to tyranny on principle! Anyway, the upshot was that Sparta now stood on a new footing

---

[43] H (v.74) seems to imply that the entire aim was concealed from the allies. But it is hardly possible to believe that Athens was not at least named as the destination.

in relation to her allies, and it was not to her advantage.

It was not to be expected that Cleomenes would respond to Aristagoras' plea for help in 499. A settled policy of opposition to Medism and to Persian expansion simply had not been reached; Sparta's previous overseas adventure – the attack on Polycrates – had been an unmitigated fiasco; and a war with Argos was in prospect. Herodotus dramatises Aristagoras' appeal exceptionally well: his inflated and unrealistic proposals characterise him nicely but also manage to convey some genuine historical information in a lively and entertaining form. Cleomenes' delayed reply is classically 'laconic'. As in the Maeandrius episode, the king does not succumb to Aristagoras' corrupt overtures, only this time the intervention of his little daughter Gorgo is needed to make quite sure. But it is impossible to say that Cleomenes does not come out of this scene well, on Herodotus' own showing. He makes it clear that the Athenian decision to help Aristagoras was (in his view) quite disastrous; plainly therefore Cleomenes was right. The reasons for his attitude to the Ionian revolt have already been fully discussed;[44] he is not merely judging it according to the outcome.

Herodotus narrates Cleomenes' war with Argos, not in its chronological context, but floating in time as it were: the campaign, and the act of sacrilege Cleomenes committed in the course of it, are brought in to explain his final insanity and death. However, the date can be fixed with reasonable precision. Herodotus links the campaign with the double oracle referring to Miletus and Argos[45] If the oracle is *post eventum*, then Cleomenes' campaign is definitely synchronised with the fall of Miletus in 494; if, as I believe and have argued in Chapter 2, it is genuine, it will have been a response given in 499 to the Argives, enquiring whether or not to support Aristagoras, and so any date in the 490s might be possible. But the campaign does not seem to belong to the last phase of Cleomenes' reign; and the beginning of the decade seems too early if the Argives had indeed not recovered from their disaster by 480;[46] so c. 494 looks right after all.

Herodotus also, presumably for the same reason, does not discuss the cause of the war, merely remarking that Cleomenes had received an oracle from Delphi prophesying the capture of Argos. Very possibly, but that could only have been in answer to an enquiry on his part: he had obviously determined to invade Argive territory. But why? Modern commentators have come up with different possible answers, and it is a testimony to the shallowness of our knowledge of the period that no one explanation seems so compellingly right that it has driven others out of the field. It does not seem to me particularly likely that it was a first manifestation of Cleomenes'

[44] Ch. 4, pp. 117-125.

[45] vi.77 and 19; see Ch. 2, pp. 62 f.

[46] vii.148 f.

policy of opposition to Medism: that only really seems to spring into being in 491, when Aigina's submission to Darius' envoys threatened to bring Persia to Sparta's own back door; nor is there any particular reason for supposing that Argos in the mid-490s was thinking along the lines that she was in 481/0.[47] The one thing to be certain of was that in any foreign war Argos would take the opposite side to Sparta, unless she could wring improbable concessions from her, like a half-share in the command.[48]

Possibly it was in some way connected with Arcadia: that highland region had Argos on its north-east border, and a combination of the two might have been almost fatally dangerous for Sparta. The bizarre episode of Cleomenes' visit to Arcadia in 491/0 suggests that there was a measure of disaffection with the Spartan supremacy: was Cleomenes in 494 trying to nip a grand anti-Spartan coalition in the bud? Herodotus' account[49] leaves us grievously unsatisfied and longing to know more.

Again, it might have been in response to an appeal for aid from the lesser towns in Argos' sphere of influence – Mycenae and Tiryns preferring alliance with distant Sparta to subjection to neighbouring Argos. They sent a joint contingent to the allies at Plataea in 479,[50] though Argos regained possession of them a decade or so later. Or was Argos planning one of her periodical attempts to reassert control over those neighbours of hers that were by now allies of Sparta – Epidaurus and Troizen? (Thucydides describes how Argos had a go at Epidaurus in 419/8, without success.[51]) Or did Cleomenes merely think that Argos was looking uncomfortably strong, and that if she were not checked, Sparta's hard-won leadership of the Peloponnese would be jeopardised? The Peloponnesian War of 431, after all, was launched on the proposition that the power of Athens 'had increased, was increasing and ought to be diminished'.

Without too much confidence I incline to the last of these views, mainly on account of the sequel: as we shall see, Cleomenes adopted a murderous policy that must have been intended to cripple Argos without obliterating her.

The campaign itself need not detain us long, for Herodotus' account of it is quite efficient. Striking northwards in orthodox fashion overland, Cleomenes was checked by the unfavourable appearance of his sacrifice at

---

[47] Though R.A. Tomlinson, *Argos and the Argolid* (Routledge, London, 1972), p. 95 f., points out that unobtrusive contacts between Persia and the Greek states are highly probable, even though they have made no mark in the histories. 'To Argos, whose authority and territory had been eroded by Spartan success . . . the temptation of Persian support was doubtless considerable.'

[48] vii.148.

[49] vi.74.

[50] ix.28; the status of Tiryns in 479 is actually a bit more complicated owing to its occupation by the 'slaves' (vi.83).

[51] Th.v.53 ff.

the crossing of the river Erasinos, a little way over the border in Argive territory. Although Cleomenes did not take the formalities of religion at all seriously – Herodotus treats us to a brief catalogue of his acts of sacrilege[52] – most other Spartans did, and we would be unwise to think that Cleomenes could in some way lean upon his soothsayers so as to produce the answers that he wanted. In particular, if it got out among the troops that bad omens were being ignored, the effects on morale can be imagined. (Cleomenes' force on this occasion, incidentally, was Spartan only; Herodotus makes no mention of allies but only helots in attendance.) He was however at least partly prepared for such a check because he was able instead to embark his force on Sparta's east coast and sail to the Argolid, somewhere near Nauplia (now the pleasant seaside town of Nafplion).

Fairly near there the battle of Sepeia was fought. The Argives fell for an 'Aigospotamoi' stratagem and lost heavily. The survivors fled for refuge to a sacred grove; some were tempted out by the promise of ransom and slaughtered; many others were burnt alive when Cleomenes had the wood fired. Herodotus says that the brushwood was laid and the fire started by helots: we may well imagine that no Spartan (apart perhaps from Cleomenes himself!) would have dared incur the guilt of personally burning down a sacred grove.

This act of treachery and ruthlessness was not only un-Greek,[53] it was in particular un-Spartan. Generally speaking, the Spartans' view of battle was that it was a contest of quality: they fought to win an admitted decision (as in an Olympic wrestling bout), not to annihilate the foe. Systematic pursuit and butchery of a defeated army did not normally figure in their scheme of things. The 'battle of the 300 champions' is perhaps an exaggerated example, but a similar attitude can be detected at Plataea in 479 (where they rejected the proposal of the Mantineans to pursue the retreating Persians), at Mantinea in 418 (Thucydides explicitly makes this point at the conclusion of his narrative) and at Coronea in 394.

Herodotus later states that 6,000 Argives lost their lives in this episode.[54] Such a total seems incredibly high, and perhaps represents a statement of one of his informants to the effect that the entire Argive army was wiped out. In any case the casualties were serious enough to permit a political revolution in Argos. The dramatic loss of hoplites – who in all Greek states represented the propertied classes – allowed a new government of 'slaves' to take over. This is not likely to mean chattel slaves who were bought and sold; it might mean serfs who resembled Sparta's helots; or even conceivably members of the free but unpropertied labouring

---

[52] vi.75 (end) and 81.

[53] See Tomlinson, *Argos*, p. 94; '300': i.82; Plataea: ix.77; cf. Th.v.73; X. *Hell.* iv.3.20 f.

[54] vii.148.

class. In democratic Athens of course these *thetes* formed the bulk of the citizen body; elsewhere they were unenfranchised, and if this last explanation is the right one the appellation 'slaves' will have been contemptuously fixed upon them by some of the dispossessed aristocrats. However this may be, if Cleomenes was deliberately aiming at an advantageous change of regime in Argos (as is quite possible), he must have been as disappointed as he had been in Athens. There is no reason to think that the 'slave' regime was any more amicably disposed towards Sparta than its predecessor had been.[55]

After a brief visit to the Argive Heraion, where he secured admission to offer sacrifice by the simple expedient of having the priest soundly thrashed by his helots, Cleomenes returned home to face trial. The charge was that he had received a bribe not to capture Argos, when it was in his power to do so. This raises some interesting questions: suppose Cleomenes had taken Argos, what would he have done with it? Not destroyed it – that would have scandalised all Greek sentiment in that age. It was in later and crueller generations that, among other places, Plataea, Olynthus and Thebes herself were erased from the map. Herodotus tells us how the destruction of Sybaris by the Crotoniates in 510 produced a horrified reaction in Miletus: Greek cities were not supposed to do that sort of thing to one another.[56]

In reality the only thing Cleomenes could have done was to install a pro-Spartan régime (there could have been no question of annexation, for what with the helots and her own restricted manpower, Sparta was almost at full stretch already) and he possibly thought that that would occur spontaneously. If so, he was wrong. The defence to the charge that Herodotus attributes to him is amusing: the wood was called 'the grove of Argos' (the mythological hero) and by taking it he had fulfilled the literal text of the oracle that he would 'capture Argos'. In the mouth of Cleomenes such scruples are frankly cynical; the Spartans characteristically regarded his explanation as entirely satisfactory! As we saw in Chapter 4, however, it was very much in Sparta's general interest that Argos remain in existence as a potential threat, in order to preserve the loyalty of her allies in the northern Peloponnese.

What was arguably Cleomenes' finest hour came in 491. Aigina had assisted Sparta under duress in the Sepeia campaign – Herodotus records that Cleomenes had 'impressed' some of her ships as transports[57] – and by 491 she was evidently a somewhat reluctant member of Sparta's formal alliance. When Aigina's rulers gave earth and water to Persia, the

---

[55] The 'slave' question is more fully discussed in Tomlinson, *Argos*, p. 97 ff.

[56] vi.21.

[57] vi.92.

Athenians, supposing that this action was aimed at them, complained to Sparta. Cleomenes lost no time in crossing in person to the island and demanding the surrender of those responsible. But his quarrel with Damaratus, dormant or otherwise, flared up again. The latter had been briefing the islanders on how to thwart Cleomenes, and on some sort of technicality hinging on the consent of both kings they succeeded in keeping Cleomenes at bay.

Damaratus may have won the engagement but he lost the war. In one of his rare expressions of praise for the man, Herodotus says that Cleomenes in Aigina was 'working for the common benefit of Greece', while Damaratus 'slandered him – not so much because he was concerned for Aigina, but out of envy and malice'. It was a fatal blunder. Cleomenes set in motion the train of events that ended in Damaratus' degradation. He showed cunning and tactical skill in taking steps to find an eligible successor to Damaratus (Leotychidas was in fact his second cousin) who would also be pliable; in using Leotychidas to impugn Damaratus' legitimacy; and in bribing Delphi to produce the answer required.

So Damaratus had to go, and Cleomenes, now with a royal colleague who stood in relation to him as a client to his patron, returned to Aigina. The islanders could no longer invoke the small print against him, and ten most distinguished hostages were taken and placed in the custody of the Athenians – of all people! Persia got no joy at all from Aigina in 490.

Cleomenes' otherwise masterly handling of the crisis was too brisk for the requirements of secret diplomacy: the truth about Delphi and the bribe came out embarrassingly soon, thus opening the last and most curious phase of his life. He fled (or was he forced to flee?) from Sparta; whether this was the result of Spartan indignation at the sacrilege (gross even by Cleomenes' standards) or at the removal of the presumably popular Damaratus is not clear. His place of first resort was Thessaly, why or with what result we do not know. That people was under the leadership of the aristocratic clan of the Aleuadae; they were later to lead Thessaly's submission to Persia before Xerxes' invasion. He next turned up in Arcadia where, with typical energy, he tried to organise a confederate body of chiefs with a view to attacking Sparta and presumably reinstating himself as head of a revolutionary government there. The Arcadians, like the Thessalians, were an *ethnos*, a people bound together by ties of race and dialect, not at all like the city-state society of Athens and Sparta; and what would have happened if Cleomenes had succeeded must remain a matter for speculation. It seems certain that the traditional forms of Spartan government and society would have been overthrown if Cleomenes had established his personal power; whether he actually went so far as to tamper with Sparta's helots is less certain; Herodotus says nothing of it.[58]

These goings-on so alarmed the Spartan authorities that they recalled Cleomenes and reinstated him as king. But now his mental condition, so Herodotus tells us, took a turn for the worse. When he started hitting in the face with his stick any Spartan he met, he was put in the stocks by his kinsmen – presumably his half-brothers Leonidas and Cleombrotus. There, with the connivance of his helot warder, he committed suicide by revolting self-mutilation.

True or false? Medical diagnosis or psychoanalysis of historical figures is notoriously difficult. Obviously the truth may have been that he was murdered, having been lured back by false promises of security. There were many, from Leonidas downwards, who would have welcomed his death. On the other hand Herodotus' account, suicide and all, has been taken seriously as an early description, reasonably accurate as far as it goes, of a variety of clinical paranoia.[59]

In discussing Herodotus' portrait of Cleomenes we must be on our guard against circular arguments: to judge the picture to be hostile because we accept the truth of Cleomenes' mental instability is no better than to accept the mental instability on the strength of a generally hostile portrait. Is there anything else to go on? Are there passages of Cleomenes' life that might have given the Spartans good and sufficient reason for posthumously condemning his memory? In attempting to answer this question we should not forget that Cleomenes left no son to rehabilitate his name, being succeeded by his half-brother Leonidas; his 'client' Leotychidas died in disgrace, being succeeded by his grandson Archidamus; and he probably had only known Cleomenes as a child and in any case could have had no reason to rewrite accepted history. The answer, if there is one, must be sought in the undoubted facts of Cleomenes' reign.

Nowadays one sometimes reads of Cleomenes being referred to as a great king, a strong and successful king, and so on.[60] In fact this is questionable. There is no doubt that he was energetic and active, and for much of his longish reign had a strong personal influence on policy, but that does not of itself constitute greatness. Often he assessed events rightly: his diplomacy over Plataea was masterly, his rejection of Maeandrius was a fair

---

[58] There are some scattered and uncertain pieces of evidence that do suggest helot trouble in 490, which are usefully and impartially summarised by Paul Cartledge, *Sparta and Laconia* (Routledge, London, 1979), p. 153 f. Probably the weightiest argument against the acceptance of them is that if there had been a helot revolt at about the time of Marathon, it is extraordinary that Herodotus should not have heard of it; or, if he had, that he did not give it as a reason for the Spartans' late arrival, much more convincing than the pretext of religion actually adopted (vi.106).

[59] Forrest, *History of Sparta*, p. 93, argues for this and suggests that Cl.'s sometimes seemingly inconsistent behaviour forms a consistent psychological picture of a man under heavy long-term mental strain.

[60] E.g. How & Wells, Appx XVII.

verdict on the man himself, and his similar treatment of Aristagoras can be similarly judged – the man was not a winner and Cleomenes did not want to back a loser. His smashing of Argos is harder to justify in itself, but – a result surely unintended in 494 – it did mean that when the Persian threat materialised, Argos was in no fit state to render any positive assistance. That campaign was of great, albeit accidental, benefit to Greece in the medium term. Finally, the way he rose to the occasion in 491 to help his former enemies in Athens against the Medisers of Aigina is an example of Spartan policy – 'working for the general benefit of Greece' – at its best.

On the other hand his handling of the Athenian question was fumbling and unsure. His misreading of the political temper of Athens led directly to the establishment of an unfriendly democratic government there, the very opposite of what was in Sparta's best interests. Then, in his attempts to dispose of the democracy, he succeeded in antagonising his fellow king Damaratus, and Sparta's most important ally Corinth. The result of the latter was the formalising of the Spartan alliance ('Peloponnesian League'), giving the allies some rights to argue about, and if necessary to veto, unwelcome Spartan initiatives. This certainly benefited Greece but it was a weakening of Sparta's power. Again, while the proposal to replace the democracy by a pro-Spartan tyranny would *ex hypothesi* be good for Sparta, the ideological somersault involved in this manoeuvre would have left her deeply discredited in the wider world, not least among those of her allies who had thrown off their own tyrannies: Sosicles of Corinth was right.

Herodotus gives us too many separate examples of Cleomenes as a profaner of religion for this side of him to be dismissed as hostile invention. It has to be accepted, I think, that a robust attitude to religious scruples was as much a part of his nature as greed and unscrupulousness were of Themistocles'; and in an age when 'enlightenment' had barely begun to dawn, when most Greeks, and certainly most Spartans, were firm believers in their gods, this must have been alarming to live with.[61] As to how far he could be allowed to go, the facts seem to speak for themselves: by bribing Delphi he went too far for Spartan opinion to overlook – when, that is, the scandal broke.

But from the Spartan point of view Cleomenes committed the ultimate crime. The position of the highly privileged Spartan citizen (Spartiate) – minority was precariously poised at the apex of an elaborate social structure. Much of the mental and physical energy of the Spartan governing class was devoted to the preservation of this order – Spartiates, Perioikoi, Hypomeiones (Inferiors), Neodamodeis (Freedmen) and helots. One of the first commandments drummed into every young Spartiate must have been: don't rock the boat. Cleomenes did rock the boat. What he did, or was

---

[61] See Ch. 2, p. 59 for a later example of popular reaction to gross sacrilege.

threatening to do, from his base in Arcadia was so intimidating that the Spartan authorities were willing, even anxious, to have him back, for all his faults, in order to halt a potentially destructive process. (Unless, of course, he was treacherously lured back in order to be murdered.)

There are parallels between the careers of Cleomenes and of his nephew Pausanias (another boat-rocker). Both were men of energy and ability. Both aspired to some sort of personal power that transcended the limits of the Spartan constitution. Pausanias perhaps had more excuse, for his power as a mere regent was a dwindling asset; whereas Cleomenes' tenure of the throne would have been unchallenged but for his final corrupting of Delphi. As we shall discuss later in this chapter, it seems highly probable that Thucydides' account of Pausanias' last days is the product of a Spartan attempt to justify his judicial murder.[62] Whether the same is true of Herodotus' picture of Cleomenes' end must remain an open question. There is no way of deciding whether the story of his suicide was the truth or a cover-up for murder.[63] But Herodotus must be acquitted of uncritical hostility in his general portrait of Cleomenes. As we have seen, his reign had its successes and its failures. Cleomenes was at times guilty of errors of judgement and of faulty political tactics, with results that were damaging to Sparta. In the age in which he lived, a propensity to sacrilege might easily – and justifiably – be construed as evidence of mental instability. But Cleomenes receives full credit from Herodotus for the stifling of Aigina's Medism, a policy which saved Athens and Greece.

No account of Cleomenes would be complete without some mention of his ready tongue. 'I am no Dorian [or 'Dorieus'] but an Achaean' neatly side-stepped the objection of Athene's priestess on the Acropolis. On his Argive campaign, as we saw, he was prevented from crossing the river Erasinos when his sacrifice to the river god produced unfavourable omens. 'Admirable of Erasinos not to betray his fellow citizens – all the same, the Argives won't escape!' and he switched to sea transport. Finally there was his exchange with Crius son of Polycritus, one of the two leaders of Aigina's ruling oligarchy, on the occasion of his first, unsuccessful attempt to arrest the Medisers. 'You won't get away with arresting a single man in Aigina' said Crius (whose name means 'Ram'); 'you can't be acting with the authority of Sparta, but must have been bribed by Athens, otherwise you'd have come with the other king to make the arrests.' 'What's your name?' said Cleomenes. 'Crius'. 'Well then, Mister Ram, get your horns sheathed in bronze: you're heading for big trouble.' Antiquity admired puns more than

---

[62] Page 202, note 115.

[63] Not even A.R. Burn's useful concept of 'public fact' can be invoked here, for Cleomenes' confinement to the stocks does not seem to have been in public view. H, incidentally, was writing of Cleom. at roughly the same interval of time as Th. wrote of Pausanias.

the twentieth century does, but this spontaneous example deserves its mention.[64]

Cleomenes could be cunning and devious, but was ruthless and single-minded in pursuit of an objective he really desired. It is a remarkable picture.

Damaratus, King and Exile

Of the circumstances of Damaratus' birth Herodotus tells us quite a lot, with copious romantic trimmings. Of him as king, however, we do not hear much. We have noticed his initial quarrel with Cleomenes on the Athenian expedition of 507/6. Herodotus says nothing of what lay behind it: was it sympathy for the Athenian democracy? Probably not, for nothing in the rest of Damaratus' career supports that. More probably it was disgust at the cynical reversal of policy by Cleomenes – to expel one tyrant and to seek to install another in less than four years. It might have been sufficient to say that the two men simply did not get on, and they probably did not; but Herodotus does go out of his way to say that there was no previous difference between them.

For 15 years the quarrel was seemingly dormant; at any rate we learn nothing of its progress until the Aigina episode, when Damaratus tried, successfully at first, to thwart Cleomenes' arrest of the leading Medisers. Herodotus criticises him for slandering Cleomenes out of spite, while the latter was working for the benefit of Greece.[65] (That is the strongest thing that Herodotus ever says about Damaratus, who is generally depicted with sympathy.) However this opposition cost him his throne when Cleomenes and Leotychidas got the question of his legitimacy opened, and, with the help of Delphi, established their case.

It is very difficult to tell what Damaratus was up to. Was he simply trying to spite Cleomenes? Or was this action definitely connected with the question of 'Medism'? His subsequent career – flight to Persia, generous gifts from Darius and so on – lends colour to the latter view; but Persia provided a refuge for all sorts of fallen potentates and it would be unwise to infer previous Medising tendencies from subsequent residence in Persia. Look at the case of Themistocles! If there is anything in this view, however, it suggests that Damaratus believed that successful resistance to Persia would be impossible; that the right policy would be to make the best terms available while Sparta was still in being, with her manpower undiminished and her institutions unimpaired. If Damaratus did take that view, he was certainly far from unique in Greece: Darius' heralds must have been

---

[64] vi.50.

[65] vi.61.

embarrassed by the quantities of earth and water they received in 491.

Damaratus was evidently popular in Sparta. When he was deposed he still had enough supporters on hand to elect him straight away into a magistracy – whether the ephorate or another, Herodotus does not specify. To judge from his dignified retort to Leotychidas' taunt – 'What's it like being a magistrate after having been king?' – the latter had never been popular enough to get elected to such an office.[66] During his reign he had won the Olympic four-horse chariot race, and Herodotus implies that he had the victory attributed to his city not himself. The second half of the sixth century saw the beginning of a long period of dominance by Sparta in this most prestigious event, and the personal and public kudos won by Damaratus can be imagined. (We saw in Chapter 1 how Athenian magnates strove to build up political capital by successful chariot-racing.) Still, none of this sufficed to save him in 491, nor did his 'high distinction in the eyes of the Spartans, both in action and in counsel'.[67] It is a pity that nothing in Herodotus' account of his actual reign bears out this glowing testimonial.

Herodotus reports, credibly enough, that Damaratus decided to get out of Sparta when it became clear to him that he was not going to be allowed to enjoy even his subordinate position unmolested. His flight, a clockwise chase round the west coast of Greece, like Themistocles' years later, kept him ahead of his pursuers and brought him to Persia, where a new chapter opened in his life.

Herodotus no doubt met and talked to Damaratus' family on the generous estates that Darius gave to him, and probably got from them an account of what they conceived to be his role in the story: his arguments which ensured the succession for Xerxes (a claim that Herodotus treats with well-justified scepticism, bearing in mind that Xerxes was Queen Atossa's son); his advice to Xerxes to split the fleet and capture Cythera (which may very possibly be authentic); perhaps the curious and not very important tale of Dicaeus the Athenian exile, in whose company Damaratus witnessed a portent of disaster for Xerxes' fleet; possibly the story of his secret message to Sparta that only Leonidas' wife Gorgo could penetrate; if that tale came from a Spartan source one feels that Herodotus would pass it on with more confidence and fewer qualifications than he does.[68]

But the most remarkable part of the story is much more likely to be Herodotus' own invention – the lifelike characterisation of Damaratus as an adviser to Xerxes. Herodotus puts into his mouth a number of speeches that are, in the familiar manner, vehicles for the discussion of issues or for

---

[66] vi.67.

[67] vi.70; this aspect of Spartan life is discussed by G.E.M. de Ste Croix, *The Origins of the Peloponnesian War* (Duckworth, London, 1972), p. 354 f.

[68] Respectively, vii.3, vii.235, vii.239, viii.65.

getting across some important non-narrative truths. It is a piece of singular boldness on Herodotus' part to use an exiled Mediser – in effect, a traitor to Greece – as a mouthpiece for historical discussion, but he carries it off with remarkable skill.

'Who are the Spartans?' asked Cyrus, when their embassy warned him to leave Ionia alone. A fair proportion of Book VII is taken up with Cyrus' second cousin, twice removed, learning the answer. Much of Xerxes' enlightenment comes from Damaratus. He first appears when the Persian host has crossed into Europe and Xerxes asks his opinion about likely resistance from the Greeks.[69] After checking that the king can take the truth, Damaratus proceeds: all the Dorians are good, but the Spartans are exceptional. 'There are no circumstances under which they will accept overtures from you that bring slavery to Greece; and again, they will oppose you even if all the rest of Greece comes to terms with you . . . they will fight you, whether there are a thousand of them, or more, or fewer.' Xerxes laughs, understandably regarding this as empty boastfulness, but Damaratus sticks to his guns.

> I knew all along that the truth would not please you . . . you know very well how fond I am of the Spartans, as things are now – they robbed me of my inheritance, they drove me into exile . . . but the Spartans, fighting individually, are as good as any man; together, they are the best that there are. They are free, but not in every respect: their master is Law, which they fear more than your subjects fear you. They do whatever it commands, and its command never varies: they must never flee from any multitude of men in battle, but must stand in the line and win or perish.

This reverence for 'Law' seems ironical in the mouth of one who had lost his throne as the result of a corrupt intrigue, but in the context this irony at least is plainly not intended: Cleomenes, the author of his degradation, was anything but a typical Spartan. (As we shall consider in the next chapter, however, Herodotus *was* intending to be ironical in a quite different sense.)

Damaratus' forecast is proved correct when there is no flight from the position at Thermopylae. He is called to Xerxes to explain the curious sight of the Spartans exercising themselves and combing their hair, despite the proximity of the Persians in force. 'They have come to fight us for the pass, and they are making themselves ready for that' – no modern soldier can miss the connection between turnout and discipline on the battlefield – 'and

---

[69] vii.101–4; Cyrus: i.152.

if you defeat them, and those who are left behind in Sparta, no other people will raise a hand against you.'[70] Again Xerxes was unconvinced, but he had the grace to admit that Damaratus was right after the Spartans' heroic stand. 'You are a good man, Damaratus . . . everything has turned out as you said it would: now – how many other Spartans are there? How many of them are as good soldiers as these – or are they all as good?' Damaratus explains by differentiating between the citizens of Sparta proper – 8,000 in number, all as good as the heroes of Thermopylae – and the Perioikoi of Lacedaemon, who, though good, are not quite in the same class. 'How am I to defeat them? As their ex-king you must know the lines of their policy.' Damaratus then advised Xerxes to detach a powerful squadron of the fleet to seize the isle of Cythera. The strategical issue here has been discussed in Chapter 4 and there is no need to re-cover the ground, except to repeat that the proposal seems credible: if it were successful, it would result in Damaratus' restoration to the Spartan throne with relatively few casualties and consequently little bitterness. The prospect of a mobile sea-borne enemy raiding their coasts in force and fomenting revolts among the helots would have brought the Spartans to terms quickly enough. But as Achaemenes' fleet even undivided was not adequate to defeat the Greeks at Salamis, his objection to Damaratus' scheme may be readily understood. In accepting Achaemenes' arguments, Xerxes nevertheless praised Damaratus' sincerity and devotion to his interests.[71]

Of the notable personalities in Herodotus, Damaratus is one of the more difficult to bring to life. He was obviously a nice chap who did not antagonise people in the way that the abrasive Cleomenes did. Nice chaps are not always gifted with political vision, however, and this Damaratus lacked. His passion for sport – one did not win the Olympic crown without passionate commitment – and the story of his robbing Leotychidas of his intended bride suggest that he may have been something of a 'blade'. His talks with Xerxes breathe an air of candour and straightforwardness; he was grateful to Persia for his generous treatment and did not abuse his privileged position. If straightforwardness was indeed a feature of his character, that would explain his opposition to Cleomenes' volte-face in 507/6.

That he sincerely loved Sparta is not in doubt, but the way he chose to preserve Sparta's institutions, at the price of acknowledging Persian supremacy, was not one that commended itself to his fellow countrymen. As an exile, Damaratus possibly deluded himself that he could secure favourable terms for Sparta under Xerxes. The secret message he is said to have sent to Sparta warning of the coming invasion is at least as likely to

---

[70] vii.209.

[71] vii.234–7; cf. Ch. 4, p. 143.

have resulted from goodwill as from a desire to gloat; Herodotus mentions both possibilities. As ruler of Sparta under Xerxes he would have been, perhaps, a Marshal Pétain rather than a Major Quisling, honestly convinced that he had secured the best deal possible for his countrymen in the face of overpowering odds, and professing to the last his devotion to his native land. As it was, he lived in Persia for 20 years and more, long enough to know Themistocles.[72]

THEMISTOCLES

Before the War

Herodotus' accounts of the Marathon campaign in 490 and Xerxes' great invasion of 480 can be faulted in some respects, as we examined in Chapter 4, but they will always remain the foundation for the historical study of those years, and for all their shortcomings do contain a great deal of solid gold to reward the enquirer. All the more disappointing, therefore, is his account of the intervening years 489–481. As regards Persia, he opens Book VII by mentioning Darius' plans to avenge Marathon – nothing very surprising in that – and the revolt of Egypt, soon followed by the old king's death. His successor Xerxes rightly concerned himself with the reconquest of Egypt before renewing the attempt on Greece. Herodotus suggests that Darius had planned to launch both expeditions at the same time. We may doubt whether that shrewd monarch entertained any such unwise notion; Egypt was much too precious a province to take any chances with. (The Greeks tended to imagine that they, and policy relating to them, were always uppermost in the thoughts of Persian kings.)

That is probably all, or nearly all, that we need to know on the Persian side; enough to tell us why the great invasion did not take place until ten years after Marathon. Had it occurred at the scheduled time, say 486 or 485, the result must surely have been disaster for Greece, as the foundations had not then been laid for Athens' sea power.

It is on the Greek side that we feel Herodotus' inadequacies most keenly. Take the case of Sparta. The decade opened with two new kings. As we saw, Damaratus was forced to make way for Leotychidas in 491, and the long and controversial reign of Cleomenes ended with his strange death soon after; his half-brother Leonidas succeeded him. The policy of Cleomenes in his last days had been staunchly opposed to Medism, and Leotychidas was effectively in his pocket. With the death of his patron, the attitude of the latter might be difficult to gauge; and what of Leonidas' views?

---

[72] Plut. *Them.* 29.

Themistocles: the 'Ostia bust,' a good Roman copy of, probably, a contemporary original. The features are not idealized, and, without being too fanciful, one may detect in them shrewdness and a touch of humour. (Deutsches Archäologisches Institut, Rome)

Of all these and other crucial matters Herodotus gives only tantalising hints. But Sparta seems to have wavered – we would dearly love to know more. Darius' heralds who demanded submission in 491 were murdered by the Spartans and, when it was known that Xerxes was preparing his great expedition, 'numerous meetings of the assembly were held where the crier proclaimed "Is any man willing to die for Sparta?"' This sequence of events, especially the many assemblies, is unparalleled in Spartan history. Two members of the Spartan aristocracy, Sperthias and Bulis, came forward as volunteers to go to Xerxes and offer themselves as expiatory sacrifices, supposedly to appease the 'wrath of Talthybius', legendary patron of heralds. Is there also a hint here that they might also have appeased Xerxes and averted the coming war? If so, this religious diplomacy failed, for Xerxes, with the usual courtly generosity, did not accept their self-sacrifice and sent them home.[73] There are hints, too, of trouble in the Peloponnese between Sparta and her allies: Tegea is a certain example, Elis a possible one. The latter was Damaratus' original place of refuge; Mardonius' seer Hegesistratus of Elis 'had done Sparta many an injury' before escaping from them; and Elis' generals brought their contingent too late to Plataea – for which they were banished. Tegea at least fought well on the loyalist side.[74]

The treatment of Athens is if anything even less satisfactory. The period was a formative one in every respect. At home the democracy, entering its third decade, was growing in self-confidence and beginning to break away from old habits of deference to the aristocracy. The law of ostracism was used successfully for the first time, and used with a frequency that would not be matched in any future decade. The Athenian people were divided by burning political issues that affected the entire destiny of the state, and their protagonists were no pygmies but men of stature and quality. In foreign affairs a war was being prosecuted with the neighbouring island of Aigina – prosecuted with no great vigour on either side, to be sure, but the attendant ill-feeling was a portent of trouble when the Persian attack should be renewed.

Little of this is treated in its context; some of it (not much) occurs in flashbacks; and in Book VII we discover why. After his lengthy description of Xerxes' forces and narrative of his march, Herodotus switches to Greece – first, the story of Sperthias and Bulis, then the gallantry of Athens, especially after the bloodcurdling oracles given to Athens by Delphi. This was Athens' blackest moment. 'The oracle specialists took it to mean that they were bound to be defeated in a sea battle off Salamis. But there was an Athenian who had recently come to the forefront: his name was Themistocles, known as Neocles' son' – and he produced a less intimidating interpretation of the oracle's words that was at once accepted as correct, and the policies that flowed from it proved to be the salvation of Athens and of Greece. What a splendid introduction to this great personality, the hero of 480! Herodotus could have mentioned him many times earlier, but delays his entry on to the stage until the moment when all hope for his city seems lost. I do not accept at all the idea that hostile sources are responsible for the *suggestio falsi*; on the contrary, Herodotus has distorted the literal truth

---

[73] vii.134–7. H's story is undated and is often put after 479, e.g. by A.R. Burn, *Persia and the Greeks* p. 321 f.; it seems more natural to place it during the period of uncertainty than after the allied victory. H's main interest in the story lies in the fulfilment of destiny—Aneristus and Nicolaus, the sons of Sperthias and Bulis, were put to death in 430 when serving on an embassy. It also gives him an opportunity for a meaningful exchange of views between the pair and Hydarnes, in which they reject the idea of friendship with the king and sing the praises of liberty.

[74] ix.37 (Tegea, Hegesistratus); vi.70, ix.77.

of history to give Themistocles the impact of a *deus ex machina*.[75]

'Recently come to the forefront' *is* misleading, except to those in whose sight a thousand years are but as yesterday. Themistocles had been archon in 493 – interestingly, the year of Miltiades' return to Athens – and had begun then the long-term project of building the port of Piraeus. He had been a general in 490 and led his tribe's regiment at Marathon. He had been a zealous and successful participant in the political infighting of the 480s: in each of the five traceable ostracisms of the decade he was a 'candidate' – and in fact far more ostraka survive bearing his name than anyone else's – but on each occasion he was able to mobilise a bigger vote against one of his rivals: Hipparchus son of Charmus, Megacles (IV) the Alcmeonid, Callixenus son of Aristonymus (if indeed that Alcmeonid gentleman was the unlucky victim in 486), Xanthippus father of Pericles, and Aristeides 'the Just'.[76]

Themistocles was not a *novus homo*; his father was a gentleman of some background, but his mother was non-Athenian. As the same was true of Cleisthenes the great reformer and Cimon the great general, we may doubt whether that was why Themistocles became a radical politician – more probably the cast of his mind so inclined him – but when he did display his political colours, his enemies did not hesitate to use the reproach of base birth against him.[77] At any rate, all those ostracised in the 480s were aristocrats and, so far as it is possible to judge, inclined towards political conservatism. What Themistocles had been working towards from 493 was a fundamental change in the nature of Athens' destiny: she was to become a sea power second to none.

After the story of the oracle and its interpretation, Herodotus continues with a flashback. 'On a previous occasion another one of Themistocles' ideas had prevailed, and most advantageously' – his proposal that the windfall profits from the state mines at Laurion should not be distributed to the citizen body (as a dividend of 10 drachmas a man) but used to finance the building of a great fleet for war – 'he said, the war with Aigina. That war . . . proved the salvation of Greece, by forcing the Athenians to become a sea power.' What passions and controversies underlay those simple words! In two other states with publicly owned

---

[75] vii.143.

[76] Them.'s archonship: Dion.Hal.vi.34. Doubts have been cast upon the early date (partly because of these words in H) but Thucydides (i.93) explicitly states that he was archon when beginning work on the Piraeus, and it is infinitely more probable that he would have been an *elected* archon, i.e. pre-487, than one drawn by lot. Ostracisms: *Ath. Pol.* 22, and for ostraka see M-L, no. 21, updated by various articles in journals. The prevalence of ostraka from the 480s is partly due to there having been more ostracisms then, but is mainly the incidental result of the Persian destruction of Athens, which effectively sealed various rubbish-tips.

[77] Facts and anecdotes about Them.'s early life and family background are to be found in Plutarch's *Life*. They do not feature in Herodotus.

mines, Siphnos and Thasos, Herodotus states (or in the latter instance at least implies)[78] that it was customary for citizens to receive a periodic dividend, and the degree of persuasion needed in Athens to get the citizens to forgo their 10 drachmas can be imagined. Themistocles, we can be sure, had his eye on the Persians' return to the charge, which he clearly foresaw;[79] but he was shrewd in basing his arguments upon the enemy close at hand and a war in being, rather than upon the remoter prospect of war with Persia which wishful thinkers in Athens may have hoped would not materialise.

Even so, the task of persuasion cannot have been easy. The war with Aigina had been dragging along in a rather desultory fashion from about 506, when that island joined the loose coalition of states that attempted, unsuccessfully, to strangle Athens' newly fledged democracy. Aigina did so informally, without any declaration of war, and, as Herodotus tells us, her not very effective contribution was to mount occasional raids on the Attic coast.[80] Athens was thinking about counter-measures when Herodotus takes leave of the topic, not to return to it until 491, the year when Aigina (along with many other island states) offered submission to Darius' heralds. Athens protested to Sparta – it is presumed that Aigina was by now a member of Sparta's alliance; Cleomenes, as we saw, swept aside the opposition of Damaratus and with the compliant Leotychidas took hostages from Aigina and deposited them in Athens. Upon Cleomenes' death the Aiginetans attempted to get their hostages back through Leotychidas, but Athens would not budge, and the war was renewed with some vigour. Herodotus details some episodes of it – Aigina's seizure of the state galley, manned by some prominent Athenians, thereby gaining counter-hostages; Athens' sponsorship of a democratic coup under Nicodromus, which failed, but had the side-effect of causing faction strife on Aigina; a victory at sea by Athens (whose fleet was bolstered by some 20 Corinthian ships sold to Athens for a nominal 5 drachmas apiece) followed by a landing on the island; a volunteer force of about 1,000 Argives under Eurybates, a noted athlete,[81] who attempted to drive the Athenians off Aigina, but most perished in the attempt; and a minor victory for Aigina when four Athenian ships were caught off watch and captured with their crews.[82]

---

[78] iii.57, vi.46.

[79] Th.i.14 makes this point.

[80] *Polemos akēryktos* is H's phrase; raids: v.8.

[81] And therefore, presumably, like most athletes of that age, an aristocrat. Since being defeated by Cleomenes of Sparta in c. 494 Argos had been governed allegedly by 'slaves', probably in fact a revolutionary government of the hitherto unenfranchised (see above, p. 173).

[82] It has long been recognised that H's account of the Aiginetan wars is unsatisfactory. Leaving aside the earlier war (v.80–9), H, reasonably enough, dates the renewal of hostilities in earnest to the period after Cleomenes' death. That fell some unspecified time after the degrading of Damaratus which must on any showing have been in 491. H narrates the various episodes summarised above (vi.85–93), then

Even so, for most Athenians the war with Aigina was little more than an annoyance, and it is not clear that a majority would necessarily have supported a policy designed to smash Aigina once and for all, regardless of cost. Moreover, even among those who, like Themistocles, foresaw a Persian comeback, it may not have been obvious that Athens should become a sea power. After all, Marathon had been a hoplites' victory, and as a triumph of Athenian arms was not likely to be improved upon. Some opposition, too, was politically motivated. Conservative statesmen must have seen that if the fleet became Athens' principal arm, the men who sat on the rowing benches – the *thetes*, the least privileged class of citizen – would gain immensely in political self-confidence; the end result could only be yet further erosion of the position of the Athenian aristocracy.

It was Themistocles' achievement to secure a majority for his ideas. He overcame the various strands of conservative opposition by the device of ostracism. After the first three recorded instances, when 'friends of the tyrants' were banished, the institution changed in its purpose: it became a vehicle for the people to choose between contending policies and their protagonists. They chose Themistocles and his controversial big navy policy. The victims were Xanthippus, a nobleman, brother-in-law of Megacles the Alcmeonid who had already been ostracised; and Aristeides son of Lysimachus, a man eminent enough to have been elected archon (eponymous) in 489.[83] Little of this appears in Herodotus: Aristeides' ostracism is mentioned in a flashback,[84] Xanthippus' not at all. But these omissions, regrettable though they may be for the systematic student of history, do serve Herodotus' artistic and dramatic purpose by enabling him to introduce Themistocles, springing (as it were) fully-armed from the head of Zeus, as the saviour of Athens in her darkest hour.

---

continues with the clear implication that they *all* occurred *before* the Marathon expedition of 490! Even if Cleomenes died more or less directly after getting rid of Damaratus (and he probably did not), the compression seems intolerable. H has been rather careless in lumping together all the incidents of this 'undeclared war'—some of them rather trivial—and it is generally agreed that most or all of the episodes referred to should be placed after Marathon. A further weakness of H's account as it stands is precisely that it does not appear to mention any details of the hostilities of the mid-480s that gave Them. his pretext for enlarging the navy. As Aigina did not lift a finger to help Persia in 490, it seems a legitimate assumption that then at least Athens still held the advantage over her in the form of the hostages, and that the war described in vi.85–93 had not yet broken out.

[83] No ancient source explicitly states that Xanthippus and Aristeides were actually ostracised for opposing Them.'s naval policy, but in Aristeides' case at least the inference is irresistible. Ironically both were to profit from it in the future, Xanthippus by his successful command in 479/8 (ix.114, 120), Ar. by his establishment of the Delian League in 478/7 (Plut. *Ar.* 23 f.). Ostracism retained this function for at least 40 years more: in the principal recorded cases, namely Them. himself, Cimon and Thucydides son of Melesias, the people were choosing between diametrically opposed policies.

[84] viii.79.

As to what would have happened had Persia not, after all, invaded, we can only guess. It is difficult, however, to imagine that Sparta would have stood by and let Aigina's navy be crushed out of existence by Athens' massive new fleet.

The Architect of Victory

The first mention of Themistocles in a purely military context is in connection with the allied expedition to Tempe in Thessaly, in which he commanded the Athenian contingent. The decision to defend Tempe was strategically correct, provided that Thessaly could be relied on – a rather large proviso. Even so, it is surprising to find him identified with a land-based operation at a time when the Athenian fleet was destined to be in action quite soon after, and we may wonder how far he really believed in the efficacy of what he was doing. However, as we saw in Chapter 4, resistance in Thessaly was stillborn for various reasons and the force fell back to the Isthmus.[85]

He must have felt more at home with the fleet at Artemisium, where he next appears as commander of the Athenian contingent. Here we find further traces of what has been regarded as a hostile portrait. The strategical importance of Artemisium and its connection with the Greek position at Thermopylae have been discussed in Chapter 4. Herodotus tells us that the natives of Euboea, fearful lest their island be abandoned to the invader, appealed in vain to Eurybiadas the Spartan commander-in-chief, and then went to Themistocles with a bribe of 30 talents. He in turn bribed Eurybiadas successfully with five talents and purchased the acquiescence of Adeimantus of Corinth with three. The balance, needless to say, he kept for himself.

There is little need to agonise over the historicity of this story. As we saw in Chapter 4, there was minimal prospect of the Greeks withdrawing from Artemisium as long as the position at Thermopylae was held; to do so would be to consign Leonidas' forces to certain death. We also examined the particular reasons why Athenian tradition, at any rate, blackened the memory of Adeimantus. The whole story has an Athenian ring to it, and at the time that Herodotus was writing, no Athenian would have regarded Themistocles' conduct as anything other than entirely commendable. He made a handsome profit out of the Euboeans – tribute-paying allies of Athens in the 430s – and he bought at an embarrassingly cheap price the commanders of two states that were then at war, or on the verge of war, with Athens. It is the others who are made to look simpletons, and dishonest ones at that; Themistocles even implies that Adeimantus might

---

[85] vii.173.

be open to corruption by Xerxes.[86]

The next time we hear of Themistocles is in a more serious strategical context. Here Herodotus introduces us to a new side of the man, as a practitioner of psychological warfare. The fighting at Artemisium was now over and the allies, though giving as good as they got, had been quite roughly handled on the third day, and although their continued presence was vital to the safety of the men at Thermopylae, it was clear that the Greek fleet would not be in any fit condition to renew battle the next day. Fortunately, the decision to withdraw was rendered less agonising by the arrival of certain news that the Persians had broken through at Thermopylae. Themistocles had in the meantime devised a stratagem. He first ensured a square meal for the sailors by telling them to 'sacrifice' as many sheep as they liked belonging to the Euboeans; the latter were rather unwisely bringing their flocks down to the shore, presumably with the intention of evacuating them. Fires were lit on the beach and the islanders were the involuntary hosts at what would have been a most welcome feast of roast mutton. Themistocles undertook to choose the moment to withdraw. Herodotus does not explicitly say that the start of the retreat would have been 'covered' by the fires, but he probably did not need to. It was a familiar device, but still a good one; the Greek retreat was unmolested.

The Athenians brought up the rear, with a special fast squadron under Themistocles' personal command. With these he stopped at the watering places on the Euboean coast and left large notices on the rocks addressed to the Ionians (and presumably any other Greeks) in Xerxes' fleet, urging them to desert Persia for the loyalist side. (Herodotus gives what purports to be the text of what Themistocles had written, and a verbose, conversational passage it is. We may be sure that the reality was a good deal more terse!) As Herodotus points out, there was a subsidiary aim in this: even if the appeal failed to produce any defections, it might cause Xerxes to suspect the Ionians of disloyalty and consequently to keep them out of the front line. Herodotus has prepared us for this stratagem by the familiar technique of direct speech: before the expedition left Asia, he makes Uncle Artabanus advise Xerxes not to take an Ionian naval contingent to Greece for fear of just such a change of side.[87] Xerxes roundly rejects this notion of his timid kinsman and defends the Ionians against the charge of disloyalty; and it must be said that Themistocles' plan did indeed fail in its main aim. Herodotus records just four ships from Naxos and one from Tenos changing sides and none from Ionia proper. (One from Lemnos had already defected before this episode.[88]) How far the subsidiary aims were realised is difficult

---

[86] viii.5.

[87] vii.51.

[88] Naxians: viii.46 (but they had evidently not been at Artemisium); Tenians: viii, 82; Lemnians: viii.11.

to tell. Some Ionian contingents fought well at Salamis; a few, unspecified, are said to have deliberately fought badly in deference to Themistocles' appeal. But the Phoenicians who tried to put the blame for the defeat upon the Ionians got short shrift – by implication, deservedly – from Xerxes. However, Leotychidas thought it worth trying something similar in his Ionian campaign in 479.[89]

The fall of Thermopylae and the withdrawal from Artemisium made the evacuation of Athens inevitable. It had obviously been foreseen in the 'wooden wall' oracle given to Athens, which Themistocles interpreted – and in the even more alarming first oracle too – the most likely chronological context for which is more or less where Herodotus puts them, between Xerxes' crossing of the Hellespont and his entry into Thessaly. In view of Themistocles' success in getting his view accepted, it is likely enough that he was the mainspring of the subsequent decision to evacuate the city and get the non-combatant population away to safety in Troizen, Aigina and Salamis. Herodotus does not actually state that he was; rather 'the Athenians' made this proclamation, a fair enough phrase for a decision taken by majority vote. Thucydides too, repeatedly and quite properly, attributes policies and actions to 'the Athenians', even in the days of Pericles' supremacy. It is Plutarch, who knew nothing of democracy in action, who tends to pin collective decisions upon individuals; however he is supported by sound fourth-century tradition in making Themistocles the author of the decree to evacuate.[90] He is further supported by the 'Troizen inscription' discovered in the 1950s, which if not authentic is at the very least a skilfully assembled reconstruction of the fourth century, based on some genuine historical knowledge. This squarely makes Themistocles the proposer of a comprehensive decree involving the evacuation, the manning of triremes, the posting of a portion of the fleet to Artemisium (this, if genuine, necessitating a shift in Herodotus' order of events) and treatment of those ostracised. Plutarch also makes Themistocles the one who capitalises on the disappearance of the sacred snake that was supposed to live on the Acropolis, an episode that Herodotus refers to without naming him.

And so to Salamis. We have already examined the allied strategy in Chapter 4. Here again Themistocles had to get his views adopted against strong opposition – opposition that was not necessarily either malignant or ill-informed. Although the decision to bring on a battle (if possible) in the narrows of Salamis was both strategically and tactically correct, it involved,

---

[89] viii.85, 90; cf. ix.98.

[90] viii.41; Plut. *Them.* 10, cf. Schol. on Demosthenes xix.303 (*Speech on the False Embassy*). Troizen inscr.: M-L, no. 23, where the question of authenticity is also discussed, To summarise the arguments deployed in the already colossal bibliography on the inscription lies outside the scope of this book.

as we saw, an heroic calculated risk that could only be justified by success. Again hostile hands are sometimes thought to have been at work in the account of Themistocles' role as transmitted by Herodotus: he represents him as reopening the question of fighting at Salamis only at the instigation of an outsider, Mnesiphilus; then in the conference room he borrowed the latter's arguments and added some more of his own. If this was indeed an attempt by Herodotus' aristocratic friends to detract from Themistocles' credit, it is singularly unsuccessful.[91] It is one thing to make a suggestion, it is quite another to take a momentous decision. 'I do not consider that prefixing the words "I am informed that . . ." relieves one of all responsibility' said Winston Churchill once, attacking the tendency of ministers to shelter behind the advice tendered by their civil servants.[92] Not Mnesiphilus but Themistocles would have been the one to get the blame had Salamis gone wrong. But in any case Herodotus' interposition of Mnesiphilus is historically motivated, like the curtain-lecture of Queen Atossa: each character serves as a vehicle for the expression of important non-narrative truths.[93]

Herodotus' picture of Themistocles here is magnificent – the burning urgency of the message he has to get across leads him to break the rules of procedure. He first convinces Eurybiadas the Spartan supremo, then before the assembled commanders he bursts into an impassioned address without even waiting for his superior officer to state the business of the meeting. He neatly turned aside the rebuke of Adeimantus of Corinth: 'Themistocles – at the games they whip those who jump the start.' 'Yes – but those who are left at the post win no crowns!' – and then stated his case. The speech which Herodotus puts into his mouth expresses the tactical and strategical issues with economy and force. Adeimantus again attacked him – this time with a cheap sneer: Themistocles should acquire a city for himself before expecting to advise his colleagues. This understandably roused Themistocles to fury and he denounced Adeimantus and Corinth: 'Two hundred battleships are as good as any city!', and he concluded by returning to Eurybiadas: if his advice were not taken, he said, the Athenians would withdraw their contingent and would emigrate *en masse* to Siris in Italy – 'it has belonged to us from time immemorial'. Had it? Or was he just bluffing? This is one of the minor mysteries of the day.[94] At any rate Eurybiadas did not seek to call

---

[91] Though Plut. *MH*, 869D regards this as yet another instance of 'malice'.

[92] Speech to the House of Commons, 6 Nov. 1950.

[93] The choice of Mnesiphilus is interesting: later tradition (Plut. *Them.* 2) represents him as a kind of mentor to Them. This might have been merely a blown-up inference from H; but recent discovery of ostraka bearing his name prove his existence, at least, and possible political importance. See Ch. 4, p. 133 and note 93.

[94] viii.62. There is no doubt that Them. had a vague interest in the west, and the fact that he called two of his daughters 'Italia' and 'Sybaris' (Plut. *Them.* 32) has provoked much modern discussion. But it is next to impossible to pin this interest down to anything concrete. The name of Cimon's son

the bluff. He conceded the argument and Themistocles' strategy was adopted.

Then follows the story of Themistocles' message to Xerxes. I have already recorded my opinion that this is, in its central substance, factual.[95] Without such an inducement Xerxes' navy would not have sailed boldly into the narrows of Salamis in force; they must have been fortified by the definite expectation that they would find the Greeks demoralised, with several contingents ready to defect or at least desert during the battle, as had occurred at Lade. Of all the passages in Themistocles' career that mark him out as a real-life Odysseus, none surpasses this one: the message was credible in itself, and it must have told Xerxes and his officers what they wanted to hear — for there was certainly a general desire for a naval showdown — and yet it was totally ruinous.

At this point Aristeides, recently recalled from ostracism, reported to Themistocles that the Greek fleet was surrounded — the western channel of Salamis was now blocked. This is an interesting scene which Herodotus dramatises nicely: he knows that Themistocles and Aristeides had been political enemies (though he does not go into details) and he puts into the latter's mouth a brief and patriotic address suggesting that the two of them bury the hatchet and confine their rivalry to the field of benefiting Athens. Themistocles expresses delight at his news — it means that they will be committed to fighting — and persuades Aristeides to report to the other commanders in person: 'they might believe you — they certainly won't believe me'. Themistocles was alive to the danger of overplaying his hand.[96]

Just before battle was joined it was Themistocles who delivered some words of encouragement to the fighting men. Herodotus has earned the gratitude of generations of readers by not concocting full-length pre-battle speeches, and the brief, soldierly address summarised by Herodotus, contrasting the best and the worst things in human life and fortune, is infinitely preferable to the turgid commonplaces that pad out later histories. Its very brevity and credibility suggest that it may be an authentic recollection of what Themistocles actually said.[97]

We get a brief glimpse of Themistocles' personal role in the battle, pursuing the fleeing enemy and listening to pleasantries from Polycritus of Aigina.[98] But after the battle he comes into his own again as an originator of ideas. He shows his flair for the really damaging blow by proposing to the

---

Lacedaemonius certainly reflected his father's pro-Spartan leanings.

[95] See Ch. 4, p. 134.

[96] Aristeides: viii.79 ff.; message: viii.75.

[97] viii.83.

[98] viii.92.

victorious commanders that they sail straight through the islands to the Hellespont and destroy Xerxes' bridge, cutting off the king and his army in Europe. This was a thing that Xerxes feared, and recalled the panic in Darius' army on discovering that the bridge over the Danube appeared to have gone.[99] But Eurybiadas would not on this occasion yield, and he was backed by the majority. The arguments must have seemed nicely balanced. Themistocles held out the prospect of decisive victory, teaching Persia a lesson that she would never forget; the majority, obviously and understandably regarding Salamis as a crowning deliverance, were merely concerned to usher Xerxes out of Europe with all possible haste.

The Athenian contingent had been the most eager to sail to the Hellespont and even wanted to go it alone after the high command rejected the idea. This was plainly not on – such a breach in the unity of allied decision-making would not have been tolerable – and Themistocles loyally dissuaded them from the enterprise. The speech he makes to them is, as usual, a well-composed affair that neatly balances the practical arguments, previously advanced by Eurybiadas, with religious reflections on the role of the gods and heroes, 'who are jealous that both Asia and Europe too should fall under the rule of one man, a man who was both impious and presumptuous'. This, Herodotus continues, Themistocles said with a view to laying up some treasure upon earth: 'should some harm possibly come to him from the Athenians – a thing which did in fact occur – he might have somewhere to resort to'. At any rate, his proven shrewdness carried the day and the Athenians were convinced. Themistocles thereupon got a message through to Xerxes – the party naturally included the faithful Sicinnus – to inform him that it was Themistocles who, out of zeal for the king's cause, had stopped the Greeks from sailing to the Hellespont, which they were anxious to do.

The Greeks then decided to exact money from some of the islands that had supported Xerxes or at any rate sent contingents to him, often no doubt under duress. Herodotus here gets into a bit of a muddle, for although he begins by saying 'the Greeks besieged Andros, intending to take it' he continues by attributing the demand for money to Themistocles himself, who said that the *Athenians* had come bringing with them those two powerful divinities Persuasion and Compulsion. The Andrians, whose land was beset by two equally powerful gods, Poverty and Inability, could not, or at any rate would not, pay; hence the siege. No doubt it *was* an agreed policy of the allies, but Themistocles is made to take the lead in executing it. 'He did not cease from his avaricious behaviour, but sent threatening demands to the other islands,' the threat being that if they failed to cough up, he would bring the allied forces to bear upon them. Carystos in Euboea did pay

---

[99] viii.97, cf. iv.140.

– and got her land ravaged just the same – but Paros succeeded in buying immunity.[100]

Themistocles makes his last appearance later that same year, when the commanders met at the Isthmus. The plunder had already been distributed, a generous (and quite undeserved) offering sent to Delphi, and now it was time to award the prize of valour. In the voting, the commanders (unlike cardinals at Papal elections) were allowed to vote for themselves and of course all did; most agreed to give Themistocles the second prize. 'The Greeks failed to reach a decision on this, through jealousy' – how very like the Greeks! – but Themistocles achieved a kind of personal triumph; his name was on everyone's lips. He went on a grand 'progress' to Sparta, where he was fêted and honoured with a wreath of olive (the same as Eurybiadas himself had received) and the gift of a splendid chariot. As he left for the north, he was given a guard of honour by the 300 Spartan 'knights', their *corps d'élite*. With Themistocles' stinging retort to his envious fellow citizen Timodemus of Aphidna, Herodotus takes his leave of him.[101] The absence of Themistocles from any position of command in 479 is a minor mystery and Herodotus does nothing to enlighten us.

Themistocles in History

What did Herodotus think of Themistocles? It seems to me that he fully recognised the man's greatness and regarded him as the architect of victory in 480, if any one man was entitled to be so called. In three separate fields he is shown as making a decisive contribution: policy (ship-building), morale (the oracle) and strategy (Salamis). Even those ideas of his which did not come off or were not adopted show his flair and imagination, and in war, which can so easily become a matter of routine or of automatic response, the leader who can generate ideas is invaluable. Far more credit is directly given by Herodotus to Themistocles than to any other individual leader of the two years – Leonidas, Eurybiadas, Pausanias (of whom, more later), Leotychidas, Xanthippus or Aristeides. The last-named in fact gets the barest mention as commander of the Athenian hoplites at Plataea.[102] Read Plutarch's 'Life of Aristeides' and you will see that roughly one-third of it is taken up with a narrative of that battle; and much of *that* reads like a simple reworking of Herodotus' narrative, only with 'Aristeides' substituted for 'the Athenians'. It may very well be that later tradition sought to put Aristeides on a pedestal as high as Themistocles'; Herodotus knew better.

Too much has been heard about the hostile portrait of Themistocles

---

[100] Bridges: viii.108 ff.; Andros, Carystos etc: viii.111 f., cf. 123.

[101] viii.123–5.

[102] ix.28.

that Herodotus has allegedly painted, under the influence of his friends in the Athenian aristocracy. We have already examined two supposed instances of hostility and found that in them at least it is imaginary. The charge of avarice that he levels against Themistocles, however, deserves to be taken a bit more seriously. Like just about every active politician in ancient Greece and Rome, from the Alcmeonidae, Cimon and Lysander to the Metelli, Pompey and Crassus, Themistocles was keenly alive to the importance of money and the power of patronage that it brought with it. Such anecdotes in Plutarch as touch on his finances certainly suggest that he was a free spender, with, it seems, ulterior political motives, rather than a miserly hoarder.[103] No doubt, too (again in common with many others), he quit public life a good deal better off than when he entered it. Themistocles' immense services to Athens and to Greece were as a statesman and strategist, and Herodotus feels himself under no obligation to idealise his personal qualities. His greed and unscrupulousness form the reverse side of his foresight and cleverness.

As it happens this charge goes back to a very ancient source, though not perhaps an untainted one. In 478/7 Timocreon of Ialysos (in Rhodes), a rather disreputable exile, wrote a vitriolic short poem in the form of a drinking song.[104] It takes as its pretext Aristeides' founding of the Delian League. Themistocles was excluded from all participation in this process, a thing that Timocreon recognised, correctly, as an enduring political defeat for him. 'You may praise Pausanias, you, Xanthippus, and you, Leotychidas; but as for me, I praise Aristeides, the finest man to come out of holy Athens, since Lato conceived a hatred for Themistocles . . .' He goes on to accuse Themistocles of corruption and other dishonesty; Themistocles had promised to arrange the restoration of his 'friend' Timocreon to his native town, but broke his word in consideration of a bribe of three talents, and so on. How much truth underlies this (if any does) is impossible to say. It would be altogether too flattering to Timocreon's importance to suggest that his little song has shaped the whole hostile tradition about Themistocles, but it was probably seized on by Themistocles' political enemies and given wide circulation. This would explain why the piece survived at all, for as a man of letters Timocreon ranked low.

The other thing that ought to be examined seriously is Themistocles' second message to Xerxes, after the decision not to destroy the Hellespont bridge. The first point to note is that Herodotus nowhere accuses Themistocles of treachery, actual or intended. The worst he does is to deceive the Athenians as to his future intentions *after* the decision has been definitely taken not to sail to the Hellespont. His conduct does not damage

---

[103] Plut. *Them.* 5, cf. *Lysand.* 16 ff.

[104] Page, LGS, no. 410, quoted from Plut. *Them.* 21.

the allied cause in the smallest degree: if anything, he bluffs Xerxes out of Europe all the more quickly. The whole story seems to be pretty improbable, flying (as it does) in the face of the axiom, once bitten, twice shy. Why *should* Xerxes have been expected to treat such a message seriously? And yet Thucydides, writing a generation later than Herodotus, seems to entertain no doubts as to the truth of the story.[105]

That question, however, need not detain us. What matters is the dramatic purpose of Herodotus' story. In it Themistocles' resourcefulness and dexterity are shown in the highest degree: he has been overruled in his plan to cut off Xerxes in Europe, but even that setback he turns to advantage. His need for a refuge, should he fall foul of his fellow citizens, is presented as only a remote contingency. And yet every Athenian reader in Herodotus' own day would know that Themistocles did so come to grief and did find not just a refuge but a splendid position with King Artaxerxes. They would experience a pleasurable frisson on reading or hearing Herodotus' narrative – a fine example of what Thucydides called 'a composition designed to catch the ears of an immediate public'.[106]

It is sometimes thought that Thucydides' account of Themistocles is intended, in part at least, as a correction of the picture wrought by Herodotus. A careful reading of his text, however, will show this to be false. The excellent story of the refortification of Athens in 479/8 shows Themistocles at his best: he displays, in combination, all the guile, boldness and devotion to Athenian interests that Herodotus credits him with. His exile and flight is made the vehicle of some strongly 'Herodotean' episodes, of which his preventing the sea captain from giving him away must take the palm.[107] This is Themistocles the unscrupulous at work again. The entire narrative speaks of the man's inventiveness, adaptability and capacity for survival.

Near the end of his digression, Thucydides treats Themistocles to a generalised obituary, praising in fine terms his intellectual gifts – his power of rapid decision, his ability to expound a case, but above all his foresight. As far as Thucydides is concerned, the foresight (in the context) clearly consisted of his having foreseen the enmity that would necessarily arise between Athens and Sparta, and having advocated measures to meet it.[108] But each of these qualities is found in ample measure in Herodotus also, the foresight above all – not least in the last example we considered, his second message to Xerxes. No Athenian politician, recalling the fate of Miltiades and the crop of ostracisms in the 480s, could count on absolute security of

---

[105] Th.i.137.

[106] Th.i.22. This point is very well argued by C.W. Fornara, *Herodotus* Ch. IV.

[107] Respectively Th.i.89 f., 135–8.

[108] Well recognised by Ste Croix, *Origins*, p. 175 ff.

tenure; but actually to hit on the form of insurance policy adopted by Themistocles argues foresight of a singular kind.

The developments in Themistocles' political position in the 470s, his policy of opposition to Sparta and the reasons for his ostracism make an exceptionally interesting study, but do not fall within the range of this work.[109] Themistocles was a great man by any standards, a towering figure around whose complex personality anecdotes were destined to gather in abundance: compare Plutarch's *Lives* of Themistocles and Aristeides, and the difference is readily apparent.[110] Themistocles, as portrayed by Herodotus, stands firmly in a literary and historical tradition of characters who were determined, resourceful and cunning. In history his predecessor is Peisistratus; in legend, Odysseus – survivors all!

PAUSANIAS – FALL OF A HERO

It is the comparison with Thucydides that lends much of the interest to Herodotus' portrayal of Pausanias, for, like Themistocles, Pausanias is made the subject of a lengthy digression by the later historian. In Herodotus he rates only three passing mentions before Book IX; and even in that book his role, up to the end of the battle of Plataea, is merely the formal one of command, and the tactics that he pursued there have already been discussed in Chapter 4. He is not characterised in any way, nor is he represented as originating any war-winning ideas. It is with the conclusion of the battle that he emerges as a clear-cut personality, and Herodotus' picture is finely wrought.

Pausanias was directing the closing stages of the operation when he received a visitation from a lady from the island of Cos, attended by her maids, all in their finest clothes, herself wearing masses of gold. She had been the concubine of a senior Persian officer,[111] and begged Pausanias (addressing him as 'King of Sparta') not to let her be enslaved as a prisoner of war. 'I am from Cos, and a daughter of Hegetoridas . . . the Persian took me from home by force.' She was in luck: 'Have no fear' he replied, 'your father is my closest friend in that part of the world' – and he entrusted her to the ephors for safekeeping.

---

[109] But Cartledge (*Sparta*, p. 211) tentatively suggests that Them.'s guard of honour of the 300 Spartan 'knights' (see above, p. 195) may have been designed 'to ensure that Themistocles went where the Spartan authorities wished'; if so, in 480/79 they may have suspected the future trends of his political thinking.

[110] *Aristeides* is less rich in anecdotal matter and many of its anecdotes actually concern Themistocles. It also contains a good deal more padding.

[111] Pharandates, son of Teaspis, perhaps a nephew of Darius, ix.76, cf. iv.43. Cos was part of Halicarnassus' sphere of influence in 480/79 (vii.99), hence perhaps H's knowledge of the story.

Not 'the dread, thrice-coiled snake' of vi.77, but the 'Serpent Column' (ix.81, c.f. M-L no. 27): set up at Delphi in 479/8, it was moved 8 centuries later to the Hippodrome, Constantinople, where it remains. It is about 20 feet tall. The 3 serpent heads broke off a long time ago, but one survives in the Istanbul Museum. (Deutsches Archäologisches Institut, Istanbul)

This is soon followed by the episode of Lampon of Aigina. He accosted Pausanias with a proposal that Herodotus describes as most impious: 'You have performed a great and glorious deed, and God has granted you, for saving Greece, to lay up for yourself the greatest reputation of all the

199

Greeks that we know of.' He went on to suggest that Pausanias 'avenge' Leonidas by impaling Mardonius' corpse even as Leonidas' had been impaled by Xerxes: 'That way, your reputation will be further increased and . . . you will earn the praise of every man in Sparta, and the rest of Greece too.' Pausanias' reply is magnificent – lofty, courteous, stern. 'You extol me and my country and my achievement, but you bring me to nothing by advising me to outrage a corpse . . . May I never please the Aiginetans in this, nor anyone else who approves of such conduct; it is sufficient for me to please the Spartans . . . Never come to me with such a suggestion again.' All the decency, simplicity and gravity of Sparta at her best is summed up in this.

Pausanias then had the stupendous booty collected, and Herodotus reviews it briefly and mentions the dedications made from it – the 'Serpent Column' at Delphi and the rest. Xerxes' tent, left for Mardonius to use, gave the opportunity for a diverting little scene. Pausanias ordered Mardonius' caterers to prepare a meal as they would for Mardonius; they did so, and a magnificent sight it was in the gorgeous tent; then, 'for a laugh' he got his own servants to prepare a Spartan meal and invited the allied commanders to enjoy the contrast. 'What fools the Persians are, who live like this, yet came to rob us, poor as we are!' That heroic simplicity again!

Finally, the allies moved up to Thebes, with the intention of punishing the Medising party there. Of the two ringleaders, Timagenidas volunteered to give himself up, along with some others; Attaginus succeeded in making a getaway. When his children were seized and brought before Pausanias, he refused to proceed against them: how can children have any part in 'Medism'? The other defendants had given themselves up in the expectation that they might bribe their way to freedom. But Pausanias, suspecting this very thing, had them summarily executed.[112]

A remarkable picture: Pausanias does not put a foot wrong at any point. Chivalrous, noble, humorous, a simple liver, fair-minded, incorruptible – who could ask for anything more? If only the story of Pausanias could have ended there, like a real-life Cleobis or Biton! Herodotus is aware of Pausanias' subsequent career, and as it happens the three passing mentions of him before Book IX all relate to it: the mammoth commemorative bowl that he set up at the north end of the Bosporus, presumably after taking Byzantium in 478; his alleged betrothal to the daughter of a Persian nobleman – a story which Herodotus treats with commendable scepticism; and the brief but telling mention of how the

---

[112] Lampon: ix.78 f., the meals: 82 (*epi geloti* is H's phrase); Thebes: 86 ff. Serpent Column (now in Istanbul): though it was erased by his time, H must have known of the arrogant inscription that Paus. had carved on it (Th.i.132), but for reasons discussed below is most anxious to preserve the consistency of the portrait.

Athenians in 478/7 used his arrogant behaviour as a pretext for depriving Sparta of the command of the allies.[113]

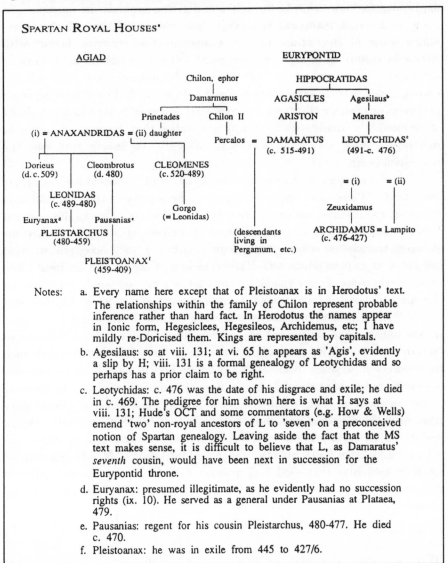

SPARTAN ROYAL HOUSES'

Notes: a. Every name here except that of Pleistoanax is in Herodotus' text. The relationships within the family of Chilon represent probable inference rather than hard fact. In Herodotus the names appear in Ionic form, Hegesiclees, Hegesileos, Archidemus, etc; I have mildly re-Doricised them. Kings are represented by capitals.

b. Agesilaus: so at viii. 131; at vi. 65 he appears as 'Agis', evidently a slip by H; viii. 131 is a formal genealogy of Leotychidas and so perhaps has a prior claim to be right.

c. Leotychidas: c. 476 was the date of his disgrace and exile; he died in c. 469. The pedigree for him shown here is what H says at viii. 131; Hude's OCT and some commentators (e.g. How & Wells) emend 'two' non-royal ancestors of L to 'seven' on a preconceived notion of Spartan genealogy. Leaving aside the fact that the MS text makes sense, it is difficult to believe that L, as Damaratus' *seventh* cousin, would have been next in succession for the Eurypontid throne.

d. Euryanax: presumed illegitimate, as he evidently had no succession rights (ix. 10). He served as a general under Pausanias at Plataea, 479.

e. Pausanias: regent for his cousin Pleistarchus, 480-477. He died c. 470.

f. Pleistoanax: he was in exile from 445 to 427/6.

Now Pausanias was very much a key figure to Thucydides, for it was his shortcomings that (in effect) launched Athens upon her imperial destiny, which in turn led to the Peloponnesian War. This is not the place to discuss Thucydides' account of Pausanias in detail; it raises numerous historical and chronological difficulties which do not concern us. What is relevant is

---

[113] Respectively iv.81, v.32, viii.3. Th.i.128 improves on H by making the lady in question Xerxes' daughter, and even quotes what purports to be Pausanias' letter to Xerxes.

the cardinal fact that Pausanias was a proven traitor, a Mediser, and everything that he was *not* in 479. He began by behaving in a tyrannical and oppressive fashion towards the allies and giving grounds for suspicion, at least, of Persian leanings; Thucydides was convinced that at this early stage, while at Byzantium in 478, Pausanias was currying favour with Persia by conniving at the escape of some Persian noblemen held there as prisoners. Later, when he returned to Byzantium, we hear of his correspondence with Xerxes, his wearing of Persian clothes and living in an extravagant manner (Plutarch for good measure even makes him a seducer of women).[114] Finally, when it was suspected that he was planning to instigate a helot revolt, he was done to death. In Sparta that was the unforgivable sin.

The discrepancy between Herodotus and Thucydides in their treatment of Pausanias cannot be explained by supposing that Herodotus is drawing upon some source favourable to Pausanias, Thucydides upon a hostile one.[115] In his passing mention of Pausanias' arrogant behaviour (hubris) Herodotus speaks as though it were a fact accepted without controversy; as it no doubt was. Rather, he is treating us to a brilliant piece of dramatic irony. Every reader in Herodotus' own day would have known the main outlines of Pausanias' later days and the facts of his fall and death. What they find in Book IX is a young hero with the world at his feet, as yet uncorrupted by luxury and power, for he has not been exposed to their temptations. The scene of the 'Persian banquet' is a skilful contrivance to introduce Pausanias to something to which he will later become enslaved – despite his jocular remark at the time. In his fine reply to Lampon of Aigina, he said 'it is sufficient for me to please the Spartans' – crushingly ironical in the mouth of one who was soon to turn his back on Spartan ways and would ultimately be put to death for plotting revolution in Sparta itself. When urging upon Pausanias the shameful mutilation of Mardonius' corpse, Lampon told him that God had granted him to lay up for himself the greatest reputation in Greece. 'What God granted, Pausanias threw away.'[116]

---

[114] Plut. *Cimon*, 6.

[115] This point is the subject of an excellent argument by Fornara, *Herodotus*, pp. 62–6. I am greatly indebted to his interpretation. Part of the trouble is that much of Th.'s narrative, i.94 ff., 128 ff., seems to come from some demi-official Spartan source concerned to justify Paus.' judicial murder. His position was invidious—as regent for his young cousin he scaled the heights in 479, but regents must in the nature of things slip away from the centre of the stage in time. It is all too credible that Paus. in 478 did begin to look around for unconstitutional ways of prolonging his personal power.

[116] Fornara, *Herodotus*, p. 64. He also suggests that the length of Th.'s digression on Pausanias may partly be explained by the fact that Th. was professedly writing for the instruction of posterity, and so may have desired to correct the impression of Paus. that H leaves us with. Not one of H's contemporaries would have been misled as to Paus.' character by the portrait in Bk ix; we certainly would be if H were our only surviving account (ibid. p. 64-6). This sets it apart from Th.'s account of Themistocles, which reads like a confirmatory postscript to H.

6. HERODOTUS – THE MAN IN HIS TIME

THE BARE OUTLINES OF A LIFE; HALICARNASSUS AND
SAMOS; THE TRAVELLER IN SCYTHIA; HIS LIFE AND
TRAVELS IN GREECE AND ITALY; HIS VIEW OF THE GREEK
STATES; THE IMPACT OF HIS WORK; HERODOTUS,
THUCYDIDES AND HISTORY

Literary biography is a major genre of twentieth-century writing. Not a
month goes by without some new full-length biographical study of an author
being discussed in the reviews – Hardy, Kipling and Orwell, to name but
three recent subjects, not to mention the ever-popular Oscar Wilde. This
sort of thing is intrinsically most interesting, but tells us, for the most part,
a good deal more than we need to know for a full understanding of the
writer's work. In antiquity this was not so. Men of letters who were also
leading actors on the stage of history receive full treatment – Demosthenes,
Caesar, Cicero – but for the rest, what remains is sketchy in the extreme.
Such of Suetonius' *Lives* of the Latin Poets as survive are informative and
readable; even so, the excellent entries on Terence, Horace and Virgil are
only of a length appropriate to a good encyclopedia article.

More typical is the 'Life' that consists of a small handful of facts,
padded out to the length of a page or so by more or less probable inferences
from the writings of the author in question. Unfortunately this is the case
with Herodotus. A brief life of this type appears under his name in the
medieval Byzantine lexicon conventionally known as the *Suda*, and that
entry is supplemented by a few stray facts preserved in other works, such as
Plutarch's *Moralia* and Aulus Gellius.[1] Herodotus' own work affords plenty
of scope for inference, and although no one could accuse him of obtruding his
personality into the narrative, it is nevertheless no very difficult task to
form an impression of the sort of man he was.

The basic facts, as recorded in the sources, are that he was born in 484
at Halicarnassus; his father was named Lyxes and his uncle was the epic
poet Panyassis; he left his city to live in Samos, out of dislike for
Halicarnassus' ruling tyrant, Lygdamis son of Pisindelis and grandson of
the celebrated Artemisia. He later returned to expel the tyrant, then
became unpopular with his fellow citizens and again left, this time to take

---

[1] How & Wells' Introduction, pp. 1–7, usefully presents and discusses the biographical tradition. Most
(not quite all) of the texts are most conveniently assembled in Hill's *Sources*, in which see Index VI
under Herodotus. The *Suda* appears in Hill, as in most older texts, as 'Suidas'.

part in the colonisation of Thuria, in south Italy (an event datable to 444/3); he lived for some time in Athens, perhaps having more than one spell there; he gave readings from his work and became friendly with Sophocles; he died and was buried at Thuria.[2]

HALICARNASSUS AND SAMOS

Not everything in this sketch is mere inference from his own work: most obviously the political background of Halicarnassus, but also the residence in Thuria. The latter is evidently a genuine tradition, for in the very opening words of the 'Histories', which form a kind of title to the work, 'Thurian' was substituted for 'Halicarnassian' in some early manuscripts and survives in citations even now.[3] Halicarnassus was an interesting place, and even without Herodotus' preface we can find several passages that testify to his special knowledge of it. A colony of Troizen, it was one of the group of Dorian cities and islands of south-west Asia Minor, forming, with Cnidos, Cos, Lindos, Ialysos and Camiros, a Dorian Hexapolis; they were united by a common religious festival in honour of Triopian Apollo, in Cnidian territory. It was reduced to a Pentapolis when Halicarnassus was expelled on the entertaining pretext narrated by Herodotus.[4]

The town had a commercial life of its own: it was one of a group of states that included Chios, Cnidos and the Rhodian towns, which built and ran the temple called the Hellenion. This was at Naucratis in Egypt, a concessionary port where Greeks traded by agreement with the Pharaoh. The three states with the biggest trade interests in Egypt – Samos, Aigina, Miletus – each had a temple of its own there.[5]

That fact that Herodotus writes in the Ionic dialect would be inconvenient but for the existence of an inscription from Halicarnassus, dating from the 450s (in which incidentally Lygdamis is named); it is in Ionic, not Doric.[6] As the same goes for the Hippocratic medical writings from Dorian Cos, we may conclude that these communities were most strongly influenced, linguistically and perhaps culturally, by their neighbours to the north. The names on the inscription also show what a

---

[2] The *Suda* adds that H learned the Ionic dialect on Samos and wrote his history there. Neither statement can be true: much of his work demonstrably belongs to later periods of his life; the dialect question will be discussed later. The statement that Lygdamis was Artemisia's grandson is also questionable, if indeed her son was a 'young man' in 480 (vii.99); perhaps he was a younger son, therefore grandson of the Lygdamis who was Artemisia's father. The points in this summary that do *not* come from the *Suda* are the date of his birth and the facts of his residence in Athens and friendship with Sophocles.

[3] See apparatus criticus to i.1 (OCT).

[4] i.144.

[5] ii.178.

[6] M-L, no. 32.

cosmopolitan place Halicarnassus was: a number of Carian-sounding names appear on it. Herodotus in his youth probably had more opportunity than most Greeks actually to know 'barbarians' as neighbours and friends; hence, perhaps, the fair-minded attitude toward non-Greeks that led to his being styled *philobarbaros* by Plutarch[7] – and probably others before him.

The history of Halicarnassus was evidently rather tranquil: its absorption by Persia produced neither the heroics of Phocaea nor the oracular interest of Cnidos; it is not mentioned in the narrative of the Ionian revolt and there is no indication that it took part at all – surprising, when the neighbouring communities of Termera and Mylasa certainly did so,[8] as did the Carian hinterland.

But in 480 the town swam briefly into the mainstream of history – or at any rate of Herodotus' narrative, which comes to much the same thing. It was under the rule of a local dynasty (*tyrannis* is Herodotus' word): the usual Persian policy operated here. The tyranny was then, uniquely for that age, in the hands of a woman, that most celebrated widow Artemisia, who like Boudicca had assumed power on her husband's death; Herodotus implies that her son, though young, was old enough for command, but that her bold spirit would not let her relinquish her position.[9] She held a kind of sub-satrapy and her little squadron of five ships was drawn from Cos, Nisyros, Calydna and Halicarnassus itself. Her membership of Xerxes' 'war cabinet' was more probably in recognition of her personal qualities than the automatic right of a petty commander. As we saw in Chapter 4, Herodotus depicts her as giving Xerxes good advice on matters of strategy, and saving herself from pursuit at Salamis by the deliberate sinking of the flagship of her Carian neighbour, Damasithymus of Calynda.[10]

Very possibly Artemisia succeeded in putting about a post-war version of events that put her in a favourable light, but even so Herodotus' picture is strongly sympathetic: he praises the excellence of her contingent and emphasises the confidence that Xerxes placed in her; even the incident at Salamis – discreditable by almost any standards – is narrated with some relish and open admiration for the way she undeservedly won Xerxes' approval.[11] Themistocles himself could not have bettered this combination of unscrupulousness and luck. All this supports the contention of Chapter 3,

---

[7] Plut.*MH*, 857A: malice!

[8] v.37. These were probably Hellenised Carian towns: 'Heracleides son of Ibanollis of Mylasa' (v.121) is an instructively international name, and Histiaeus son of Tymnes of Termera (vii.98) is explicitly named among the Carians.

[9] A parallel example of a sub-satrapy lapsing to a widow can be found at the end of the century: Mania inherited her husband's position in the Troad, with the approval of the satrap Pharnabazus (X. *Hell.* iii.1.10 ff.).

[10] Distinguish between Calynda, Carian town, and Calydna (later Calymnos), Dorian island.

[11] Artemisia: vii.99 (her squadron); viii.68, 102 (advice); viii.87 f. (at Salamis).

that Herodotus is no doctrinaire enemy of tyranny: he may have helped to expel Artemisia's descendant Lygdamis, but that did not blunt his patriotic feeling of pride in the mettlesome exploits of one who had, albeit briefly, put Halicarnassus on the map.[12]

A few other stray references seem to stem from Herodotus' special knowledge. It was a Halicarnassian *condottiere* named Phanes who deserted Amasis of Egypt and brought valuable military intelligence to Cambyses; Herodotus attributes to him the plan that got Cambyses' expeditionary force safely across the desert to the gates of Egypt. It was another Halicarnassian soldier, Xenagoras son of Praxilaus, who stopped Artayntes from murdering Xerxes' brother Masistes in a fit of rage. Only Artemisia's Halicarnassians would have known that the ship they sank belonged to a near neighbour. Scylax of Caryanda – a town very near Halicarnassus – was a member of Darius' survey party round the Indus; Herodotus almost certainly got the story from his family, or even from the man himself. Scarcely further away was Myndus, and it was a Myndian captain – another Scylax – whose harsh treatment sparked off the quarrel between Aristagoras and Megabates, which in turn led to the outbreak of the Ionian revolt. Gelon's envoy to Xerxes, whom Herodotus praises for his utter integrity, was Cadmus, a native of nearby Cos; so was the unnamed lady who, at Plataea, gave Pausanias a chance to display his chivalrous instincts; and it was the men of Cnidos who attempted to repatriate Gillus to Taras. These last episodes are not in themselves very important, but Herodotus includes them because they are interesting and do add something to the pictures of Darius and Pausanias.[13]

The fact that Herodotus lived for a time on Samos is something that we would have had no difficulty in inferring from his work. As we considered in Chapter 3, when events make Samos the focus of Persia's attention Herodotus has at his disposal a copious body of high-grade, relevant information – as well as some good *logoi* for colouring. His account bears all the marks of an interested eye-witness: he lists, for example, various dedications in the Heraion, the most massive of Greek temples in his day – the painting of Mandrocles' bridge, two wooden statues of Amasis of Egypt and a magnificent bronze bowl of colossal size: dedicated by the merchant Colaeus, it was a tithe of the 60–talent profit he cleared on one fantastic voyage. He saw a notable inscription in the Samian Agora, and is familiar with the names and works of Samos' greatest artists; he slightly exaggerates the dimensions of Eupalinus' tunnel and watercourse, but no

---

[12] Cicero offers a somewhat similar example of local patriotism: much of what C. Marius stood for in politics was abhorrent to him, but more often than not he refers to his fellow townsman (and distant kinsman) from Arpinum in respectful terms, e.g, *Pro Rab. Perd.* 27 ff.; *de Div.* i.59.

[13] Phanes: iii.4, 7; Xenagoras: ix.107; Scylax of Myndus: v.33; Cadmus: vii.16. For other episodes, see Ch. 5, pp. 121, 123, 153.

more than any layman might who was judging with the naked eye. His knowledge even extends to unofficial history: when Xerxes' nephew Sataspes was executed, a eunuch servant of his made off with much of his fortune, and fled to Samos only to be robbed of it by a certain Samian – 'I deliberately forget his name – but I know it.'[14]

Two other interesting passages are history's first mention of Aesop the fable writer, who had been a slave of a Samian named Iadmon; and the note on Pythagoras, the pioneer mathematician and mystic, whom Herodotus calls 'one of Greece's most considerable sophists' (here, evidently, 'teachers').[15] He rejects the story that Salmoxis was Pythagoras' slave, but it does allow him an opportunity to give a good mention to Samos' most distinguished intellectual. (He later moved to Croton in Italy.)

More generally, he is broadly sympathetic to Samos and the Samians. To give two examples, he puts the best possible face upon their conduct at Lade: he could easily have represented it as treachery of the blackest dye; indeed, he might have been expected to. But their response to Aeaces' overtures was, according to Herodotus, conditioned by the state of the Ionian forces they saw around them – demoralised and undisciplined, with no prospect of beating the Persians (and even if they did, Darius would return to the charge with a fleet five times as big!) – so they determined to save their city from an otherwise inevitable sack and destruction. Secondly, he singles out for commendation two Samian officers who fought gallantly at Salamis – on Xerxes' side. A possible example is his tart comment on the timorous allied naval strategy in 479: this may well have been inspired by impatient Samian friends who could not understand the delays.[16]

How long Herodotus lived on Samos cannot be reckoned. But what seems certain is that it was during his period of residence there that he embarked upon what was to be the first of his careers – travel. We cannot say precisely when he conceived the idea of composing his history or indeed the idea of any literary composition, but it is clear that he determined early on to satisfy his curiosity about the world both of Greece in its widest extent and of the 'barbarians' beyond its borders, and to record material of interest for future use in one form or another.[17]

This is a convenient point to mention some of the features of his travels as they appear in his work. First, it must not be supposed that Herodotus was an explorer in any geographical sense. Though his horizons

---

[14] Colaeus: iv. 152. For the rest, see Ch. 3, pp. 85 ff. and note; Sataspes: iv.43.

[15] Aesop: ii.134; Pythagoras: iv.95.

[16] For these examples, vi.13, viii.85, viii.132; for the last, cf. Ch. 4, p. 148.

[17] The question of how H's work may have originated and evolved into what we now possess has been intensively and not always profitably discussed. The most authoritative contribution, the starting point of most recent debate on the subject, is that of Jacoby in RE, Suppl. II, 1913. Cf. also J.L. Myres, *Herodotus, Father of History* Ch. II, and C.W. Fornara, *Herodotus* , Ch. I.

were infinitely broader than those of most Greeks of the age, and though he had visited more lands than all but the tiniest handful, he never broke new ground and never learned native tongues; his occasional remarks on native philology or grammar are usually infelicitous. Greek merchants had of course covered his ground long before, and many of Herodotus' contacts in foreign parts will have been established through the agency of these ubiquitous figures. Herodotus shows considerable interest in the processes and commodities of trade: Arabian spices, linen from Egypt and the Black Sea, corn grown specifically for export by Scythian tribesmen and the horns of wild oxen from Thrace are among the various trade goods that he mentions.[18] Details like the navigability of the Nile and Euphrates, and the size and type of boats that use them, are the sort of thing that his commercial friends will have helped him with,[19] little realising the contribution they were making to the study of ancient economic history.

THE TRAVELLER IN SCYTHIA

There is no need here to give a full account of all Herodotus' travels in Egypt, the Middle East and so on; it will be enough to discuss one example. Probably the earliest of his important expeditions was that to the north of the Black Sea, the home of the Scythians. He travelled by way of the Hellespont and either on the way out or back turned aside for a brief survey of parts of Thrace. Several stray details in different parts of his narrative suggest the eye-witness with a keen interest in the unusual: to give two examples, the story of the heroön of Protesilaus, and the gross sacrilege committed upon it by Artayctes the Persian, is hardly likely to have been common property; and the same goes for the little mention of how the natives of western Thrace treated the road over which Xerxes passed with reverence, and never ploughed or sowed it.[20] The journey by merchant ship up from the Bosporus to the joint mouth of the Hypanis (Bug) and Borysthenes (Dnieper) must have been dreary and uncomfortable, but Herodotus was abundantly rewarded by what he found at the end of it, for his Scythian excursus contains some of his most impressive ethnological work.

At the mouth of the Borysthenes stood a Milesian colony, founded in the second half of the seventh century. It was usually known by the name of the river though its official name was Olbia ('Prosperity'), and Herodotus records that its Greek citizens liked to refer to themselves as Olbiopolitans to distinguish themselves from the native Borysthenites. Some Greeks over

---

[18] Goods: iii.111, ii.105, iv.17, vii.126.

[19] Rivers: ii.29, 96, i.194.

[20] Protesilaus: ix.106; Thracians: vii.115.

the years had gone native, however, and Herodotus mentions a tribe of mixed Scytho-Hellenic race living inland of Olbia.[21] At Olbia Herodotus found an informant in the person of Tymnes, who acted as agent for the Scythian king Ariapeithes; as the only other Tymnes we hear of was the father of Histiaeus of Termera (Halicarnassus' near neighbour) we may wonder whether this useful person is yet another instance of the Halicarnassus connection.[22]

Archaeology has shown that much of Herodotus' observation of the customs of Scythia was of first-rate quality. His circumstantial account of Scythian royal burials, for instance, has been very largely vindicated. More curiously, so has his account of the vapour baths, caused by seeds of hemp (cannabis) being placed on red-hot stones inside a small wigwam-like structure. Examples of these have actually been discovered, not in southern Russia as it happens, but at a Scythian burial ground in western Mongolia – poles, leather covering, stones and even seeds in position! Herodotus says that this was for the purpose of purification after burial, but his own remarks on the ecstatic pleasure of the Scythians in their vapour baths give the truth away.[23]

He penetrated inland some way, sailing up the Bug or the Dnieper, the navigability of which he remarks upon, and was shown a colossal bronze bowl at a place called Exampaeus, 'six times as big as that dedicated by Pausanias at the entrance to the Black Sea'.[24]

We have mentioned the sympathy for barbarian ways that was to earn Herodotus the reproaches of the bigoted, and we saw in Chapter 5 how he, like Darius, endorsed Pindar's views on the sovereignty of custom. Some of his remarks on Scythia are particularly interesting from this point of view. He tells two similar stories to illustrate Scythian xenophobia. The details of the first came on the authority of his friend Tymnes: the sage Anacharsis, most travelled and most cultivated of all the Scythians, had visited the Milesian colony of Cyzicus in the Sea of Marmara. There he was impressed by a festival in honour of the Mother of the Gods (Cybele) and vowed that he would perform her rites himself on his safe return home. This he did in all due form; but he was seen and denounced to his brother, King Saulius, who came up and shot him dead; 'and now the Scythians deny any knowledge of Anacharsis, and all because he went off to Greece and picked up foreign ways'. This took place in the middle of the sixth century; the king was the father of that Idanthyrsus who led Darius' force such a dance in c. 514 and

---

[21] iv.17–18.

[22] Tymnes: iv.76, cf. p. 205, note 8.

[23] Burials: iv.71; cannabis: iv.73 f. For H and Scythian archaeology see, most recently, Tamara Talbot Rice, *The Scythians* (Thames & Hudson, London, 1957); she singles out the vapour-bath example.

[24] Exampaeus: iv.81.

probably grandfather of Tymnes' employer Ariapeithes.

The second story belongs to Herodotus' own lifetime, the best part of a century later. The victim this time was King Scyles; he was the son of Ariapeithes by a Greek lady from Istria, near the Danube's mouth – yet another Milesian colony. His philhellene tendencies went a long way further than Anacharsis': he had been brought up by his mother to read and speak Greek, and on becoming king had bought himself a fine property in Olbia, and from time to time would go there unescorted, and live, dress and worship as a Greek. The townspeople there helped him to conceal this from the native Scythians, but 'evil was destined to befall him': word got out that he had been initiated into the rites of Dionysus and some Scythian officers were able to watch the king participating in a Bacchic orgy: Herodotus had previously explained that the Scythians regarded such worship as a disgrace to Greece – fancy inventing a god who induced insanity in men! A revolt was raised against Scyles, he fled to Thrace, whence he was extradited and put to death.[25]

'Thus do the Scythians guard their own traditions, and such are the punishments they inflict upon those who seek to introduce alien ways': that is all the comment that Herodotus feels the need to make at the conclusion of the narrative. He does not condemn or criticise the Scythians, even though in each instance the worship of Greek gods was what caused the trouble. They were fully as entitled to their views as the Greeks were to theirs. Such an attitude on Herodotus' part must have been extremely rare in his day.

HERODOTUS' LIFE AND TRAVELS IN GREECE AND ITALY

It was probably in the mid-440s that Herodotus came to live in Athens for a time. A treaty had been made with Persia, the Thirty Years' Peace freshly signed with Sparta, the building of the Parthenon was under way and Pericles was almost – not quite – at the height of his powers: his last rival, the aristocratic and athletic Thucydides, son of Melesias, was still a force on the political scene. Athens was his base for tours in mainland Greece, and in addition to the battlefields (the topography of which, as we saw in Chapter 4, receives scrupulous attention) Herodotus got to know Delphi well and recorded many of its monuments: some of these are still extant, including the statues of Cleobis and Biton, the Siphnos treasury and the Serpent Column (which, by a pardonable slip, he calls the three-headed serpent).

---

[25] Anacharsis: iv.76; Scyles: iv.78–80.

A relief from the treasury of Siphnos, Delphi, justifying Herodotus' assertion that 'it was as good as the richest to be found there' (iii.57). (École Francaise d'Archéologie, Athens)

It is also usually the mention of dedications in temples, and the anecdotes attached to them, that testifies to his other visits, for example to Thebes, Aigina and Tegea, where he saw interesting items from the sixth century: in the temple of Ismenian Apollo at Thebes, a gold shield, spear and tripod sent by Croesus; at the temple of Aphaia[26] on Aigina, some ornamental prows from ships captured in a sea battle off Crete against the Samian exiles, c. 525; and at Tegea, the shrine of Athene Alea contained the fetters that the Spartan captives wore after their disastrous campaign in the 560s, as well as a spectacular trophy from the battle of Plataea.[27]

One of the most interesting of his minor visits was to the Spartan village of Pitana. There he gained some valuable historical information from Archias son of Samius, who passed on the family tradition relating to the Spartans' unsuccessful Samian campaign in the 520s. In his account of the Plataea campaign of 479 Herodotus names Amompharetus as 'commander

---

[26] *Athenaie* (Ionic-style) in MSS. But no major temple of Athene is known on Aigina; that of Aphaia on the other hand is described by Pausanias ii.30. The fine building now on the site, however, dates from a few years after the incident mentioned, c. 500 BC.

[27] Thebes: i.53, 92; Aigina: iii.59; Tegea: i.66, ix.70. Cf. p. 67.

of the Pitanate *lochos*' (battalion) – for which Thucydides ticks him off: 'there never was any such unit'. Possibly Herodotus made a technical slip in relation to Spartan military organisation, but no one can say that his opinion was uninformed; indeed he was very probably right. Thucydides was no pundit on Spartan military organization, as his fumbling over the Spartan numbers at Mantinea (418) makes clear.[28]

Of Herodotus' life in southern Italy we need not say much except to remark that there is some material in his book that suggests unusual knowledge of those parts. Thuria was founded by Athens, but as a Panhellenic colony, in the territory of Sybaris, which had been destroyed c. 510 by the neighbouring colony of Croton: Sybaris was famed for luxurious living, Croton for medicine, wrestling and puritanism. Herodotus tells us more than the strict claims of relevance demand about Democedes the Crotoniate physician and his relationship with Darius, and about the last adventures of the Spartan prince Dorieus who helped the Crotoniates in their war with Sybaris. To these may be added the curious little digression on Micythus regent of Rhegion, who dedicated some statues at Olympia and ended his days in exile at Tegea.[29]

It is generally accepted that Herodotus returned to Athens in the late 430s. He refers to four episodes in the opening phase of the Peloponnesian War: in 431 the Theban attack on Plataea and death of Eurymachus, the expulsion of the Aiginetans from their island by Athens, and the sparing of Decelea by the invading Peloponnesians; and, in 430, the execution of the Spartan ambassadors Aneristus and Nicolaus, along with Aristeas son of Adeimantus of Corinth.[30] Each of these references is introduced to tie up loose ends of some earlier story and, apart from the Aigina episode, their details are too minor to have become known to someone living in southern Italy. How long he stayed before returning to Thuria, where he is said to have died, we cannot say.

HERODOTUS' VIEW OF THE GREEK STATES

Mention of Herodotus' life and travels in Greece gives us an opportunity to discuss his views of the different states of Greece. It is quite reassuring to learn of his travels; some of the places he visited were hostile to Athens at the time he was writing, and he might otherwise have been at the mercy of strong Athenian misrepresentation. As it is, Aigina and Tegea get full credit for their respective roles in 480 and 479. The former does, however, come in for some sneers, doubtless inspired by Athens, in the narrative of 479. It

---

[28] Pitana: iii.55, ix.53; Th.i.20, v.68

[29] Democedes: iii.129–37, cf. pp. 109 and 162; Dorieus: v.41–8, cf. pp. 165 f., Micythus: vii.170.

[30] Respectively vii.23, vi.91, ix.73, vii.137; and cf. Th. ii.2–6, 27, 67, Th. calls the last-named 'Aristeus'.

was an Aiginetan named Lampon who advocated the mutilation of Mardonius' corpse and was stingingly rebuked by Pausanias. Then the Aiginetans were said to have traded upon the ignorance of the helots who gathered up the booty at Plataea, thereby laying the foundations of their prosperity – a comical notion that no reader of Herodotus can have taken seriously. Finally he suggests that the Aiginetan tomb at Plataea was a mere cenotaph erected ten years later, to disguise their absence from the battle proper: the fact may be correct, the attribution of motive is probably quite false.[31]

The Theban contingent is given credit for courageous and effective fighting on the Persian side at Plataea, although the general picture of Thebes is unfriendly. This is probably not just a matter of Athenian hostility, though the mutual antipathy of Athens and Thebes was one of the facts of Greek life. Admittedly we saw in Chapter 4 that the libellous treatment of the Thebans at Thermopylae was probably due to Athenian resentment against the family of the commander Leontiadas. But Thebes was not popular in Greece, not only because she had been the most active and zealous of all the Medising states, but because of her tendency to bully her neighbours, in Herodotus' period most obviously Plataea and Thespiae. Thucydides states that it was almost entirely for the gratification of Thebes that Sparta sanctioned the destruction of Plataea in 427.[32]

Corinth is an interesting case – an enemy of Athens from 433 onwards, and Aristeas son of Adeimantus a persistent thorn in Athens' side.[33] Yet as we saw in Chapter 4 the Corinthians in general do not get a wholly bad press for their part in Xerxes' war. Herodotus as good as denies the slanderous Athenian allegation of cowardice at Salamis; the bitterness is reserved for their commander Adeimantus – another example of hereditary resentment. The Corinthians are among the minor contingents at Plataea who Herodotus says advanced 'in no order . . . and died without honour' – an unjust comment on their tactical role – but at Mycale they distinguished themselves and received their due credit. Corinth also emerges well from earlier episodes: it was the Corinthians who twice quashed Spartan schemes to undo Athens' democratic revolution, and they gave Athens solid and valuable aid in her war with Aigina in the 480s.[34]

After Herodotus' treatment of Thebes, the other principal Medising states, Thessaly and Argos, could consider themselves let down rather

---

[31] Sneers: ix.78–80, 85. H is in fact perfectly well aware of Aigina's past greatness in the world of commerce. As we saw, he mentions the Aiginetans' own temple at Naucratis in Egypt; and Sostratus of Aigina he describes as a trader 'beyond compare' (iv.152).

[32] vi.108, cf. Th.iii.68; also Th.iv.133 (Thebes destroys Thespiae's fortifications) and vi.95 (she supports an unpopular government there).

[33] For Adeimantus, and Leontiadas of Thebes, see Ch. 4, pp. 135 f. and 129 f.

[34] On these episodes, see pp. 141, 170, 187 and vi.89.

lightly. This may partly be because they lent less effective aid to Xerxes – in Argos' case none whatsoever – and partly because the general trend of their policy in the middle and late fifth century was favourable to Athens; in fact both were at times formally allied to her. But neither state was as generally unpopular as Thebes was. Nor could anyone have seriously expected Argos to join the allied coalition. Fourteen years was insufficient for her to have made anything like a full recovery from the crippling losses inflicted by King Cleomenes at Sepeia;[35] and it was in any case barely conceivable that Argos would actually accept orders from Sparta.

Herodotus quotes a total of three versions purporting to explain Argos' conduct in Xerxes' war: the third, alleging that Argos called in Persia to redress the balance against Sparta, he mentions so briefly as effectively to dismiss it. The two preceding versions have in common the central fact that Argos asked for an equal share in the allied command with Sparta and was refused. The Argives' own account – Herodotus tells it in *oratio obliqua*, repeating three times that it is an Argive version – puts the city in the most favourable light, willing to join the alliance on equal terms of command despite the warnings of Delphi and the losses of Sepeia, and only prevented from doing so by Spartan intransigence. The version current in the rest of Greece alleged overtures from Persia to Argos before the war, and suggested that Argos' claim to joint command was made in the sure knowledge that it would be rejected, thereby providing a pretext for keeping out of the war. This was supported by evidence of diplomatic contacts between Argos and Persia in the reign of Artaxerxes.

It is the latter version that Herodotus appears to accept, for he says 'As to all this, I express no opinion beyond what the Argives themselves say . . . I see it as my duty to record what is said, but it is by no means my duty to believe it – a principle which can be applied to my entire work.' But he interrupts this by saying that if every man were given an opportunity to meet and exchange his troubles with another, he would take a good look at his neighbour's troubles and be only too glad to take his own back home with him – 'and on that basis, the Argives are not the worst offenders there have ever been'. Thus Herodotus accepts the guilt of the Argives, but palliates it by saying that others (the Thebans?) were worse – a piece of reasoning that Plutarch so misunderstands that he cites this entire passage as yet another example of Herodotus' 'malice', at the expense of Argos![36]

Plutarch also attacks Herodotus' treatment of the Phocians: 'The Phocians were the only people [in central Greece] who did not Medise, for no other reason, as far as I can see, than their hatred of the Thessalians; they

---

[35] See Ch. 5, pp. 173 f.

[36] vii.148–52; Plut. *MH*, 863C-D.

would have Medised, I think, if Thessaly had supported the allied cause.'[37] On the face of it, certainly unfair, for Phocis sent a contingent to Thermopylae (which, however, failed to do its job) and afterwards the Phocians saw their land terribly ravaged; some continued to wage guerrilla war around Mount Parnassus, while their contingent with Mardonius in 479 served under duress.[38] All the same the comment may be a true one! Something quite similar, after all, obtained between Argos and Sparta: whichever side Sparta was on, Argos was almost sure to be on the other one. Even today in country parts of Greece one can find villages where the men vote *en bloc* for one political party because it is known that the next village gives its corporate support to the opposition. Neither the Phocian nor the Locrian contributions at Thermopylae, incidentally, earned them a mention on the Serpent Column, the inscription of which was simply headed 'These fought in the War'.[39]

But it is Herodotus' view of the Big Two, Athens and Sparta, that must be of the greatest interest. His adult lifetime saw the breakdown in their alliance – a development precipitated by the helot revolt of 464 – and the so-called First Peloponnesian War; the Thirty Years' Peace and the strains to which it was subjected before it broke down after only 14 years; and the opening phase of the great Peloponnesian War, Thucydides' war. We have already discussed his handling of leading personalities on both sides and his account of their military efforts from 490 to 479. All we need do here is to consider his general view of the two cities and try to judge where, if anywhere, his sympathies lie.

Though the exact terminal dates are not firmly ascertainable, Herodotus' residence in Athens certainly included some of the brilliant years of the Periclean peace. When and why he left for Thuria we do not know – perhaps it was in 440 when Athens fell out with his beloved Samos.[40] What is interesting, however, is that none of the glamour of Athens in the 440s has rubbed off on his work. He mentions a dedication on the Acropolis set up c. 506 after Athens' victory over Boeotia and Chalcis, which archaeology suggests was destroyed by the Persians in 480 and restored in, probably, 457. But of the great programme of public works that got under way in the years of peace, and of the masterpieces of Pheidias, he says nothing, despite his obvious interest in

---

[37] viii.27–33; Plut. *MH*, 868B-E.

[38] ix.17, 31.

[39] The names inscribed on the column tally very closely with H's list of forces at Salamis and Plataea: every name on the col. appears in H, but he adds one ship each from Lemnos (a deserter), Seriphos and Croton, 200 hoplites from Pale, and the Mantineans who were too late for Plataea: viii.43–8, 83; ix.28–30, 77.

[40] How & Wells, pp. 6–8, discuss evidence that points to 446–440 being the exact years that H lived in Athens.

the visual arts.[41]

Perhaps more surprisingly, he is untouched by the great contemporary movement of Athenian literature. There is, as we have seen, independent evidence of his friendship with Sophocles, and there are some striking similarities between passages in their works, but it is at least as probable that Sophocles is echoing Herodotus as vice versa. (The date of *Oedipus Tyrannus* is of course not known, but the most plausible supposition is that it was inspired by the plague at Athens and therefore dates from the early 420s, too late to have any influence on Herodotus' work.) In any case Herodotus mentions neither Sophocles nor Euripides, the other living master of tragedy. And yet his interest in poetic literature was great. He not only knew his Homer and Hesiod,[42] he was well read in the early lyric and elegiac poets: he quotes effortlessly and without any parade of learning from Archilochus, Sappho and Alcaeus, and Solon, as well as the much more shadowy figures of Aristeas of Proconnesus and Olen of Lycia; Arion of Methymna and Anacreon earn interesting mentions without quotation.[43] Of the poets whose lives overlapped with his own he quotes from Simonides (twice), Aeschylus and Pindar, and gives a good mention to the pioneer dramatist Phrynichus – dead, all of them, long before Herodotus' work began to take shape.[44] It is as though Herodotus' literary and artistic tastes were fixed in his youth and remained, cut in bronze as it were, unchanged throughout his life.[45]

The purpose of all this is to suggest that if Herodotus is to be convicted of partiality to Athens, it cannot be because he was captivated by the brilliance of Athens in his own day. In fact he very probably was not. Though he certainly approved of democracy in so far as it was a guarantee of freedom, he cannot have approved of everything done at Athens in its name. We have already discussed the Delphic ambiguity of the lion that symbolised Pericles,[46] and Herodotus cannot have approved of Pericles' citizenship law of 451. This law was a breach with Athenian tradition – it would have disqualified Themistocles and Cleisthenes, among others – and blighted the hopes of any metic who might have aspired to Athenian civic rights. Athens afforded Herodotus a home and an appreciative audience for his readings, and he moved in Athens' most exalted social circles – but that

---

[41] Acropolis dedication: v.77. Cf. M-L, no. 15 for fragments of both the original and the restored inscription; the latter, differing in the order of the lines, is the one that H saw and copied.

[42] Homer: ii.116 f. etc; Hesiod: iv.32.

[43] Respectively i.12, ii.135, v.95, v.113 (Solon); iv.13, iv.35, i.23, iii.121 (Anacreon).

[44] Respectively v.102 and vii.228, iii.38, ii.156, vi.21.

[45] Interestingly, H shows some acquaintance with sophistic patterns of thought, even though the heyday of the sophistic movement had not yet arrived. For examples, see Ch. 2, p. 68. Sophistry was not entirely, or even chiefly, an Athenian phenomenon.

[46] See Ch. 1, p. 32; on H and democracy, Ch. 3, pp. 100 f.

was all.

It is even less likely that he approved of Athens' growing imperialism under Pericles. The loss of freedom (in one or other of its senses) experienced by an increasing number of allies must have struck him as an abuse of power; or rather perhaps as an abuse of the victory that the gods granted in 479; for Athens had benefited from that to a far greater extent than any of the other loyalists. More poignantly, he must have seen that a decisive clash between Athens and Sparta over the question of hegemony could not be postponed for long; and, as he proclaims at the opening of his work the doctrine that no human prosperity is of long duration, he would not have been surprised by developments. Indeed he would have regarded the narrative of Thucydides, Books VI and VII, as the fulfilment of scripture.

His genuine admiration for Athens, therefore, is squarely founded upon her glorious record against Persia in the wars of 490 and 480/79. Writing in the days of strong imperialism, he says 'Here I feel bound to put forward a view that will be offensive to most people; but it seems to me true, so I shall not keep it back. If the Athenians . . . had abandoned their country, or had remained and surrendered to Xerxes, no attempt would have been made to resist the King at sea,' and any fortification of the Isthmus by the Spartans would have been pointless. 'As things are, one would not be wrong in maintaining that the Athenians were the saviours of Greece: whichever side they inclined towards was sure to prevail. They chose that Greece should survive, free . . . and it was they who, after the gods, drove back the King.'[47]

What a splendid panegyric! And yet there are two significant points. One is that Herodotus knows that the view is unpopular, true though it be – Athens was deeply disliked in the Greek world at large at the time of the outbreak of the Peloponnesian War.[48] The second is that the portion omitted in my translation contains a remarkable eulogy of Sparta – less eloquent, but forceful for all that. However well they fortified the Isthmus, 'the Spartans would have been abandoned by their allies – perforce; and thus abandoned, they would have performed heroic deeds and died gloriously. Or else, before that happened, they might have seen the rest of Greece Medising and so would have made terms with Xerxes: in either case, Greece would have fallen to Persia.' There is a subtle difference of treatment: Herodotus holds out the possibility that Athens might have Medised from the start; by not doing so, she won the war for Greece. But he appears to assume that Sparta would never do so, even if all others defected; only as an afterthought does he admit the possibility that she would, and then only

---

[47] vii.139.
[48] Th ii.8.4.

217

after finding herself isolated.

As we saw in Chapter 4, Herodotus is under the potent spell of the Spartan myth in his narrative of Thermopylae, which does to some extent exercise its influence over the surrounding passages too; some of the remarks put into Damaratus' mouth, for example, point the same way. One should beware of reacting with cynicism, for Sparta's actual war record speaks eloquently in her favour. However, Herodotus is not uncritical and is aware of some of the more sinister sides to Spartan life. For instance, in the story of the Minyae at Sparta – a context at least half mythological – he slips in the telling remark that the Spartans carry out their executions by night, never by day. This obviously refers to the hateful Spartan custom of covertly doing away with helots who might threaten the state's security; Thucydides records a particularly gross occurrence of this in the mid-420s.[49] And as we saw in Chapter 3, Herodotus could be critical of the secret processes of decision-making at Sparta, a thing which almost caused the Athenians to abandon the loyalist cause.

Some of Herodotus' comments on the two states are made in a dramatic but indirect way. Without naming Herodotus, but very obviously intending to contrast his own history with his great predecessor's, Thucydides (who is all too aware that his own work will seem dull, owing to the absence of a story-telling or 'romantic' quality in it) states that it was intended to be 'a possession of permanent value, rather than a composition designed to catch the ear of an immediate public'. The immensity of this claim is liable to be missed, because obviously Thucydides' work has been of permanent value, but then so has that of Herodotus, Sophocles, Aristophanes and the rest. The point is that Thucydides was the first writer who thought that he did not *need* to catch the ear of his contemporary audience; plainly he considered that Herodotus had in some unspecified ways departed from the literal fidelity of an historian in order to achieve that purpose.

What was it in Herodotus' work that Thucydides had in mind? Informed guesswork may perhaps come up with some answers: it seems to me that any passage of history which Herodotus has in some way shaped in order to make a contemporary point, or to cause a pleasurable frisson among his readers, has a claim to be considered under this heading. Some of these we have met already: the story of Phye of Paeania, a hit at the sophisticated pretensions of Periclean Athens; the satirical defence of the Alcmeonidae – his friends, whose disloyalty however he is well aware of;[50] the cunningly orchestrated portraits of Themistocles and Pausanias, heavy with overtones of their subsequent careers. Along with these I would put the

---

[49] iv.146, cf. Th.iv.80.

[50] See Ch. 1, p. 30 f.

obviously unhistorical episodes of Solon and Croesus, Polycrates and the Ring, and Xerxes' cabinet meeting, the three great theological passages fully discussed in Chapter 2. The fineness of their composition raises them above their surrounding contexts, and in each of them Herodotus is using the external trappings of dramatised historical narrative to put over what he sees as profound truths about the human condition.

But more interesting still are ironical passages that bear upon the contemporary political scene. A few examples will suffice. At the close of Book VIII, with the campaign of 479 about to begin, Mardonius made a serious and determined attempt to seduce Athens away from the loyalist side by skilful political warfare on the part of Alexander of Macedon. The Athenian reply is ringing Churchillian stuff:

> We too are aware that the power of Persia is many times greater than ours . . . but we long for freedom, and will defend ourselves by all the means in our power. As for making terms with the barbarian, do not attempt to persuade us: we shall never be persuaded. Take back to Mardonius this message from the Athenians – that so long as the sun continues on his present course, we shall never make terms with Xerxes; we shall fight him . . . trusting in the gods and heroes . . . whose temples and statues he destroyed by fire. Never show your face in Athens again with such a proposal.

A Spartan embassy, which had nervously sought to dissuade Athens from yielding, receives a similar reply, concluding thus: 'Rest assured of this, if you were not sure already, that so long as a single Athenian survives, we shall never come to terms with Xerxes.'[51]

This is splendid rhetoric for public consumption, but, as Herodotus goes on to point out only a few paragraphs later, Athens in secret diplomacy was still keeping open the option of Medism in order to put pressure on Sparta – quite justifiably, no one would now dispute.[52] But for Herodotus' readers, there is a deeper irony. To be sure, Athens never did make terms with Xerxes. But she did do a deal with Artaxerxes, and no very glorious deal at that: the Greek communities of Cyprus were abandoned to their fate, the general rights of the king over all Asia (including Ionia) were conceded, but Athens, freed now from the fear of Persian armed intervention, continued to draw tribute from Ionia and the rest of the Delian League; using it, what is more, to rebuild the very shrines that Xerxes had burnt to the ground.[53]

[51] viii.142–4.

[52] ix.7.

[53] By implication, I accept the 'Peace of Callias', and these are what I consider its main terms to be. This is not the place to argue the somewhat complex question.

The onset of the Peloponnesian War also causes some disturbing echoes. In the speech just referred to, the Spartan envoy is made to say, *inter alia*, 'It would be intolerable for the Athenians to be responsible for the enslavement of the Greeks, seeing that you have long since been seen as the liberators of many.' Fair enough in 479: but no reader of Herodotus could miss the phrasing. Sparta may have launched the Peloponnesian War in order to cut Athens down to size, but her publicly proclaimed purpose was the liberation of the Hellenes from Athenian tyranny – a hope falsified, alas! in the event, but no doubt sincerely believed by many in 431.[54]

Again, in the days of waiting before Plataea a dispute arose between Tegea and Athens as to who should have the secondary post of honour in the allied line. The Tegean spokesman justified his claim by a lengthy citation of mythology. The Athenian reply was a good deal briefer on mythology; their spokesman continued, 'But it is not much use recalling all this; for men who were then brave might now be degenerate, and those who were then insignificant might now be better men. So, enough of ancient history!' – and he goes on to base his claim on the glory of Marathon. Again, fair enough in 479. But in 432 the identical point was being made *against* Athens by Sthenelaïdas the Spartan ephor: 'If the Athenians did well against the Persians then, but are acting badly towards us now, they deserve double punishment for becoming bad having once been good.'[55] Admittedly this is in a speech in Thucydides, and Thucydides' speeches record what ought to have been said rather than what actually was said; even so this laconically expressed argument has the ring of authenticity; in any case, on Thucydides' own showing, it is the *sort* of argument that is all too likely to have been used against Athens then.

Nor does Sparta escape. As we saw in Chapter 5, Damaratus, in preparing Xerxes for the ordeals to come, praises the Spartans for various qualities, but in particular their reverence for and obedience to Law (*nomos*).[56] It is a not very important irony that this is put into the mouth of one who was swindled out of his royal position in Sparta. Set in the context of 432–429 it looks decidedly hollow. The Thirty Years' Peace of 446 contained a clause that disputes be referred to arbitration – to use the Greek formula, 'just judgement and oath'; in other words, the disputing parties swear beforehand to abide by the decision of the agreed arbitrator.

Now of course in all diplomacy there is an element of gamesmanship, and arbitration is no exception. Few states would be very willing to submit

---

[54] Th.i.124.3, i.139.3, ii.8.4–5.

[55] ix.27, cf. Th.i.86.

[56] The chief command of Spartan 'Law', according to Damaratus, was never to abandon one's post in battle but to win or fall (vii.104; see Ch. 5, p. 181). In 425 BC, when H's work was newly published, the Greek world was somewhat stunned to learn that a considerable Spartan force had in fact laid down its arms on Sphacteria island. This can only have been an unforeseen bonus for H (cf. Th.iv.40.1).

to arbitration if they were sure that the judgement would go against them; still, most fifth-century treaties included such a provision. In 432 Athens offered to submit to arbitration on the disputes over Potidaea and the rest, and (in a Thucydides speech, but quite credibly) King Archidamus, a personal friend of Pericles and an advocate of caution, declared 'It is not lawful [nomimon] to proceed against a party who offers to submit to arbitration as though he is in the wrong.'[57] But this sage advice was swept aside by the ephor Sthenelaïdas and a large majority vote in the Spartan Ecclesia; the treaty was torn up and war declared. So much for arbitration and the Spartans' respect for 'Law'! They knew they had the weaker case, but were confident that they would prevail in war.

The point is put more generally into the mouth of a barbarian. Mardonius, in his address to Xerxes at the cabinet meeting, says, 'Since the Greeks share a common language, surely they should settle their differences by the use of diplomacy, or anything at all rather than war' – a fair criticism, many would think, and poignant reading in the 420s.[58]

We will end with a remarkable example of this dramatic irony. Herodotus knows that the Peloponnesian Wars, both that of the 450s and Thucydides' war, were fought over the question of supremacy in Greece[59] and he regards this development as flowing inevitably from the Persian War and the way the allied victory was shared. He never idealises the relationship of Athens and Sparta in 490 and 480/79. On the contrary, the strains, misunderstandings and occasional accusations of bad faith are realistically treated: allies drawn together under the pressure of some dire threat from outside really do behave like that, but if the pressure is strong enough they will stay together and win. The political and military difficulties of that alliance in Xerxes' war were not all that different from the problems of Anglo-French co-operation in 1914–18, nor of the Russian alliance and the 'Second Front' controversy from 1941.

Herodotus gives us an excellent and entertainingly dramatised picture of this in the episode of the allied embassy to Gelon of Syracuse: the humorous and masterful tyrant is contrasted with the anxious and prickly ambassadors. Such an embassy was certainly sent, and tradition preserved the name of one of its members, Syagrus of Sparta. Yet again, however, the narrative is unhistorical: with a major war with Carthage looming, there can have been no question of Gelon offering aid to the homeland, and so Herodotus allows his imaginative gifts full play. After some preliminary fencing, Gelon makes an offer of forces on a breathtaking scale – provided that he has the supreme command in the war. The Spartan Syagrus rejects

[57] Th.i.85.2; for the formula, Th.v.18.4 (Peace of Nicias).

[58] vii.9b.

[59] vi.98.

this out of hand: 'Agamemnon would groan aloud if he heard that Sparta had been deprived of her command by Gelon and the Syracusans! . . . If you don't like the thought of being under orders, don't come to our help.' Gelon's response is to settle for command in one element, preferably the navy. This time the Athenian envoy leaps in and – at rather greater length than the Spartan, but with a similar dash of mythology in support – quashes the idea. The only naval command Athens would accept other than her own was that of Sparta.

Gelon dismisses them with a witticism and a rebuke. 'My Athenian friend: it seems that you have the generals, but will have no men for them to command. So – since you make no concession, but want to possess the whole – you should get back to Greece without delay, and tell her that for her, the Spring has been taken out of the year.' This fine closing phrase is not obviously relevant in 481/0; the Greeks after all won the war. But it was quoted by Herodotus directly from a funeral oration of Pericles, in reference to the slain youth of Athens,[60] probably the actual oration delivered in 431. (The phrase does not appear in Thucydides' composition, but that is not disproof.) As the Peloponnesian War was ultimately a conflict of two sides who 'were unwilling to make any concessions, but desired to possess the whole', the contemporary relevance of the Gelon episode is all too easily appreciated.[61]

THE IMPACT OF HERODOTUS' WORK

The appearance of Herodotus' finished work before an Athenian public whose appetite was whetted by the memory of his earlier readings was a matter of great interest. No ancient writer says so, but more eloquent than any such statement is the fact that Aristophanes immediately draws upon Herodotus for material to parody and for general entertainment value. His first extant play is *The Acharnians* of 425. The fact that this excellent comedy has two substantial passages of clear allusion to Herodotus, assuming knowledge of his work among the audience, is evidence that the *Histories* were freshly published then, for Aristophanes tends to reserve his satire for what is prominent and in the public eye; obscurity earned no laughs. Herodotus is not named and there is no physical parody of him (unlike the cases of Socrates, Euripides and others), so he was probably not in Athens in 425.

Thucydides tells us that in late 425 negotiations with Persia were in the air, both at Athens and Sparta.[62] In *The Acharnians* a party of Athenian

---

[60] Aristotle, *Rhet*.iii.10, i.7.

[61] This point has been well argued by Fornara, *Herodotus*, pp. 82–4, to which I am much indebted.

[62] Th.iv.50.

ambassadors return from the Persian court – after an absence of eleven years. What hardships they had endured! They slowly made their way up the Cayster (the route of the Athenians to Sardis in 498), in covered carriages (just as Xerxes did); their hosts compelled them to drink neat wine out of gold and crystal goblets (like Xerxes and Mardonius); and when the king entertained them, he treated them to oxen baked whole ('Poppycock!' interjects Dicaeopolis) – exactly as Herodotus describes a Persian gentleman's birthday celebrations, with the option of a whole horse, ass or even camel baked instead; and finally Aristophanes brings on stage Pseudartabas, the 'King's Eye', remembering that the boy Cyrus, when playing at being king, had appointed just such an official.[63] (It was in fact a genuine Persian appointment.)

There Herodotus' subject matter is being pressed into the service of Aristophanic merriment; no less entertaining is the famous parody of his preface. Herodotus opens with a light-hearted look at the *cherchez-la-femme* school of historical criticism; he briefly rehearses the legends of abduction that were supposed to provide an origin for the antipathy of Europe and Asia, and dismisses them. Aristophanes is thus in effect parodying a parody when he supplies a comic origin for the Peloponnesian War in the form of Simaetha the courtesan: when she was kidnapped from Megara by some tipsy Athenian youths, Megara retaliated by the theft of two girls from Aspasia's courtesan school. This was the signal for Pericles to propose the 'Megarian Decree', and so on.[64]

There was evidently still some mileage to be obtained eleven years later, for in *The Birds* of 414, Pisthetairus tells the chorus to build themselves a city like Babylon, fortified with walls of baked brick; and when, a few scenes later, word reaches him that the wall of Cloudcuckootown is complete, 600 feet high with room for *two* chariots to pass on top, we realise that Aristophanes has simply doubled two of the salient statistics that Herodotus quotes for the real Babylon.[65]

A few echoes are traceable in the tragedians. Leaving aside the correspondences of thought already discussed, there are some passages in Sophocles worth mentioning, because they suggest some familiarity with odd parts of the Histories. Orestes' remarks (in *Electra*) on the advantages of a return to life after supposed death are reminiscent of the story of Salmoxis – the version, that is, retailed by the Hellespontine Greeks; and when (in *Oedipus Coloneus*) Sophocles makes Oedipus complain of his sons – 'just like the men of Egypt who sit at home weaving, while the women are

---

[63] Ar. *Ach.* 65–94; cf. v.100, vii.41, vii.119, ix.80, i.133, i.114.

[64] Ar. *Ach.* 524–34. Presumably on the principle that many a true word is spoken in jest, this glorious parody has caused many, from Plutarch onwards, to suppose the Megarian Decrees really were the cause of the war, despite the plain evidence of Thucydides' text.

[65] Ar. *Av.* 1125–31, cf. i.178 f. (H actually says '200 royal cubits').

the breadwinners!' – he obviously has in mind Herodotus' well-known passage on the topsy-turvy roles of the sexes in Egypt.[66]

Euripides provides less of substance. 'Call no man happy till he be dead' evidently became a commonplace and is found more than once in his dramas.[67] More interestingly, the plot of *Helen* takes its cue from the version of the myth that Herodotus narrates in his Egyptian history; and when, in *The Suppliant Women*, Theseus inveighs against tyranny, he seems to have got some of his ideas from reading the story of Thrasybulus and Periander.

HERODOTUS, THUCYDIDES AND HISTORY

Thucydides was about a generation younger than Herodotus and never names him. The only historian he does mention is Hellanicus of Lesbos, and that with dismissive contempt.[68] (If Hellanicus' account of the years 478-439 really did compare unfavourably with Thucydides' own in respect of fullness and chronological precision, we can bear the loss of his work with perfect equanimity.) But there are clear indications that he regarded Herodotus as his only serious predecessor in the historical field and aimed to appear distinctively different from him. After putting the story of Harmodius and Aristogeiton into perspective (in agreement with Herodotus), he then makes two specific corrections of points of fact in Herodotus' work. So small are the details involved that there is no doubt that Herodotus is the authority being criticised: the Spartan kings and their proxies and the 'Pitanate' battalion in the Spartan army. As we have seen, on the first of these Herodotus does get into a linguistic muddle with the surely unintended result that the kings are given two votes each; as regards the latter, he may not have made a mistake at all. One feels that if these were the worst mistakes Thucydides could find, Herodotus did not do at all badly. More seriously, Thucydides had fault to find with Herodotus' presentation – at least, we confidently assume that it is Herodotus that he is referring to; we have discussed earlier his view of compositions aiming to catch the ear of an immediate public.[69] Thucydides saw no future for imaginative dramatic invention in history. No 'Solon and Croesus', no 'Appeal to Gelon', no 'Damaratus and Xerxes' for him, even though each of these passages contains important non-narrative truth; and no reshaping of past events to make a contemporary point.

And yet in one respect Thucydides could be said to have strained at the

---

[66] *El.* 62–4, cf. iv.95; *OC*, 337–41, cf. ii.35. Both plays are later than H's work.

[67] E.g. *Troades*, 509 f.; Helen: ii.112–15; Supplices, 445–9, cf. v.92.

[68] Th.i.97.

[69] Th.i.20–2, cf. pp. 218-222; see also Ch. 1, pp. 18 f, for a separate correction of H by Th.

gnat and swallowed the camel. It would be quite wrong to make Thucydides the author of a complete methodological revolution. His mode of gathering information was exactly the same as Herodotus' – oral. True, he does sometimes quote documents, the texts of treaties, mainly in Books V and VIII; but then so does Herodotus, copiously – inscriptions at historical sites, and oracles of Delphi that have a bearing on important events. To see the truth of that, one only need look at the episodes that Thucydides handles after a lapse of 60 years or so – roughly the interval that separates Herodotus from much of his material. Nothing could be more 'Herodotean' in treatment than the story of Themistocles and the refortification of Athens, an episode narrated with infectious relish. The same goes for the digression on Pausanias' last days: details like Xerxes' 'delight', the role of the message bearer and the ephor's tip-off in the street give the story its period charm. Thucydides actually 'improves on' Herodotus by making Pausanias a suitor for the hand of Xerxes' daughter rather than Megabates'. Themistocles' later days are similarly treated: his adventurous flight (complete with pretty ethnological detail from Epirus) and his letter to Artaxerxes are well worthy of Herodotus.[70]

But it was probably because, on the one hand, Thucydides saw no alternative to oral evidence and, on the other, he saw its limitations clearly, that he decided to confine himself to events of his own time for the main body of his work. Partly as a result, the two historians have utterly different views of their relationship with the reader. Herodotus, as any casual reading shows, makes it clear when he is making statements on the responsibility of some person, party or community other than himself; material assembled by more remote hearsay, especially in relation to distant lands that he has not visited, is also generally presented in such a way as not to mislead. When there are two or more versions of some event in circulation, he generally feels it his duty to present them without overtly committing himself to one, though sometimes doing so by clear implication. (The episodes of the Medism of Argos and the Corinthians at Salamis are examples of this.) This is one of the features of Herodotus' work that gives it its open-textured quality (*fusus*, Quintilian called him) that has always been found attractive.

With Thucydides the case is quite different. He sees it as the historian's duty to make up the reader's mind for him; and the simplest way of achieving that is to eliminate, as far as possible, alternative versions. Leaving aside the remoter episodes discussed earlier, one of the most impressive things about Thucydides' work is the tremendous air of authority with which the narrative is put across – *his* authority. He never lets his guard slip; we very seldom even glimpse the sources behind him.

---

[70] Respectively Th.i.89–93, 128–34, 135–8.

When he states that he has cross-checked his oral information, and implies that he admits into his text only what passes his strict tests of acceptability, we believe him. But it is obvious that he could only have satisfied his own criteria with a history of his own day; cross-checking of remoter events was not possible.

Another respect in which Thucydides represents an advance on Herodotus without being revolutionary is in his handling of cause and motivation. As we saw in Chapter 4, Herodotus is aware of some of the factors that lie behind great events – imperialist ambition, for instance; his grasp of this question is a good deal more secure than he has sometimes been given credit for. But lesser events do not always get such satisfactory treatment: the Persians invade Samos because Syloson once gave Darius a cloak, Miltiades attacks Paros in order to pay out a personal enemy, and so on. In Thucydides the causes of lesser events are still personal, but more generalised: things happen in certain ways because Cleon and Brasidas, Alcibiades and Nicias, are the *sort* of men they are – a useful step forward.[71]

Thucydides' superiority to Herodotus as a critic of military tactics is too obvious and well-known to need discussion, though (as we saw in Chapter 4) Herodotus has a good grasp of the broader issues of strategy. One technique of historiography which Thucydides could fairly claim to have revolutionised, however, is the handling of chronology. Herodotus made a brave pioneering effort to bring Greek and Oriental chronologies into some sort of relationship: the opening paragraphs of Book VII, for instance, give a good idea of the time taken by Xerxes' preparations after Darius' death, and 'the archonship of Calliades' pins the invasion down to 480.[72] But there remains a certain hit-and-miss quality about it. Thucydides, with his systematic scheme of summers and winters, independent of the different calendars of the contending states, showed how it could be done. (Even so, one wonders how successfully he could have projected this method back into the past: the chronology of the 'Pausanias and Themistocles' digression is notoriously vague and difficult.)

But there are points of resemblance too. One is their interest in medicine. Herodotus records all sorts of medical details: the Egyptians' custom of purging themselves periodically with emetics – 'on the supposition that all illnesses that men are prone to stem from the food they eat'; Democedes' successful treatment of Darius' torn ligaments; the cauterising of the veins of the head in Libya, to prevent catarrh; the 'female disease' (whatever that may have been) among the Scythians; the absence of any professional medical care in Babylon; and the unusually thick skulls of

---

[71] iii.140; vi.133; cf. Th.v.16 etc.
[72] viii.51.

the Egyptians.[73] Not surprisingly, Thucydides cannot match this versatility; but his powerful account of the Plague of Athens suggests knowledge that goes beyond a mere layman's interest. He also mentions the debilitating attack of nephritis that Nicias suffered at Syracuse, which undoubtedly affected his judgement.[74] As Athens was no medical Mecca, this point is worth noting.

More generally, Thucydides borrowed from Herodotus the technique of direct speech and developed it. We discussed in Chapter 4 the way in which Herodotus puts short speeches into the mouths of his characters, often not as a mere literary device, but in order to convey non-narrative matter.[75] As is well known, Thucydides' speeches are generally the vehicles for 'issues' – explanations of motive or of policy; sometimes self-justification on the part of the speaker; in the case of the Funeral Speech, painting an eloquent picture of Athens and the Athenians before the decline set in.

The average speech in Thucydides is a good deal longer than the average Herodotean example, and more generalised, not to say philosophical, in content.[76] Thucydides also claims to have taken trouble to achieve verisimilitude in one sense or another; though they are his own compositions they aim to reproduce what the speaker ought to have said, or at least might have said, on the given occasion; there will be no wholly imaginative compositions such as appear in Herodotus. And yet for this a price has to be paid. There is inescapably an air of artificiality about many of Thucydides' speeches. They look like what they are, carefully contrived set pieces, with none of the Herodotean spontaneity.[77] They are often composed in ferociously difficult Greek and we can be sure that no one ever actually spoke in that style. Even in his own day Thucydides cannot have been an 'easy' writer, and whenever he is handling ideas rather than factual narrative his mastery of the language's resources seems imperfect. This criticism applies also to his accounts of the plague, the revolution in Corcyra, and (more briefly) the character of Themistocles, for in each of these passages he is grappling with abstractions. One lesson that Thucydides failed to learn from Herodotus was the importance of lucidity and readability.

In the field of the emotions the two differ greatly, a thing which one would be inclined to put down to personalities rather than to any desire on the part of Thucydides to be different. Herodotus has a peculiar bitter-sweet quality: no reader can miss the notes of sadness and pity that are struck

---

[73] Respectively ii.77, iii.129 f., iv.187, i.105, i.197, iii.12.

[74] Th.ii.47–54, vii.15.

[75] p. 109 and note 29.

[76] The longest in H, Sosicles' at v.92, is a vehicle for the transmission not of ideas but of *logoi*.

[77] Exactly as Quintilian observed (x.i.73): Thuc. excelled in *contiones*, H in *sermones*. The rest of Quint.'s epigrammatic review is equally just to both.

from time to time in his work; and yet this is lightened by passages of champagne-like sparkle and humour – Cyrus and the Spartan envoys, Aristagoras' appeal to Cleomenes, the tales of the Alcmeonidae, Mardonius and Xerxes' cabinet, the exploits of Artemisia and many another; even some jokes, such as a remark of Anacharsis that he rejects but cannot resist quoting.[78]

It would be untrue to deny Thucydides a sense of humour, but it is not very pervasive and tends to be reserved for slightly malicious use against his dislikes. No one could fail to laugh at Cleon's discomfiture in the Ecclesia in 425; but the posthumous jibe at Cleon and the remarks on the fecklessness of democracy are more calculated to raise a mirthless smile.[79] On the other side, Thucydides maintains an air of detachment for much of the time, truly remarkable for a contemporary and an Athenian involved in the events, and this lends further authority to his narrative; consequently when real tragedy does strike, in the latter part of Book VII, it does so with terrific impact.

One vital difference between Herodotus and Thucydides remains to be discussed, and that is their subject matter. One might have supposed that the Father of History fixed for all time to come what lay within the compass of the historian – but not so. It was Thucydides, the most influential historian who ever lived, who did that. Ethnography and geography are heavily pruned (some notes on Thrace and Sicily survive), art and literature fall away; religion – still a powerful and formative influence on the minds of men – is either ignored or slighted. War, diplomacy and politics are what remain in bulk; and the ins and outs of domestic politics do not interest Thucydides all that much until he embarks on his model account of the events of 411.

He thus sets the pattern for the rest of ancient history. Xenophon, Polybius, Caesar, Sallust (whom Quintilian flatteringly compares with Thucydides) and Tacitus all fall to some degree into the mould. Even in the case of Livy, though his treatment of events is often Herodotean, his subject matter is that of Thucydides. The tradition can be traced down the centuries. It is there in Guicciardini's *Storia d'Italia* of the mid-sixteenth century: so busy is he in chronicling the ups and downs of the Italian princely houses, the French, Spanish and Austrians that he does not name the artist responsible for a great bronze statue of Pope Julius II thrown down in a riot at Bologna.[80] It is there in Kinglake's monumental *Invasion of the Crimea* (though his better-known masterpiece, *Eothen*, is a

---

[78] 'The Greeks are too busy to attend to any intellectual matters—all except the Spartans, who are the only ones able to conduct a reasonable conversation' (iv.77).

[79] Th.iv.27 f., v.16, viii.1.

[80] Michelangelo!

Herodotean work), in Churchill's *World Crisis* and dozens of others.

Some parts of the Herodotean tradition were kept alive, however. Caesar, in his well-known excursus on the Gauls and Germans,[81] showed that ethnography was still of legitimate interest to the historian. Tacitus introduced such matter into *Agricola* (on Britain) and his *Histories* (on the Jews), and his *Germania* is a full-length ethnographic treatise. Plutarch had a range of interests that could at least be compared with Herodotus', but he never essayed full-scale historical composition. Herodotus' work, seemingly, stood on its own.

And yet time has wrought a strange vindication of Herodotus. Ethnography of his type – travellers' accounts of strange peoples – was reborn at the Renaissance with the expansion of Europe's horizons to the New World. The nineteenth century saw a further upsurge in this field, especially in relation to Africa. To cite one example out of many, much of J.H. Speke's *Journal of the Discovery of the Source of the Nile* is work after Herodotus' heart. And then the twentieth century has seen a reappraisal of the importance of social, economic and cultural history, modern, medieval and ancient. Such subject matter as formed part of Herodotus' varied tapestry is now the object of systematic and sympathetic study. When a book like *Montaillou* (Emmanuel Le Roy Ladurie) earns critical acclaim and arouses wide public interest, we can say that Herodotus' claim to be the Father of History is more true today than it has ever been.

---

[81] *Bell.Gall.*vi.11–28.

APPENDIX ONE: HERODOTUS AND THE IONIANS

Herodotus' alleged prejudice against the Ionians has been looked at in Chapter 4, but it is not entirely confined to his account of the revolt, nor can it be dismissed as wholly imaginary. It is only the Ionian cities of the Asian mainland that are meant in this connection, for Chios, Samos and most obviously Athens are exempt. Yet the claim of Athens to be the mother-city of the Ionians is asserted at the beginning, in the middle and at the end of his work. In discoursing on the state of Ionia at the time of the Persian conquest he speaks of 'those who started out from the *prytaneion* [town hall] in Athens'; Aristagoras bases his appeal to Athens on the fact that Miletus was a colony of hers; and after Mycale, the Peloponnesian proposal to resettle the Ionians in mainland Greece is successfully resisted by the Athenians on the grounds that they are 'colonists of their own'.[1] Herodotus also mentions the Apaturia – the phratry (kinship-group) festival that was common to Athens and nearly all the Asian Ionians. It seems to follow that whatever the basis for his feeling is, it is not racial.

Herodotus represents the Ionian communities as playing no very glorious part in the fall of the Lydian kingdom. Urged by Cyrus to revolt in Croesus' rear when the latter opened his invasion of Cappadocia, they refused – understandably: they supposed, like Delphi, that Croesus would win. By tendering their submission after the issue was decided, they invited Cyrus' grimly humorous reproof. He treated them as enemies, but adroitly separated Miletus from the rest, evidence of disunity that Herodotus pounces upon: 'All the Hellenic race was weak at that time, but the Ionians were far and away the weakest of the Greek peoples, and of least account. Apart from Athens, there was no Ionian community worth talking about.'[2]

A similar note is struck in the narrative of Darius' Scythian expedition. The Ionian forces at the bridge under Histiaeus of Miletus and his colleagues pretended to accede to the Scythians' suggestion that they destroy it and strand Darius, but did no more than go through the motions. 'The Scythians judge the Ionians, as free men, to be the most cowardly and faint-hearted in the world; and reckoning them as slaves, they say they are the most attached to their masters and utterly disinclined to run away.'[3] The jibe gains force from being put into the mouth of a brave and successful barbarian people, but is doubly unfair: it stigmatises the Ionians as a whole for what (on Herodotus' own showing) was a carefully calculated act of self-

---

[1] i.146; v.97; ix.106.

[2] i.143.

[3] iv.142.

interest on the part of the commanders; and the majority of the commanders were not Ionians anyway, though Histiaeus no doubt set the tone.

As fair-mindedness is widely and rightly agreed to be one of Herodotus' most characteristic qualities, this calls for explanation. The disunity, infirmity of purpose and ultimate treachery that marked the revolt are probably adequate to account for Herodotus' generally harsh judgement on that enterprise;[4] and it is possible that this feeling would spill over into the other passages dealing with Ionia. At any rate I see no reason for supposing that in them Herodotus is writing from a Dorian standpoint, Dorian though he was by birth: his text simply does not suggest that Dorian-Ionian antagonism was strong enough to demand that sides be taken.

A more probable reason is the fact that the Ionians of Asia had forgotten what freedom was, and that was the commodity that he most prized. For most of the sixth century they were under barbarian rule, first Lydian, then Persian; after the brief episode of the revolt they were back under Persia, then, on liberation, they passed into Athens' alliance, as second-class allies from the start, contributing a money tribute rather than maintaining armed forces of their own as Chios, Samos and others did.

There remains, however, one curious point. Herodotus ends his entire work with a little moralising anecdote of Cyrus: to Artembares' suggestion that the Persians, now that they were lords of the Middle East, should move to a less rugged land, he replied 'By all means, but be prepared no longer to rule, but to be ruled: for soft lands generally produce soft men' – recognising the wisdom of which the Persians elected to stay in their own harsh and barren homeland.[5] This forms a beautifully appropriate conclusion to a work that deals with the themes of war and empire – and at the very moment that Athens is embarking on her imperial career with the capture of Sestos: if one is not to be ruled by others, sacrifices, sometimes great ones, must be made. But it also has a peculiar relevance to Ionia. For in his early sketch of Ionia he states that the mainland Ionians happened to have founded their cities in the most perfect climate in the known world – not so cold and wet as points north, nor so hot and dry as points south.[6]

I would not suggest a deliberate cross-reference on Herodotus' part; rather, a straightforward statement of belief. He was not alone in assuming a link between a mild climate and the lack of warlike qualities; the idea is found, developed at some length, in a quasi-scientific work that was roughly contemporary with Herodotus, the Hippocratic treatise *On Airs, Waters and*

---

[4] See Ch. 4, pp. 117-125.

[5] ix.122.

[6] i.142.

Places.[7] With this question effectively pre-judged in his mind, Herodotus would have believed from the start that the mainland Ionians were an unwarlike body, a belief he had no great difficulty in substantiating from a study of their recent history.

---

[7] Hp. *Aer.* 12–24.

APPENDIX TWO: SCEPTICISM AND DELPHI

My approach to the question of Delphic oracles and their authenticity has been generally cautious: in Chapter 2 I have tended to accept oracles where there appears to have been no motive for forgery and no inconsistency involved. Thus the 'Cypselus' oracles look like the weapons of political factions, and at least three, perhaps all five, of the 'Croesus' oracles were put about to raise Delphi's prestige, or to save it. In the latter class, the early 'Cyrene' oracles are self-condemned, and acceptance of the 'Pelasgians of Lemnos' example would involve projecting Delphi's history impossibly far into the past. But most of the oracles relating to the Persian Wars seem to me to be acceptable, as well as some examples from the sixth century. This broadly traditional view has been challenged in recent years and perhaps should be defended. One influential book was R. Crahay, *La Littérature Oraculaire chez Hérodote*;[1] a more recent contribution to the controversy is Joseph Fontenrose, *The Delphic Oracle*.[2]

Crahay deals with all oracles, Delphic and others, in Herodotus, but is excessively sceptical of the authenticity of the verse oracles. In a temperately worded but quite damaging review of the book George Forrest wrote 'If one believes much more to be true than Crahay allows, it is only because Delphi's undoubted reputation seems to demand that the oracle did at times play some real part in important political events; because the hypotheses involved in belief are often no more extravagant than those of Crahay or other sceptics.'[3]

Fontenrose goes even further, wading knee-deep in carnage. He aims to judge the authenticity of oracles by objective criteria. He divides oracles into historical, quasi-historical (i.e. purporting to be historical), legendary and fictional. To earn the label 'historical', an oracle must fall within the lifetime of the earliest writer to attest it. Having thus drawn up a list of 75 examples, he establishes from them his criteria for the acceptance or rejection of the individual quasi-historical examples, of which there are no less than 267. He examines historical and legendary 'modes' – commands, warnings, predictions (whether clear, ambiguous or conditioned) and 'topics' – cults, sacrifices, legislation, war and so on; the formulation of questions and the occasions of consultation. With the help of copious statistical analysis he eliminates nearly all the quasi-historical oracles, admitting as genuine or possibly so a tiny handful: from Herodotus, five – the unquoted

---

[1] Les Belles Lettres, Paris, 1956.

[2] University of California Press, Berkeley, 1978.

[3] *CR*, VIII, 1958.

one given to Lycurgus concerning the Spartan constitution; the two instances when the Pythia was corruptly influenced – by Cleisthenes the Alcmeonid and King Cleomenes; 'Pray to the Winds'; and that in which the god complained of the Aiginetans' victory offering after Salamis.[4]

Of the numerous examples that do not meet his criteria, Fontenrose rejects that given to Sparta about the death of a king as being an 'oracle of folkloric origin' – comparing, fairly enough, the legendary self-sacrifice of King Codrus of Athens – without ever mentioning its possible relevance to Leotychidas and Damaratus. He rejects the 'Siphnos' example because of what he calls its 'Birnam Wood theme', an ambiguous warning. But the only awkward detail in Herodotus' story is his statement that the Siphnians failed to understand the last line, 'a wooden ambush and a scarlet herald' – not a very difficult conundrum. He rejects the 'Teisamenus of Elis' story, though on the facts given by Herodotus it cannot be *post eventum*. In his catalogue of oracles he marks the two long utterances given to Athens in 481/0 as 'doubtful';[5] his text argues against acceptance on the grounds of their unlikeness to 'historical' oracles, though (p. 126) he is not blind to the historical problems raised by doing away with the entire story of Themistocles and the interpretation of 'wooden wall'.

This critique of Herodotus must be taken seriously. As it hinges upon method, it is through method that any attempt to rebut it must proceed. First, the observant reader who has persevered thus far will have been surprised to find the oracles of 481/0 classed as quasi-historical, in as much as they fall within Herodotus' lifetime on almost any computation. The consequences for Fontenrose's argument that would flow from their acceptance, however, are so embarrassing that he bends his own rules (p. 8, note 10) and banishes them to the quasi-historical category. (It should be noted, however, that to the 'historical' class Fontenrose hospitably admits oracles in Diodorus that fall within the lifetime of Diodorus' presumed source Ephorus.)

There are no 'historical' oracles earlier than c. 440, and only eleven between then and the end of the fifth century (five of which are from Thucydides). Fontenrose's case thus rests squarely upon the assumption that what Delphi said and did not say in that and later epochs is evidence for the sort of things it did and did not say in the period ending in 479. That seems to me by no means self-evidently true, nor even particularly probable; at any rate no more so than the supposition that Delphi, having (as it were) caught a chill in 480, confined itself to less contentious subject matter and less controversial phraseology thereafter.

Fontenrose would deny to Delphi any serious political involvement

---

[4] Respectively i.65, v.62 f., vi.66, vii.178, viii.122.

[5] Respectively vii.220, iii.57, ix.33, vii.140 f.

(and therefore of course any 'Medism' in 480), regarding the oracle as a consultant authority on matters of cult and ritual. Let us therefore examine his handling of one oracle that would seem to fall clearly under that heading, one that even Crahay accepts – that given to Cleisthenes of Sicyon when he was seeking sanction for banishing the cult of Adrastus: 'Adrastus is King of Sicyon; you are a stone-thrower' – meaning probably that in comparison with the legendary hero, Cleisthenes was a mere skirmisher.

Fontenrose argues that 'It is unlikely that the Delphic Oracle would insult such a powerful consultant [as Cleisthenes]. Rebukes are found only among narrative oracles', and narrative oracles, needless to say, are rejected *en bloc* under the quasi-historical and legendary categories. As regards the first point, we do not know how secure Cleisthenes was in his tyranny at the time of consultation to be able to make any confident judgement of the unlikelihood of the response. As for the second, to reject a particular example on the strength of a generalisation which depends for its truth upon the rejection of the example is an argument of perfect circularity. It recalls J.B. Bury[6] rejecting Plutarch's story of Elpinice mediating between Cimon and Pericles, on the grounds that 'Women played no part in the history of Athena's city'; or, a more recent gem, J.P.V.D. Balsdon[7] denying Suetonius' story of Caesar being given a forestry commission ,as his province, because 'Senators often behaved with childish folly, but not with such childish folly as that.'

Ambiguities and riddles are not found in the 'historical' catalogue, according to Fontenrose, and he therefore rejects all examples containing any such material in Herodotus and elsewhere. He even adds (p. 236) that Delphi's reputation for ambiguity 'is wholly modern: Delphi had no such reputation in antiquity. Herodotus quotes ambiguous and obscure oracles, but never says that ambiguity was a Delphic characteristic.' Not in so many words, to be sure; but he twice uses the word *kibdēlos* (deceitful) to describe ambiguous oracles, that encouraging Croesus to attack Persia (as it stands, spurious) and that promising Tegea to the Spartans (in my opinion, authentic); and the story of the Thebans applying to 'their nearest' rests upon the *assumption* of Delphic ambiguity on the part of the unnamed Theban speaker.[8]

But even this part of Fontenrose's case is weakened by one example that he and all others accept as historical: that of 427, quoted or paraphrased by Thucydides,[9] telling the Spartans to 'bring back the seed of

---

[6] HG[3], p. 359.

[7] J.P.V.D. Balsdon, *Julius Caesar and Rome* (English Universities Press, London, 1967); Cleisthenes' oracle, v.67.

[8] Respectively i.75, i.66, v.79. On i.75, see note 11 below.

[9] Th.v.16.

the demigod son of Zeus from the foreign land to their own; if not, they will plough with a silver ploughshare'. That is as enigmatic as anything in Herodotus, and the cognate words for 'plough' and 'ploughshare' (eulaka)[10] are found nowhere else in Greek. In any case the Spartans construed it as a threat of some kind and did in due course recall their exiled King Pleistoanax. Fontenrose senses a difficulty here. Ah yes, he says in effect, but this example doesn't count. It was 'a suborned response and as such might show unusual phrasing' (p. 87, note 62). Might it? Thucydides does not state it as a fact that persuasion or pressure was brought to bear on Delphi to produce it, but let us for argument's sake accept the allegation: I find it very hard to believe that a response that was corruptly procured would draw attention to itself by phrasing or style that was seriously out of line with what was customarily uttered by the Pythia.

Fontenrose makes many interesting and thought-provoking points on folklore, oracular collections and other topics, but I am not convinced that he has made out his case. Though it is a good thing that we should have our cherished beliefs and preconceptions challenged from time to time, I think that the relatively conservative position adopted in Chapter 2 has plenty of life left in it. In particular, if Delphi really was little more than a glorified Citizen's Advice Bureau handing out unambiguous instructions in prose on questions of religion, sacrifice and so on, it is difficult to avoid asking oneself what on earth all the fuss was about.[11]

---

[10] Liddell & Scott's Lexicon (9th edn, revised by H. Stuart Jones), s.v., suggests that a dearth is indicated. Neither Fontenrose nor, surprisingly, A.W. Gomme's Commentary on Thucydides, vol. iii (Oxford University Press, 1956), p. 663, offers a solution to the riddle.

[11] Fontenrose's book has been criticized scarcely less severely by Peter Green in Classical Bearings (Thames & Hudson, London, 1989), ch. VI, a revised and expanded version of a review that originally appeared in the New York Review of Books; his criticisms and mine overlap at more than one point. Green produces an interesting defence of the oracle misread by Croesus (i.53): Delphi had sized Croesus up as 'a self-promoting and greedy adventurer' crudely attempting to buy divine favour, and utterly without the self-knowledge needed to interpret the oracle correctly. The text of the oracle itself (Green argues) was clear, 'that the forthcoming conflict would be decisive one way or the other . . . , that one side or the other would be totally destroyed'. It is refreshing to read a well-argued defence of a conservative position like that.

BIBLIOGRAPHY

Andrewes, A. *The Greeks* (Hutchinson, London, 1967)
– *The Greek Tyrants* (Hutchinson, London, 1956)
Archaiologikon Deltion, no. 23

Barron, J.P. *The Silver Coins of Samos* (Athlone Press, London, 1966)
Bicknell, P. 'Studies in Greek Genealogy', *Historia*, Einzelschrift 19
Bradeen, D.W. 'The Fifth-century Archon-list', *Hesperia*, 1963
Brunt, P.A. 'The Hellenic League Against Persia', *Historia*, 1954
Burn, A.R. *The Lyric Age of Greece* (Edward Arnold, London, 1960) – also the Greece of colonisation, tyranny and similar archaic phenomena.
– *Persia and the Greeks* (Edward Arnold, London, 1962). The most highly recommended modern treatment of its subject. Greatly preferable (for instance) to C. Hignett, *Xerxes' Invasion of Greece* (Oxford University Press, 1963).
– *Pericles and Athens* (English Universities Press, London, 1948)
Bury, J.B. *History of Greece*, 3rd edn, revised by Russell Meiggs (Macmillan, London, 1951): a fourth edition, further revised and reset, is now available, but page references are to the third, cited as Bury, HG^3. Still the best medium-length narrative account in English of Greek history down to the death of Alexander: by no means superseded by N.G.L. Hammond's book of the same title (Oxford University Press, 1959). Originally produced in 1900, it reflects the predispositions of the age in its heavy concentration on military, political and diplomatic history at the expense of social, economic and cultural, and in its concomitant overvaluing of Thucydides in comparison with Herodotus.

Cartledge, Paul *Sparta and Laconia* (Routledge, London, 1979) is a fuller and more detailed treatment, including considerable archaeological material, than Forrest's admirable short book. Several controversial questions are discussed in readable form.
Cawkwell, George introduction to Rex Warner's translation of Xenophon: *The Persian Expedition* (revised edition, Penguin Books, Harmondsworth, 1972)
Crahay, R. *La Littérature Oraculaire chez Hérodote* (Les Belles Lettres, Paris, 1956)

Davies, J.K. *Athenian Propertied Families* (Oxford University Press, 1971)
Dodds, E.R. *The Greeks and the Irrational* (University of California Press, Berkeley, 1951)

Ehrenberg, V. 'Origins of Democracy', *Historia*, 1950
Eliot, C.W.J. *The Coastal Demes of Attica* (University of Toronto Press, 1962)
– 'Where Did the Alcmeonidae live?', *Historia*, 1967
Evans, J.A.S. 'Histiaeus and Aristagoras', *American Journal of Philology*, 84, 1963
– 'Notes on Thermopylae and Artemisium', *Historia*, 1969

Fontenrose, Joseph *The Delphic Oracle* (University of California Press, Berkeley, 1978)
Fornara, C.W. 'The Athenian Board of Generals, 501–404', *Historia*, Einzelschrift 16
– C.W. *Herodotus: an Interpretative Essay* (Oxford University Press, 1971). A short book (98 pages) whose title gives a fair idea of its scope. Fornara aims to view Herodotus from the context of the age for which he was writing – the period around the start of the Peloponnesian War – and to my mind is entirely successful.
Forrest, W.G. *The Emergence of Greek Democracy* (Weidenfeld & Nicolson, London, 1966). Full of valuable insights on tyranny, oligarchy, Cleisthenes' reforms etc., and most readably presented.
– *History of Sparta*, 950–192 B.C. (Hutchinson, London, 1968). A short, readable work, recommended as an introduction to its subject. For more detailed treatment, see bibliography to Chapter 5.

Gomme, A.W., A. Andrewes & K.J. Dover *A Commentary on Thucydides*, vols. III and IV (Oxford University Press, 1956 and 1970)

Green, Peter *Classical Bearings* (Thames & Hudson, London, 1989)

Guthrie, W.K.C. *The Sophists* (Cambridge University Press, 1971)

How, W.W. & J. Wells *A Commentary on Herodotus* (Oxford University Press, 1912, slightly revised 1928). At the time of writing, the only systematic paragraph-by-paragraph commentary in English and still of great utility. If in the endnotes I sometimes quote from How & Wells in order to disagree with them, that is a tribute to their continuing *auctoritas*.

Kent, Roland G. *Old Persian* (American Oriental Society, New Haven, 1950). This splendid volume is out of print and, I am told, very hard to come by now. If there is anything comparable in print, I have not seen it. Kent contains, most relevantly for the purposes of this chapter, a full text and translation of Darius' great Behistan inscription, cited as DB I–V, the numbers denoting columns. It is a highly informative official version of the opening phase of Darius' reign which tallies with Herodotus at many points, e.g. the names of six out of the seven conspirators, Cambyses' murder of Smerdis and the usurpation of the Magus (whose real name, Gaumata, is given). Herodotus seems to derive his account indirectly from it, and for once it may be necessary to discount possible 'official' distortion and self-justification on Darius' part.

Kirk, G.S. *The Nature of Greek Myths* (Penguin Books, Harmondsworth, 1974)

Lang, Mabel 'Herodotos and the Ionian Revolt', *Historia*, 1968

– 'The Murder of Hipparchus', *Historia*, 1955

Lewis, D.M. 'Cleisthenes and Attica', *Historia*, 1963

Lloyd-Jones, H. *The Justice of Zeus* (University of California Press, Berkeley, 1971)

Maspero, G.H. *Histoire Ancienne de l'Orient* (Paris, 1895)

Mitchell, B.M. 'Herodotus and Samos', *Journal of Hellenic Studies*, 1975

Momigliano, A. *Studies in Historiography* (Weidenfeld & Nicolson, London, 1966). A collection of the author's papers, of which three are of special interest and value: 'The Place of Herodotus in the History of Historiography','Some Observations on Causes of War in Ancient Historiography', and 'Historiography on Oral and Written Tradition.'

Myres, J.L. *Herodotus, Father of History* (Oxford University Press, 1953)

Olmstead, A.T. *History of the Persian Empire* (Chicago University Press, 1948) – heavy going.

Parke, H.W. & D.E.W. Wormell *A History of the Delphic Oracle*, 2 vols. (Blackwell, Oxford, 1956). The first volume is the history, the second is a catalogue of all attested responses.

Pearson, Lionel 'Credulity and Scepticism in Herodotus', *Transactions of the American Philological Association*, 72, 1941

– *Popular Ethics in Ancient Greece* (Stanford University Press, California, 1962)

Powell, J. Enoch *A Lexicon to Herodotus* (Cambridge University Press, 1938)

– 'Notes on Herodotus – II', *Classical Quarterly*, 1935

Pritchett, W.K. 'New Light on Plataea', *American Journal of Archaeology*, 61, 1957

– 'New Light on Thermopylae', *American Journal of Archaeology*, 62, 1958

– 'Toward a Restudy of the Battle of Salamis', *American Journal of Archaeology*, 63, 1959

Ste Croix, G.E.M. de *The Origins of the Peloponnesian War* (Duckworth, London, 1972). Despite its formidable bulk and appearance, a readable, at times sparkling, work of authority. Ste Croix has many illuminating things to say on earlier history and draws copious illustration from Herodotus.

Snodgrass, A.M. *Archaic Greece, the Age of Experiment* (J.M. Dent & Sons, London, 1980). An admirable work that treats much of the social history of the period described by Herodotus from an archaeological standpoint. It appeared when the writing of the present work was well advanced and sent me back to reconsider several points.

Talbot Rice, Tamara *The Scythians* (Thames & Hudson, London, 1957)

Tomlinson, R.A. *Argos and the Argolid* (Routledge, London, 1972) deals, *inter alia*, interestingly with Cleomenes' campaign from the Argive point of view.

Wade-Gery, H.T. 'Miltiades', in his own *Essays in Greek History* (Blackwell, Oxford, 1958)

Wardman, A.E. 'Herodotus on the Cause of the Greco-Persian Wars', *American Journal of Philology*, 82, 1961

Waters, K.H. 'The Purpose of Dramatization in Herodotos', *Historia*, 1966

– 'Herodotos and the Ionian Revolt', *Historia, 1970* – an answer to Mabel Lang's article cited above

– 'Herodotos on Tyrants and Despots: A Study in Objectivity', *Historia*, Einzelschrift 15

Wells, J. 'Herodotus and the Intellectual Life of His Age', in his own *Studies in Herodotus* (Blackwell, Oxford, 1923)

INDEX OF NAMES

PRELIMINARY NOTE

1. Entries like 'the Peloponnese' and 'the Isthmus' are only indexed when they are the centre of attention in the text.

2. 'Athens', 'Persia', 'Sparta' and 'Xerxes' are indexed selectively: for further material see under the names of individual Athenians, etc., and the battles of the Persian Wars.

3. Not indexed are some minor mentions of persons and episodes treated more fully elsewhere in the work; parallels from Roman and modern history; mentions of persons as relatives of other named figures (e.g. Neocles father of Themistocles) or whose sole appearance is in a genealogical table (e.g. Megacles III).

Apollo 50, 53, temple at Thebes 63, 211; *see also* Delphi, Delphic responses
Apollonia *see* Evenius
Arcadia, -ans 172, 175, 178; too many for Sparta 66; *see also* Mantinea, Tegea
Arcesilas III of Cyrene, murder of 111
Arcesilas IV of Cyrene, hymned by Pindar 21
Archias of Pitana 211
Archidamus, Spartan king 142 n. 125, 165, 176; in 432 98, 221; marries his aunt 165
Archilochus, poet 216
Ardys, Lydian king 50
Argos, Argives 114-6, 167, 171-4; broken reed in 480/479 116, 147, 177, 213 f.; Delphi advises
    neutrality 64; geography of 114 f.; obscure oracle to 62 f.; 'slave' regime 173; war with
    Sicyon 23, 80; *see also* Eurybates
Ariapeithes, Scythian king 209 f.
Arion of Methymna, poet 78, 216
Aristagoras of Miletus 117-122, 157; at Athens 83; at Naxos 49, 160; at Sparta 62, 115; a windbag
    100; resigns tyranny 74
Aristeas of Proconnesus 216; Delphi and 60
Aristeas son of Adeimantus, Corinthian officer 135, 212
Aristeides son of Lysimachus 135, 186, 188, 193, 195; founds Delian League 188 n. 83; Timocreon
    praises 196
Aristodicus of Cyme 55
Aristogeiton *see* Harmodius
Ariston of Byzantium, tyrant 40
Aristophanes, comic dramatist 222 f.
Aristophilides, king of Taras 160
Aristotle 79
Arrian, historian 109
Artabanus, brother of Darius, his pessimistic advice 52, 54, 112, 143, 158, 190
Artabazus, Persian advocate of political warfare 138
Artaphernes, brother of Darius, satrap 49, 84 f., 121, 160; and Ionian revolt 118, 125; kills
    Histiaeus 95, 164
Artaxerxes, king of Persia 214, 219, 225; gives Themistocles refuge 197; murders brother 49
Artayctes, Persian officer 208
Artaynte, fateful figure 49
Artayntes, Persian general in 206
Artemisia of Halicarnassus 203-6; naval exploits in 480 135, 143, 146
Artemisium, battle of 130-2, 143-5, 189
Artystone, Darius' favourite wife 157
Aryandes, satrap of Egypt 108, 111; Darius puts to death 160 f.
Astyages, Median king 105
Athens, -ians 17-47 *passim*; and Aigina 177, 212 f.; and Gelon 221 f.; archers at Plataea 139;
    captured in 480 133; deceived by Aristagoras 100; democracy at 95 f., 100 f.; dislikes
    Thebans 167, 213; empire 118, 201, 231; grim oracles given to 56, 64, 185, 234; H on 215-
    222; mother-city of Ionians 230; oligarchy in 411 97 f., nn. 133-4, 103; pressurises Sparta
    147; rejects Medism 121, 217; tyranny at 81-5; waives command 149
Athos, mount, and Persian strategy 107, 125
Atossa, wife of Darius 109 f., 157, 162, 180
Attaginus, Theban Mediser 200
Attica 23, 29; poor cavalry country 137; *see also* 'Plain, Coast, Hill'
Atys, son of Croesus 51, 56

Babylon 106, 223; Darius and 108, 152 f., 156
Bacchiadae, Corinthian aristocracy 75, 77 f.; untypical of later oligarchies 96
Bacis and Musaeus, alleged oracles of 57
Bagaeus, Persian gentleman 161
Barca, Aryandes' capture of 111; inmates deported 157 n. 16
Bias of Priene, sage 73, 117; dissuades Croesus 86
Biton *see* Cleobis
Boeotia, -ans 167, 170; at Plataea 140-2; *see also* Thebes
Borysthenes, river *see* Olbia
Bosporus 40, 107, 161.; visited by Pausanias 200

Cylon, Athenian nobleman 18-20; Delphi's advice 61

Cyprus 119, 124; Athens abandons 219

Cypselus of Corinth 19, 36, 77 f.; non-Dorian 80; oracles relating to 66, 77, 233

Cypselus (II) of Athens, archon 36 f.

Cyrene 166; Delphi and 66, 233; *see also* Arcesilas, Demonax

Cyrus, king of Persia 106, 111 n. 33, 181, 223, 231; an argument for monarchy 71 f.; and Croesus
    93 n. 114, 150; and Ionians 116, 230; humour of 105, 151; prophetic dream 152

Cythera, island 143, 180, 182.

Damaratus, Spartan king 73, 75, 164 f., 179-183, 220; and Darius 163; Delphi bribed to depose 61,
    179; Delphi urges restoration 65; Olympic victor 180; popular in Sparta 180; praises Sparta
    73, 150; quarrels with Cleomenes 99, 170, 175; Xerxes' adviser 143, 180-2

Damasithymus see Calynda

Darius, king of Persia 152-164 *passim*; advocates monarchy 68, 71 f.; and Athens 125; and
    individual Greeks 90, 93-5, 162-4.; before reign 152 f.; death 183; delighted by advice 93;
    finance 118; generosity 155; imperialism 109 f., 160; reign begins evils 149; Scythian
    expedition 40 f., 108, 157-60, 194, 230; uxorious 157 n. 17

Dascyleion, seat of Hellespontine satrapy 89

Daurises, Persian general 124

Deinomache mother of Alcibiades 33

Delos 83, 148; portentous earthquake at 149

Delphi, Delphic oracle: allegedly bribed by Alcmeonidae 35, 84, 168; and by Cleomenes 61, 175,
    234; backs wrong side 63-5; dedications at 78, 210; geographical advantages 60; offerings in
    480/479 60, 200; role in 481/0 64 f., 234 f.; temple destroyed 27

Delphic responses 57-67, 233-6; ambiguities 61-4, 235 f.; colonisation see Cyrene, Demonax,
    Dolonci, Dorieus; cults and purification 59 f., 235; *see also* Aesop, Agylla, Aigina, Aristeas
    of Proconnesus, Cleisthenes of Sicyon, Evenius, Lemnos; political and public 60-67; *see also*
    Argos, Cnidos, Crete, Croesus, Cylon, Cypselus, Damaratus, Miletus, Pleistoanax, Siphnos,
    Tegea; private 58 f.; *see also* Glaucus, Miltiades I, Teisamenus; spurious 63, 65 f.

Democedes of Croton, physician 109, 160, 162

Demonax of Mantinea, sorts out Cyrene 61

Demosthenes, Athenian general in 420s, 113, 158 n. 19

Dicaeus of Athens 180

Didyma *see* Branchidae

Dienekes of Sparta, a wit 130

Dionysius of Phocaea, 'razor's edge' speech 123 and n. 63

Dodona, oracle of Zeus 60, 63

Dolonci, the 37

Dorians, the 80, 181; Cleomenes not one 169; H one 204, 231

Dorieus, Spartan prince 165 f., 169; neglects Delphi 61

Doriscus 107

Eëtion *see* Cypselus of Corinth

Egesta, borrows trick from Oroetes 89

Egypt, -ians 86 f., 107, 111 n. 33, 152, 208, 224; and Darius 152 f.; at Salamis 134; revolt in 480s
    183

Eion 44, 107

Elis, -eans, bad relations with Sparta 185

Epaminondas of Thebes, tactical innovator 114

Ephesus, -ians 104, 123 f.

Epidaurus, target for Argos? 172; *see also* Procles

Epixyes, Persian satrap 95 n. 121

Erasinos, Argos' patriotic river 173, 178

Eretria 125-7, 157

Ethiopia, Cambyses' invasion of 107

Euboea *see* Artemisium, Carystos, Chalcis, Eretria

Eupalinus of Megara, engineer 88, 206

Euphrates, river of Babylon 106, 208

Euripides, dramatist 69, 71 n. 6, 216, 224

Eurybates, Argive athlete 187

Eurybiadas, Spartan admiral 130, 133, 189, 192-5

Eurymachus, Theban officer 129, 212 *see also* Leontiadas
Euryptolemus, an Alcmeonid 33 f.
Evagoras of Sparta, Olympic victor 39 n. 68
Evenius of Apollonia, seer 59
Exampaeus, H visits 209

Gaumata *see* 'Smerdis'
Gela *see* Gelon, Hippocrates
Gelon of Syracuse 91; in 480 92, 206; twits allied ambassadors 92, 116, 221 f.
Gillus of Taras 162, 206
Glaucus, moralised upon by Leotychidas 55, 58
Gobryas, Persian nobleman 154, 158 f., 162
Gongylus of Eretria, exile in Persia 75
Gorgias, sophist 67 f.
Gorgo, daughter of Cleomenes: interprets message 180; marries uncle 165 n. 34; precocious advice 171
Gorgus of Salamis (Cyprus) 124, 131
Gyges, Lydian king 49 f., 60; sin expiated by Croesus 53
Gyndes, river 106

Halicarnassus, H's birthplace 203-6, 209; *see also* Artemisia
Harmodius and Aristogeiton, tyrannicides 28, 74, 84, 224; *see also* Hipparchus
Harpagus, Median general under Cyrus 86, 116
Hecataeus, geographer 120
Hegesipyle, Miltiades' wife 41
Hegesistratus of Elis, seer in Persian service 185
Hegesistratus of Samos 148
Hegetoridas of Cos, his daughter rescued 198
Hellanicus of Lesbos, incompetent historian 224
Hellespont, the 54, 108, 194; Athens' interest in 38; *see also* Ionia – revolt in 490s
Heracles, Spartan kings' ancestor 169
Heraion at Argos, Cleomenes' sacrilege at 116, 174
Heraion at Samos 85, 87; noted art-gallery 107, 206
Herodotus: compared with Thucydides 224-8; influence of 222-9; interests of: inscriptions 130, 206, 215, 225; medicine 226 f.; poetry and drama 216; trade 208; visual arts 85 nn. 80 and 81, 107, 206, 210 f.; life and travels of 203-212; *see also* Index of selected subject-matter
Hesiod, poet 49, 216
'Hill' *see* 'Plain, Coast, Hill'
Himera, battle of 92
Hipparchus son of Peisistratus, his murder 26, 84
Hipparchus (II) son of Charmus 42, 186
Hippias, tyrant of Athens 84 f.; Archon in 526 25; Artaphernes backs 121; at Marathon 65, 75, 85, 127, 160; Medising tendencies 40 f.; not restored in 503 170; relations with Sparta and Argos 167-9
Hippocleides son of Teisander, his ill-timed dancing 19, 35
Hippoclus of Lampsacus 40 f., 168
Hippocrates, popular name in sixth-century Athens 24 f.
Hippocrates nephew of Pericles, general in 424 17
Hippocrates of Gela 91, 163
'Hippocratic' medical writings 204, 231 f.
Hippodamus of Miletus, town-planner 76
Histiaeus of Miletus 40 f., 93 ff., 159, 230 f.; Darius and 94 f., 164; in Ionian revolt 117, 157
Homer 216; Authorised Version 48; banned by Cleisthenes 80; H borrows technique 109; on pollution 59
Hydarnes, Persian general 44, 129 f., 185 n. 73
Hystaspes, father of Darius 153

Ialysos in Rhodes 196, 204
Idanthyrsus, Scythian chief, leads Darius a dance 158
Imbros 41, 93
India, explored by Darius 161

Intaphrenes, Persian nobleman 154 f.
Ionia, -ans 125, 230 ff.; Cyrus, Harpagus and 116; high tribute to Darius 118; in Xerxes' fleet 131, 190; not transplanted 157; revolt in 490s 41 f., 117-125, 206; H's view of 117, 124 f., 230-2.; revolt in 479 148; subject to Athens 219, 231; untalented mathematicians 158
Ion of Chios, poet 76
Isagoras, Athenian politician 28, 33, 169; not a Philaid 36
Isodice, wife of Cimon II 33
Isthmus, the 99, 133 f., 146 f., 195

Justin, historian, disappointed in H 128

'Kroisos', Athenian noble youth 24

Lacedaemon see Sparta
Lacedaemonius son of Cimon, general in 433 17, 44, 192 f., n. 94
Lade, battle of 56, 91, 122-4, 207; precedent for Salamis? 134, 193
Lakiadae, Miltiades' deme 37
Lamachus, Athenian general in 415 128
Lampon of Aigina 199 f.
Lampsacus 38, 40; see also Hippoclus
Laurion, Athenian silver-mines 186
Leipsydrium, failure at 26 f.
Lemnos 41, 44, 90, 93, 190; mythical Delphic oracle 59, 66, 233
Leobotes son of Alcmeon 33
Leonidas, Spartan king 65, 129 f., 176, 183; corpse outraged 54, 200
Leontiadas, Theban officer 129, 213
Leotychidas, Spartan king 65, 148, 179 f., 191; Cleomenes' client 175 f., 183; robbed of bride 165, 182; Timocreon approves 196; see also Glaucus
Leros, island 120
Lesbos, -ians, at Lade 122 f.
Libya see Aryandes, Dorieus
Lindos in Rhodes 204
Lycaretus of Samos 42, 90
Lycidas, lynched in Athens 100
Lycophron son of Periander 79
Lycurgus, leader of 'Plain' faction 21 f., 33, 82
Lycurgus, Spartan lawgiver, brings good government 73, 98, 234
Lydia see Alyattes, Croesus, Gyges
Lygdamis, tyrant of Halicarnassus 203 f.
Lygdamis of Naxos, tantalising figure 76
Lysagoras of Paros, enemy of Miltiades 44
Lysander, Spartan general 116, 196

Macedonia 125, 160; in fourth century 109, 114, 138; see also Alexander
Maeandrius of Samos 89 ff., 156, 167; proclaims isonomia 73 f.
Magnesia, coast of Thessaly 108, 144
Magnesia, Ionian city 53, 89, 118; Themistocles' last home 75, 197
Magus, Magi, the see 'Smerdis'
Mandrocles of Samos, engineer 107, 162
Mantinea, -eans 61, 173; battle of (418), offers useful parallels 137, 140, 173, 212
Marathon: battle of 42 ff., 126 ff.; Peisistratus lands at 127
Mardonius, Persian general in 479 136-142, 200, 219; and Ionia 118, 162; brash in council 54, 111; in Thrace 125, 160; laughs at Greek warfare 113, 221; strategy 146 f.
Masistius, Persian officer 139
Massagetae, Cyrus and 111 n. 33, 153
Media, Medes 105, 152, 157; at Thermopylae 129
Megabates, Persian nobleman 119, 206; Pausanias woos daughter 225
Megabazus, conqueror of Thrace 94, 125, 160; Darius praises 156
Megabyzus (Megabyxus in OCT), advocate of oligarchy 71 f.
Megacles the Archon 18 f., 97; H shifts blame from 34
Megacles (II) son of Alcmeon, leader of 'Coast' 22-5; a tricky politician 35, 82

Scyles, Scythian king and philhellene 210

Scyllias of Scione, diver 131

Scythes of Zancle, friend of Darius 92, 163

Scythia, -ians 208-210; Cleomenes and 168; Darius' expedition 108, 110, 157-160; Histiaeus and 94; Miltiades and 40 f.; on Ionians 230 f.

Sepeia, Argos crushed at 115 f., 173

'Serpent Column' at Delphi 199 f., 210, 215

Sesostris, Pharaoh – better man than Darius? 152 f.

Sestos 38, 40, 150 n. 144

Sicinnus, Themistocles' trusted servant 194

Sicyon, -ians 79, 142; see also Cleisthenes

Sigeum 37, 41, 79, 85

Simonides, poet 78, 216

Siphnos, -ians 187, 210; shrewd Delphic oracle 67, 234

Siris, claimed by Themistocles 192

Sisamnes, Persian judge flayed by Cambyses 161

'Smerdis' the Magus 71, 89; a popular usurpation 154 f.

Smyrna see Alyattes

Socles see Sosicles

Socrates 69

Solon, Athenian statesman 20 f., 35, 38; effects of reforms 22, 81 f.; preaches to Croesus 50-2; quoted by H 216

Sophocles, dramatist and friend of H 204, 216; some parallels in 54-6, 59, 223 f.

Sosicles of Corinth, his discourse on tyranny 74, 77 ff., 170

Sostratus of Aigina merchant 213 n. 31

Sparta, -ans: Athens blackmails 147; attack Polycrates 87; Cyrus and 151; deceived over Tegea 67, 114, 235; Delphi urges regicide 65, 234; duped by Alcmeonidae 28; gift to Croesus 86; H admires 98, 217 f; Helots 114, 138, 173-7, 213, 218; honour Themistocles 195, 198 n. 109; jealous of citizenship 58; mixed constitution 73 f., 97; murder Darius' heralds 184; myth of Thermopylae 124, 129; oppose tyranny 27, 77, 87, 167-9; piety 80 n. 54, 168, 175-7; prickly reaction to Gelon 221 f.; respect for Law 220 f.; social divisions 177, 182; too late in 490 127, 176 n.58; two-faced in 479 99; wars with Argos 62 f., 167 f., 171-4

Sperthias and Bulis, Spartan heralds 184 f. and n.73

Stesagoras brother of Miltiades II 38 f.

Sthenelaïdas, Spartan ephor 98, 220 f.

Strattis, tyrant of Chios in 480 75

Susa, Persian capital 153, 157

Syagrus, Spartan envoy 221

Sybaris, destruction of 166, 174, 212

Syloson, tyrant of Samos 86, 90, 153, 156

Syracuse 96, 128, 135; splendour of her tyranny 89; see also Gelon

Talthybius, legendary herald 184

Tanagra, staunch for Thebes 62

Taras 160, 162

Tearos, river, Darius' boastful inscription at 158

Tegea, -ans: bad relations with Sparta 185; Delphi's error 66 f., 114, 235; disputes precedence with Athens 139, 220; H visits 211 f.; see also Chileos

Teisamenus of Elis, seer 58, 234

Tellus of Athens, happiest man ever 51, 55

Telmessi of Lycia 63

Tempe, vale of., wrong place to defend? 144, 189

Tenos, -ians 134 n. 100, 190

Teos, Teians 116

Termera 205, 209

Thasos 44, 160, 187

Theagenes, tyrant of Megara 18, 81

Thebes, -ans: an oligarchy 96; attempt to outwit oracle 62, 235; at Thermopylae 129; bad relations with Athens 167, 213; destroyed in 335 174; H visits 211; in 479 137 f., and n. 113, 200; see also Apollo

Themistocles son of Neocles 42, 147, 185-198, 225; and Aristeides 188, 193; dramatic entry 185;

founder of Athenian sea-power 186, 188; in 480 128, 134, 188-193, 195; in Magnesia 75, 197; unscrupulous 189, 194-6

Theodorus of Samos, artist 85 n. 81

Theomestor, tyrant of Samos in 480 75

Thera, -aeans, linked with Sparta 166

Therma, Xerxes at 107

Thermopylae, battle of 108, 129-132, 145.

Thersander of Orchomenus, banquet anecdote of 56 f., 138

Thespiae, -ians 62, 129, 213 n.32

Thessaly, -ians: aid Hippias 84 f. and n. 77; ally of Xerxes 107, 125, 144, 175, 189, 213 f.

Thrace 40, 125, 160; H visits 208

Thrasybulus of Miletus, authority on tyranny 39, 77 f., 93, 224

Thucydides, historian: compared with H 224-8; confirms H on Themistocles 197, 225; cynical view of religion 57, 69; descended from Miltiades 41 n. 79; no admirer of democracy 70, 121; on Cylon 18 f.; on fear of pollution 59; on H 23, 31, 211, 224; on Hippias' Medism 40; on Pausanias 201 f. and n. 115; on Pericles 34; on sea-battles 135; on Sparta and tyranny 27; on war and its causes 103 f., 111; realism on Persian numbers 109; rejects determinism 49; speeches and pseudo-prophecy 22, 143 n.126, 220, 227; supports H on Hipparchus 28, 84, 224; see also Mantinea, battle of

Thucydides son of Melesias, Athenian politician 34, 210

Thuria, a home for H 68, 166, 204, 212

Thyrea, fought over by Argos and Sparta 115

Tigris, river 106.

Timagenidas, Theban Mediser 200

Timo, priestess at Paros 59

Timocreon, minor poet, hates Themistocles 196

Timodemus of Aphidna, put down by Themistocles 195

Timonassa, Hippias' Argive step-mother 167

Tiryns see Mycenae

Tissaphernes, satrap of Sardis in 412 89

Tolmides, Athenian general see Cythera

Troizen 172, 204; inscription found at 191

Tymnes, agent at Olbia 209

Xanthippus father of Pericles 32, 35, 186, 188 and n. 83; successful in 479/8 142 n.125, 148; Timocreon praises 196

Xenagoras of Halicarnassus, officer in Persian service 206

Xenophon, Athenian soldier and writer 69 n. 79, 108; *Hellenica* dull stuff 104

'Xenophon' *Athenaion Politeia* 17, 72, 96

Xerxes, king of Persia: advised by Artabanus 52, 143; and by Artemisia 93 n.114, 146, 205; and by Damaratus 180-2; and 'hubris' theme 53 f.; at Salamis 134-6; at Thermopylae 129; compared with Darius 159; harem intrigues 49, 157; invasion 107; mentioned 184, 196 f., 225; owed throne to Damaratus? 180; wants war 111 f.

Xypete see Agryle

Zopyrus, Persian nobleman, at Babylon 156, 161